EMILY HANCOCK

THE GIRL WITHIN

E. P. DUTTON · NEW YORK

Published in the United States by E. P. Dutton,
a division of Penguin Books USA Inc.,
2 Park Avenue, New York, N.Y. 10016.

Published simultaneously in Canada
by Fitzhenry and Whiteside, Limited, Toronto.

Library of Congress Cataloging-in-Publication Data

Hancock, Emily.
The girl within / Emily Hancock. — 1st ed.
p.   cm.
Bibliography: p.
Includes index.
ISBN 0-525-24774-2
1. Women—Psychology. 2. Girls—Psychology. 3. Maturation
(Psychology). 4. Self. 5. Sex role. 6. Women—United States—Case
studies. I. Title.
HQ1206.H238   1989
155.6'33—dc19   89-1288
                                                        CIP

Designed by Steven N. Stathakis

10 9 8 7 6 5 4 3 2 1

First Edition

*This book
is dedicated
to my son,
Tad*

CONTENTS

ACKNOWLEDGMENTS

This book never would have been conceived without the stunning conceptual work of Jean Baker Miller and Carol Gilligan, who directed the original study and nurtured my interest in women's psychology.* Marcia Westkott's challenge to "male" research methods in social science research provided me at the start with a sound and fruitful approach to the interview process when I began my doctoral work. During the seemingly interminable hiatus between the completion of my dissertation and the emergence of *The Girl Within*, Marcia maintained that my ideas were important when I myself was unsure. Her candid analysis of various versions of the manuscript and her

*I was supported at Harvard while doing doctoral research by two Radcliffe grants for graduate women; a Woodrow Wilson Research Grant in Women's Studies; a Peter Livingston Research Grant; and a Danforth Fellowship.

encouragement at critical junctures kept the project viable when my work on it flagged.

As this book began to take form, Naomi Lowinsky and Marilyn Steele helped me discover and amplify my own voice in its chapters. When it neared completion, Sally-Ann Bemis and Robert Harris affirmed that voice. With Robert, I nearly always had the first word of the day; with Sally-Ann, I often had the last. Each confirmed that the book carried the message I wanted it to carry. In the interim, Jane and Joe Wheelwright were real mainstays. I will long remember Joe going over an early version of the manuscript with me. He had written hysterically in the margins and explained his comments starting at the last page and working forward. Going thus from the end to the beginning gives the author a unique appreciation of her work!

Many others contributed important elements. Dorothy Witt's experience as a children's librarian (combined with her extraordinary capacity to understand my struggles as a writer) resulted in the invaluable examples of eight-, nine-, and ten-year-old girls in children's books. Dorothy Duff Brown helped clarify my book's organization by holding me to my original vision of it as an arrangement of female portraits. William B. Anhalt, Catherine Wurdack, and my late father, Theodore M. Hancock, made real contributions, as did the women in *The Girl Within* therapy workshops and study group.

Felicia Eth sustained me with her steady interest and good sense. Her generosity of spirit, her enthusiasm, and, best of all, her candor saw me through many an upheaval. Carol Mann, my agent, deserves special thanks for putting my manuscript into the hands of the perfect editor, namely, Meg Blackstone. Meg endeared herself to me the very first time we met when she called my book "the anti-Christ of self-help books." It was simply wonderful to work with an editor who, from the start, shared my vision of the book.

Finally, I thank the women who were the subjects in this research for delving so deeply into the truth of their experiences. I admire each one of them for the courage with which they have led their lives and for the honesty with which they have related their life experiences. Their contribution is indeed a profound one, and I am delighted that their life stories are now in print.

1

REDISCOVERING
THE GIRL WITHIN

This book is about a phenomenon both discouraging and hopeful: women's loss and rediscovery of the "true self." This finding, which came out of my doctoral research at Harvard, was not what I was looking for. I was studying contemporary women of various ages and occupations, wondering what I would find when I asked them to describe their psychological histories as adults. The answer came as a surprise to me as well as to the women I interviewed.* At the buried core of women's identity is a distinct, vital self first articulated in childhood, a root identity that gets cut off in the process of growing up. The women in my study came fully into their own and became truly themselves only when they recaptured the girl they'd been in the first place—before she got all cluttered up.

I did not know about this girl within—the self-possessed child who serves as a touchstone for women's identity—when I began the

*See Chapter 12 for a description of the subjects in the study and its methodology.

biographical studies that make up this book. Nor did she leap out at me when I completed my doctoral research.[1] Initially unaware of how directly a woman's childhood sense of self would be implicated in her adult identity, I had set out simply to sketch in the outlines of women's psychology, partly in response to a crush of studies about men and partly to balance what had become a lopsided picture of "human" development—a picture that had left women's voices out. I wanted to get beneath the "what" of women's experiences—externally observable features like marriage, motherhood, and the so-called empty nest—to the "how" of women's development. To do that, I engaged twenty self-reflective, highly developed women who were willing to delve into the details of their lives.

It was through the process of telling me about their experiences as adults that women stumbled almost by chance on the girl they had long ago left behind. They themselves were distressed to find that they had lost her—a disturbing insight that often came to them unbidden when they confronted the contrived self that had stolen in to take her place. They were unprepared to find that the task of a woman's lifetime boils down to reclaiming the authentic identity she'd embodied as a girl. Although the details differed among women in the study, each who described her experience in depth spoke of this striking phenomenon—the inner girl, lost and reclaimed.

This radical finding gives rise to provocative questions: How is this girl lost or buried in the first place? What is her importance to a woman's adult identity? And how is it possible that these women apparently managed to lead responsible, effective lives—marrying, having children, in many cases pursuing careers, going along just as though they had a solid sense of self—until they suddenly found that they had lost their "real" self and come to rely on the trappings of a self instead?

These were questions I could not ask the women in my study, for I came upon this self-possessed girl and discovered her authority a good three years after finishing my doctorate. I was invited then to join a colleague giving a presentation at a retreat for the wives of an elite family. My colleague knew that I had interviewed women about their lives as adults, and she knew that I came from an old, established clan. She thought I would be able to speak these women's language— and be of help to her. She cautioned, however, that they were not psychologically minded and warned that any material that might direct them to peer beneath the surface of their socially correct, upper-crust lives would be unwelcome. Their happiness, in fact, depended on not looking too closely at inner satisfaction or its lack. Initially hobbled by these constraints, I racked my brain for a way to present my research on women's lives. I searched for a presentation that would not rock the boat.

As I struggled with that hapless assignment, I went back to the life studies I had collected and thought again of their many facets. One, I realized, was an intriguing recollection a woman named Megan* (see Chapter 5) came upon when her marriage went awry. Jolted by her husband's affair just after the birth of a new baby, she realized suddenly that she had no identity of her own. She had counted on marriage itself to provide her with a sense of self. Frightened when she found that such an assumption had led her instead to abandon her own quest, she faced the difficult task of building an identity. This she was able to do by making choices, decisions that sprang from a newfound sense of who and what she was. Making those choices reminded her of a critical experience she'd had at the age of nine. It was then that her family had moved from New York City to the suburbs, interrupting Megan's confirmation studies. Without the aid of her parents, she had arranged with the nuns to send her lessons so she could complete them by herself.

This act of independence was lodged in Megan's girlhood image of herself. "I can remember walking on a fence, all around a park, thinking I really liked being nine years old and I wouldn't mind being nine forever. I was finding out about the world, not doing anything particularly momentous, just thinking those thoughts to myself as I walked along the fence. I remember having a real sense of joy, of confidence about negotiating the world on my own. The image I have is of a child with a long string to hold on to, one she can move freely around. I felt secure and self-contained. I had a sense that 'I can get by in the world, even if it means I am alone. There's a way for me to negotiate it. I can do it.' "

Vulnerable in her new motherhood and distressed by the crisis in her marriage, Megan harkened back to this spirited, purposeful, playful girl. She recaptured the initiative she'd embodied, rediscovering the forgotten autonomy she needed for adult independence. Megan had carried those materials in the memory of herself as a girl even as they became unfamiliar to her in the process of growing up.

*The names of the women in the study have been changed to protect their privacy.

Now that girl served as a touchstone for the woman she would become. Retracing her steps and finding in the girl a child she could rely on led Megan to the roots of her womanly strength.

When I described Megan's experience to the women at the retreat, it struck a resonant chord. One by one, they recalled what they'd been like at age nine and began to speak excitedly of their girlhood ventures. But melancholy followed on the heels of excitement as each in turn realized that she had early put this girl aside, replacing her vitality with feminine compliance. So compelling was these women's recognition of the girl—and her loss—that I began to wonder if other women in my study also traced their identities to such a child.

I raced home from the family compound and ripped through the files containing the narratives of my twenty subjects—and found the self-possessed, authentic girl embedded in each account. Woman after woman had unearthed the memory of the girl, not as we embarked on her life story but rather as she described the crises of adulthood. All of a sudden, the "girl within" appeared to be more than a fluke.

Who is the girl within? What deep truth does she possess? Poised between the make-believe of preschool and the thrall of adolescence, the eight- to ten-year-old occupies an intermediate zone of childhood, a space between fantasy and reality that fosters creative self-ownership.[2] A child of eight enjoys a wholeness of self, a unity with the cosmos, a natural radiance—the unity and radiance of the golden ball that appears in so many fairy tales.[3] Nature and society conspire to allow a girl to flourish, and harmony and integrity abound. Playful yet purposeful, girls of this age have opened the gate to the age of reason. Practically old hands at school, they are already reading and calculating, playing group games, acquiring athletic skills, and absorbing the rules of their young society. The rapid development of a girl's mind, the acceleration of her know-how, the shift in the way she thinks at this time,[4] are acknowledged by cultures and religions around the world.

At nine, Megan was confirmed in the Catholic church, as her account reminds us. She was expected to appropriate a set of principles she herself had learned and considered. When she has the good fortune to grow up in a family that encourages her independence and applauds her achievements, a girl this age meets the world with confidence. A soaring imagination combines with competence and adventurous longing to take her far from home, in both imagination and reality.

Although dwarfed by the likes of Huckleberry Finn in a literature rife with daring boys, a scattering of such adventurous girls survive in children's books. Among fictional girls this age, Louise Fitzhugh's Harriet the Spy is most inventive.[5] Unfettered by feminine convention, Astrid Lindgren's wacky Pippi Longstocking embodies an essential "girl."[6] Claudia Kinkead, in *From the Mixed-Up Files of Mrs. Basil E. Frankweiler*, while far saner, is both clever and free: she runs away from home with a younger brother and goes to live secretly at the Metropolitan Museum of Art, where they explore the mysterious sculpture of the school of Michelangelo and endeavor to prove that it is really his.[7] With astonishing competence Claudia sees to feeding herself and James, finds an ancient bed in the museum to sleep in, and above all works out a way to elude the night watchman on his rounds. Ruth (see Chapter 8) led that sort of interior life. More out of sheer necessity than to pursue adventure, she teamed up with her brother and took her authentic identity underground to elude a malevolent mother. "My mother is not a lady around whom one would wish to be vulnerable. If you let a chink show, the arrows were poised. If you complained, she went straight for the jugular. I put my vulnerability away early because it was a suicidal act to have it out in her presence." Hiding from her mother as Claudia hid from the night watchman, Ruth protected her vulnerability—and preserved her integrity—in the vault of her authentic personality. There, with the help of her brother and her brains, she sustained, nurtured, and protected herself until she could grow up.

Ten-year-old Lucinda in Ruth Sawyer's *Roller Skates* goes to live with two able but slightly loopy maiden teachers while her parents take a European cure.[8] Stripped of family, Lucinda creates new relations among the people she comes to know while skating: the driver, a policeman, and a Russian émigré who will become a famous violinist. She renews her connection to an uncle who invites her into Shakespeare's plays. While her bemused guardians watch her make her willful, exuberant way, uselessly admonishing themselves to put her on a shorter tether, Lucinda has the talent and good fortune to explore the world and herself. When her parents do return, she puts on good clothes and proper manners—secretly coveting her brilliant year. One almost finds her in the history of Willa, a writer in this study (see Chapter 6), who left her rural beginnings in the 1930s at just about the time *Roller Skates* was published. Intent on exploring the big cities, she navigated as a single woman when doing so required the courage to depart from convention.

Born at the edge of the American frontier in an uncivilized Wisconsin of the 1860s, Carol R. Brink's character Caddie Woodlawn is a noble heroine.[9] She begins in frail health; a sister of hers has died. Her father, determined that Caddie will live, wrests her from the world of hearth and home. He lets her run in all weathers out-of-doors with her robust brothers. She gains not only a strong body but a new independence of mind and an outreaching spirit. Caddie depends on that strength of spirit when spirit and strength count greatly. The white settlers of the region, believing rumors of an Indian plot to wipe them out, plan a first strike. Caddie knows the Indians as friends. Their leader, John, has fed her and shown her Indian ways. Just before the settlers' attack, Caddie steals away from home on horseback, rides through the snow, crosses the river over perilously thin ice, and at last reaches the Indian encampment. She warns John with words and sign language that he must take his people into hiding. He in turn escorts her back home, an equally dangerous deed, and there gains her father's promise that there will be no attack. Caddie is eleven, still a girl in the terms of this work, for she is not as yet bound into feminine conventions.

Jillian (see Chapter 7) was a father's girl like Caddie. Her mother died when she was three; her father remarried when she was eight. Rejected by her stepmother, she was turned out of the house at dawn to fend for herself. Undefeated by these circumstances, she took a fishing rod her father had fashioned for her and headed down to the beach. There she clambered out onto a big rock in the middle of the lagoon to fish for herring. A lone European and the only girl on the New Zealand beach, she was not entirely alone: Maori fishermen observed her and came to teach her how to catch what she was after. Ultimately Jillian gained an inroad into the native culture and through fishing learned patience and freedom, qualities that she would rediscover in midlife, when she moved to China for a year.

These examples are not meant to cast all girls this age out of the same adventurous mold, for surely they are as various as people of any age or either gender. In fact, children's literature is sodden with pretty, perfect, useless girls. We all know passive, will-less girls rendered inert by a host of deprivations—familial or social. Helen (in Chapter 4), for instance, was destroyed by divorce at age thirty-five. She was unable to find the autonomous, eager child of her past to bring strength to her present catastrophe, perhaps because that child was never allowed to exist. The deep pessimism of Helen's adult life may have been a resounding echo of the whisper of a hopeless childhood. But competence, imagination, and strength of character may find a way to surface in a girl even when her childhood is treacherous, as it was for many in the chapters of this book. And apart from those with either adventurous or difficult beginnings lie still other sorts of girls: chatty social runabouts; docile, dreamy introverts; athletes driven toward Olympic goals; little mothers nursing any orphaned nestling. All abound in American culture.

A completely different sort of girl is the little coquette. She can't wait to wear lipstick, put on high heels, paint her fingernails, and seduce boys. Childhood seems wasted on her, a mere dressing room for adolescence—that wondrous, ghastly stage on which the child's voice grows faint while the clamor of the tribe thrums her into a manic chorus of conformity. And yet the coquette is herself creative and smart; she may do as well at putting together a sexy little costume as her more androgynous contemporary does in building a tree house. She ardently studies her subject matter—romance, clothes, make-up—with a thoroughness that would render a scholar wobbly with envy. If she gives herself over to female ruses at the expense of honoring herself, however, she is likely to lose her identity in a wash of female empathy, as Carol (Chapter 8) did when she found herself playing mistress to a series of dependent men. If she aspires to co-quetry but does not have what it takes, she may despair of expressing any of her femininity. That's what happened to Jo (Chapter 7) when she realized as she started school that the syndrome she'd been born with made her ugly.

Citronella in Elizabeth Enright's *Thimble Summer* is a toned-down fictional version of the coquette.[10] Utterly at one with her ro-mantic destiny, she has a pal of another type, Garnet. Citronella's best friend and the central figure in the book, Garnet works in the fields with her father and brother. Her daily rounds take her to school, to the library, and often to the tree house she has built herself. There she and Citronella make up stories. Citronella's are of pretty girls wooed by handsome princes. Garnet's are of wild animals and ex-plorers breaking trails in new lands. When Garnet's brother Jay tells her she must stop doing men's work on the farm and start to help her mother in the kitchen, Garnet cries, "Mean Jay!" Such a forthright outburst might have empowered Sophie (Chapter 6), protecting her from the female confines of her era. Instead it took decades of stag-nation before despair impelled Sophie to "burst out of the vise" she had been caught in, to find "the inner soul of a person"—through a suicide attempt.

True-to-life Birdie of Lois Lenski's *Strawberry Girl* is luckier in being urged to do the very things she wishes to do—planting, tending, harvesting, and selling beautiful, juicy strawberries.[11] She hasn't Garnet's playfulness, for her imaginative life has had to make way for respectability. Her family is too bent to the struggle to civilize a patch of land to care much for flights of fancy. But Birdie also loves school and learning. Her competence at home and school grows in one long, upward sweep. Katherine (Chapter 3) was just such a girl. Although her family was as privileged as Birdie's is bereft, as a girl she ate lunch out of the garden too. When she grew up, she tended her children just as she was tended, cultivating the gardens of their personalities.

Some girls, clipped and bookish, spend this era sharpening their wits, committing their experiences to memory, a treasury to draw on throughout their adult lives. Eudora Welty must have been this kind of girl. She wrote of her free-ranging fourth-grade independence in *One Writer's Beginnings*: " 'Through the Capitol' was the way to go to the Library. You could glide through it on your bicycle or even coast through on roller skates, though without family permission. I never knew anyone who'd grown up in Jackson without being afraid of Mrs. Calloway, our librarian. . . . My mother was not afraid of Mrs. Calloway. She wished me to have my own library card to check out books for myself. She took me in to introduce me and I saw I had met a witch. 'Eudora is nine years old and has my permission to read any book she wants.' . . . So two by two, I read library books as fast as I could go, rushing them home in the basket of my bicycle." And later, "Of course the greatest confluence of all is that which makes up the human memory—the individual human memory. My own is the treasure most dearly regarded. . . . I am a writer who came of a sheltered life. A sheltered life can be a daring life as well. For all serious daring starts from within."[12]

In her memories of childhood, author Annie Dillard recalled this as a period sharply demarcated from her heedless earlier years: "Children ten years old wake up," she wrote in *An American Childhood*, "and find themselves here, discover themselves to have been here all along. . . . They wake like sleepwalkers, in full stride . . . like people brought back from cardiac arrest or from drowning, . . . surrounded by familiar people and objects, equipped with a hundred skills. They know the neighborhood, they can read and write English, they are old hands at the commonplace mysteries, and yet they feel themselves to have just stepped off the boat, just converged with their bodies, just flown down from a trance, to lodge in an eerily familiar life already well under way."[13]

Rosabeth, a thirty-year-old woman in this study, was such a Renaissance girl. She has drawn on her store of girlhood skills for a lifetime. She captured this girlhood experience when she recalled an inner dialogue at age eight that is nearly identical to Megan's recollection at age nine: "I remember I had a wonderful childhood. I was popular and I loved people, I loved the world, and I loved school—and everything was just terrific. And I remember going out of the third-grade classroom and standing right beside a pear tree. It must have been spring. I was talking to God, and I said, 'I know I have a choice, I can stay eight always,' and that was my feeling, that I could. And I said to God, 'I know that I will never be as happy as I am now. Everything is perfect, but I want to keep going. I want to get older than eight.' I can remember that so distinctly.

"My model of happiness then was that I was good at absolutely everything. I was interested in almost everything I knew about. I was a kind of Renaissance eight-year-old, if you will. I had no weak subjects, including recess and sports! That, for me, was equated with happiness. The seeds of self-ownership were there."

Rosabeth too lost herself in the process of growing up—despite her girlhood confidence. But she too reclaimed her girl within. She said of her adult identity: "It came from the child I had been. I'm not quite as happy as I was when I was eight, but I'm so close. And my satisfactions come from the same kinds of things—knowing a lot about subject matters, the way things work, enjoying a lot of people, being well-liked. Doing things well, being active. Being in touch with nature. I really have to say that I was a very wise eight-year-old."

What waylays the girl within? What becomes of her élan? How is her self-ownership negated? How do we lose our grip on the self-possessed, playful, purposeful girl as we grow up?

Although there is no single experience of girlhood, the scores of women I have talked with give a surprisingly uniform account of growing up and losing her. They recall this girl as one who can finally make the world her own. Liberated at last from the confines of the family, she is proud of her newfound ability to order and direct her life. It is at this age that a girl gets her first wristwatch, sets her own alarm clock, chooses her clothes in the morning, packs her own lunch.

A tomboy at heart, this girl has many capabilities and is superbly competent. The faster she can run, the higher she can jump, the more she is admired. Being a girl is secondary to being an athlete, a wizard at word games.[14] Sharpshooter and ballet dancer, spelling champion and botanist, applauded for being both smart and strong, she is a mistress of excellence.

Even if her circumstances are limited, a girl this age can aspire to far-reaching objectives in her imagination—an inner realm no one else is privy to. There, if nowhere else, her ambitions are boundless; anything is possible. Contradictions do not deter her: Future lawyer and archaeologist, she will practice law during the winter and go on digs when summer comes. Rancher and junior astronomer, she will tend the flock by day and watch the stars by night. The night sky is wide, her horizons broad. Would-be oceanographer, explorer, astronaut—she is, ideally, supported in her future vision of herself. Even if she lacks the support of others, her goals are rarely subject to criticism; her choices do not yet include losses. Only later will her interests begin to matter and to count; only later will one choice preclude another. Heady with the power that comes from genuine competence, she brims with initiative. A sense of well-being permeates her experience. Unfettered by feminine conventions, a real-life Pippi Longstocking, she can think, she can plan, she can do.

Now as never before, her parents recognize how very different she is from the little girl she was at four or five. They support her independence, encourage her unfettered freedom. Impressed with her self-reliance, they no longer restrict her to the household. Her mother, in fact, breathes a sigh of relief as the opposition of the preschool years—an opposition she is bound to encounter again when her daughter becomes adolescent—ebbs away. If the girl is the couple's youngest child, her father may now reclaim his wife's attention, as she takes a long-awaited respite from the immediacy of mothering.

Her father, in fact, is this girl's special ally. Ideally, he provides her with the nuts and bolts that support her feeling of being "in business for herself."[15] Ideally, he helps extend her ambitions and interests into the future, giving form and credence to her dreams: if she is intent on charting the heavens, he gives her a telescope; if she aspires to medicine, he borrows an anatomy book from a doctor friend.

Paradoxically, this is the time in a female's life when she is most likely to be allied with her father yet *least defined by the patriarchy.* For this short period, the culture permits her respite from its construction of the female. Liberated from feminine constraints, her world encompasses male and female, work and play, independence and dependence—without subordinating either to the other. At the center of a universe in perfect harmony, she is master of her destiny, captain of her soul. She is, in short, the subject of her own experience.

But suddenly, well before puberty, along comes the culture with the pruning shears, ruthlessly trimming back her spirit. Adults who left the girl to her own devices anticipate her blossoming femininity and nip her expansion in the bud. As the culture draws the line between little and big, play and work, female and male, its agents feel, despite themselves, obliged to intervene. Old templates of female as nurturer persist, making a girl's boundless initiative threatening. Too often, the teacher who applauded the ambitious archaeologist warns that archaeology requires five languages. The little rancher given a lasso for her birthday is informed, in the gentlest way perhaps, that only men are cowboys. The anatomy book that affirmed her interest in medicine is subtly replaced with a nurse's watch suitable for taking a pulse, as parents who indulged her scientific aspirations suddenly uproot them. Once tolerated as inconsequential, the little girl's projections of herself into adulthood are now unwelcome. Her elders deflate her "grandiose" ideas, deem them unrealistic. Myriad ways are found to pinch the girl back and shape her.

Conformity marks the era of the older girl, in spite of changing times. Seldom permitted to be a tomboy once her features begin to change, she is expected, even now, to "behave like a young lady." Taken out of the tree house of her earlier days, the girl is turned to the human environment and expected to cultivate social graces. The feminine mandate to care for others persists beneath the modern whitewash, stifling her impulse to climb, to run, to scale a ridge— and to otherwise follow her active pursuits. Whereas her childhood competence knew no bounds, her feminine effectiveness is channeled into the interpersonal realm as she approaches puberty. In this realm, where little is under direct control, muddled feedback clouds her clarity; the pure effects of her actions grow dilute amid social nuance. While her brother is encouraged to flex his muscles and test his mettle, she is turned to feminine compliance. Previously abroad in the world of nature, the older girl must come inside.

As she trades her blue jeans for a skirt, her father, just yesterday her staunch supporter, pushes her out of his lap and draws back to let her mother take over again. Returned to the women's world, she is drawn into the "cave of womanly doings," as Liz of Chapter 9 put it. Even these days, her mother may subtly shape her activities to fit feminine stereotypes, training her daughter in the same roles that have defined *her* as wife and mother. The official culture—a patriar-

chal structure that places its lock on her mother, aunts, friends, teachers, *and* her father—defines her as female instead of as person. The
link between who she is and what she does is twisted. She gives up
"doing" in favor of "being" a good girl. Instead of suiting herself, she
tries to please those around her. Impressed with the importance of
others' opinions, she molds herself to what she thinks they want her
to be.

The girl-world of eight or nine thus gives way, long before adolescence, to a world divided by sex. The skills that assured her place
among peers now jeopardize a girl's popularity; a sinewy body, im-
pressive height, and forceful strength belong to the males. Sexual
dichotomies divide a girl against herself by labeling her abilities and
interests as unfeminine.

Rosabeth remembers at age thirty how the opposition between
"femininity" and her active girlhood doings operated to rob her of
what she treasured—even before she became a teenager: "I was a
tomboy when I was a kid. I climbed trees all the time. I used to
collect snakes and I loved dissecting frogs. I was always good in sports.
By fifth grade, these things were, on the whole, not true of girls:
they were considered masculine. The sense of adventure, too, was
associated with masculinity. The things I always liked got to be associated with being a boy. It made me embarrassed to be a girl."

As the male-female division sets in, a girl searches out the lives
of women in the course of her everyday doings, and sizes up their
status. Turning the pages of her schoolbooks, she still finds few females. Nearly invisible except as nurturers or sexual beings, women
have been virtually absent from the annals of science, history, politics,
the arts. Even in contemporary studies, a girl finds a dearth of women
who count. Men run the world's businesses, hospitals, schools. Where
are the female pilots, oceanographers, astronomers, governors, neu-
rosurgeons, judges?

While she may be determined, initially, to change all that, a girl
herself has second thoughts as she notes the consequences of worldly
ambition to women she may know. Too often the female doctor lacks
husband and children; the executive aunt may be similarly alone.
There is a crimp in the womanly life of women she admires; independent women with careers are suddenly sensed as incomplete. A
girl's ambition is tempered with uncertainty as she realizes that for
a female, achievement has its costs. When the uselessness of what
she learns becomes increasingly apparent, her schooling becomes
"pseudo-schooling,"[16] her goals become "as if." The once harmonious

consonance between inner choices and outer action is riddled with conflict. No longer free to project herself into the future with the egocentrism natural to her age, she works to curb her competence. Competition intensifies the conquests of her brother; in her it yields to compromise.[17] Competence enhances the male; it still desexes the female.*

An exuberant athlete at age nine, many a girl is a careful young lady at eleven, as female appendages begin to intrude on pure physical prowess: unwieldy breasts, broadening hips, softening contours clutter the taut, streamlined body of her androgynous youth. No matter how proud she may be of "becoming a woman," bodily changes hamper a girl's freedom and weaken the confidence she earlier placed in her physical skills. With a girl's earlier puberty comes a lag in growth; with a boy's comes an increase in mass. As he catches up to and surpasses her in height, weight, and muscular force, the boy, for the first time, is bigger and stronger than she. Her body softens while his hardens. As he gets stronger, smarter, louder, she feels weaker and less certain. The boy's pubertal changes portend an increased ability to dominate; the girl's imply, recurrently, the mandate to nurture and the need for restraint. His experience of adolescence is one of increased power; hers is one of increased risk. His freedoms are dramatically expanded while hers are curtailed. He is encouraged to explore; she, cautioned about her feminine vulnerability, is expected to stay close by. He is urged on while she is coerced: diminutive in comparison to her male age-mate, she can no longer fend off an attack. For him, new lands are filled with conquest; for her, safety resides at home. The world is his oyster; it holds dangers for her.

The older girl succumbs to the culture's image of the female: object to the male subject. Her childhood displays give way to hiding—skills, excellence, aspirations—first from others in order to please, eventually also from herself. The unity of her activities falls away as her own goals are cast against a "womanly" life. Female roles impinge; stereotypes take over. A young girl projecting herself into the future can't help but feel caught by contradictory imperatives: even as she dons her soccer uniform, ads for Dry Idea deodorant implore her to "never let them see you sweat."[18] Self-confidence yields

*This effect of competence, noted decades ago by Margaret Mead, appears still to operate as it did then. A 1987 cover on *Savvy* magazine proclaims that success makes a woman sexy, but the article concludes that in women, competence and power deflate a man. The author, a psychologist who specializes in human sexuality, advises a woman to do her best to hide her abilities and feign "submission" if she wants a fulfilling sexual relationship.

to self-consciousness as a girl judges herself the way others judge her—against an impossible feminine ideal. To match that ideal, she must stash away a great many parts of herself. She gives up being natural in order to be compliant. She loses her position as self; she senses that she is now "other."

In the grand scheme of things, a girl, even these days, has little choice but to take her place as a member of the "second sex," as Simone de Beauvoir named it nearly forty years ago.[19] Ironically, what de Beauvoir wrote still stands: despite the latest wave of the feminist movement, females of all ages are objectified and devalued. Advertising has multiplied the legion invitations to exploit a woman's sensuality, whether by eating yogurt, by drinking a fine liquor, or by flying away to vacation on an island beach. Yuppie watering holes to which a woman may repair after work offer up dazzling concoctions with such names as "Silk Panties." In fact, females are increasingly sexualized—at a shockingly young age. Alongside vampish women in black lace teddies and French-cut bikinis, department-store catalogs feature seven-year-old girls modeling satiny tap pants and camisoles, their little faces oddly provocative when made up with cherry rouge and lipstick. These girl-sirens are impelled to develop into adolescent *femme fatales*. Contained, adapted, and sexualized long before adolescence, a girl is cowed and tamed as her natural spontaneity gives way to patriarchal constructions of the female. In donning the masks provided by the culture, a girl easily loses sight of who and what she is beneath the feminine facade she adopts in youth.

Once I unearthed the vital girl beneath this feminine facade and became attuned to the childhood identity a female is estranged from in the process of growing up, the phenomenon of the girlhood self, lost and reclaimed, began to crop up all around me. A senior Jungian analyst, for instance, took her journey back to the age of eight, when she would sneak out the bedroom window at 3:00 A.M., while it was still dark, take a knapsack with two eggs and some bread, and go upriver a couple of miles. There she pretended to be a primitive woman: she would heat a flat stone with fire, fry the eggs, and "in a ritual manner" eat them. The memory of this repeated solitary adventure became the central metaphor for her life and work.

A contemporary of hers recalled how she and her twin brother used to hunt rattlesnake bladders on an expansive ranch where she grew up. The Chinese cook used them in recipes, and paid the children a dollar apiece for their bounty. At age eighty this analyst and writer assigned herself the task of protecting the ranch and all its animal inhabitants, including clusters of rattlesnakes that might otherwise be disturbed by visitors. Of the hundred-acre parcel she still owned, she wrote: "I am respectful of it in its wild state and consider myself its steward."[20]

A scholar of the same vintage repudiated marriage in her youth, claiming that she'd gotten her role model at age nine, when she was called Hypatia.[21] Hypatia was a famous mathematician in Alexandria during the Hellenistic age who refused suitors because she was wedded to the truth. The scholar, like her namesake, stuck with her virgin orientation throughout life, dedicating herself to the realm of the intellect.

A pediatrician in my study, skeptical of my doctoral findings, on hearing of its new thesis led me to Lynne Sharon Schwartz's *Disturbances in the Field,* a book in which the dream recollection of the nine-year-old rescues the protagonist from a siege of alienation when that rescue is urgently needed.[22] An editorial assistant in charge of a review I wrote linking the girl within to that book called to say that merely typing the review on a word processor had sent her back to a girlhood memory that provided an anchoring image.[23] An associate who initially rejected the notion of the girl within found herself mailing a photo to her homesick daughter at college. The snapshot was of the daughter and a friend dressed up as fortune-tellers ready to perform magic for lucky passersby. It was taken when they were eight. A psychotherapist who had passed off my thesis as inconsequential was suddenly disabled by an injury. Flat on her back for six weeks, she took up pencil and paper and started idly sketching. Only when an entire line of women's clothing she produced from those drawings was purchased by a major shop did she recall that she had first made fashion sketches as a third grader.

A sociology professor married for over twenty years put me in mind of Dante's Beatrice when she confided that her husband, some years older than she, had first seen and fallen in love with her from afar when she was exactly nine. A new neighbor told me that her nine-year-old daughter had made up a story called "What Is Girl?" Divorced women in my counseling practice spontaneously offered, with relief, that being on their own had led them back to the girl they'd been in the first place—before they got tangled up in male-female relationships. A *Ms.* magazine article on Marilyn Monroe suggested that in the girl she'd been and left behind lay the irretrievable loss of Marilyn herself.[24]

A psychologist I met at a health club had recently taken up skiing and white-water rafting at age forty—recapturing the athlete she'd been at ages eight and nine. Camp counselors swore by girls this age, ruing the day they were assigned to the older girls instead. And when I told people about the girl within, in a mere few sentences she rang true. At last I realized that I had found in this girl a piece of the truth. Rediscovering the girl within appears to be the key to women's identity.

2

MEN'S THEORIES, WOMEN'S LIVES

ichael and Alan Post sat down and continued the conversation they had enjoyed in the study," Doris Lessing wrote of a British woman lunching with her husband and his colleague in *The Summer Before the Dark.* "She poured the coffee into the pretty plastic cups she had used in the garden ever since next door's dog had bounced through in pursuit of another dog and had smashed a whole tray full of her best china. Having handed them coffee and chocolate wafers, she set an attentive smile on her face, like a sentinel, behind which she could cultivate her own thoughts. . . . She had, as they say, 'worked' on that smile, or on the emotions it represented."[1]

Many a contemporary American woman, excluded from worldly matters that occupy the talk of men, retreats like Lessing's woman behind an absent smile, taking her own thoughts with her. Thus protected from the very social conventions that force it out of view, her inner world becomes, with time, ever more her own. More than an amusement, it provides her with sustenance: its characters, animated by her unique creativity, readily engage her. Their intimate conversations about the personal, the close at hand, include her. They draw her into a human intrigue, where together they hash out in private earthly matters of personal consequence while the gears of society turn obliviously around them. And like a play within a play, both the outer drama and the subtext that works beneath it are "real." The workings of this inner realm and its coexistence with outer realities lie at the heart of a body of literature by feminist writers such as Lessing, and before her Virginia Woolf, writers who have been concerned with how the inner life of women has been hidden by a compliant facade.

Recently, scholars seeking the keys to women's psychology have begun to regard the inner realm as *the* realm worthy of study. A pioneer in this effort, analyst Jean Baker Miller, claims that only by exploring this realm can we understand women, as it alone can carry validity in a culture women do not themselves shape. Social scientists are coming to recognize that studying the manifest behavior of any subordinate group is futile when the task at hand is understanding the psychology of the individual. Those determined to decipher women's psychology are veering away from that study and turning instead toward what emerges as woman's sphere of freedom: inner consciousness.[2] If remnants of female authenticity are to survive, that is where they will be harbored.

A woman does not easily gain access to this authentic inner realm, the realm that is free from the patriarchal construction of who and what a woman should be. She must break through a crust of negative evaluations of the feminine in order to reach it at all. These evaluations affect her self-concept in a profoundly damaging way, even if she is a contemporary woman of accomplishment. Yet it is in this realm that a female is free to be the subject of her experience. It was precisely by delving into this realm that I came to understand women's experience and began to perceive the unusual facts of women's identity.

Identity is hardly a new topic. Erik Erikson put it in the spotlight in the 1950s, theorizing then that crystallizing a sense of self is the central task of adolescence. He asserted that successfully resolving the identity crisis of youth depends on striking out alone, taking an independent stand, and making an individual commitment to ideals that set one apart from others. This critical accomplishment between boyhood and manhood is a necessary forerunner to mastering the demands of adulthood: intimacy depends, in Erikson's view, on grasping and holding a firm, autonomous self.[3]

Although it is seldom acknowledged, Erikson's seminal work on identity, like the search of Lessing's protagonist and the women in this study, was borne of personal struggle. Himself the victim of confused origins, Erikson learned in his youth that the man he knew as his father was actually his stepfather. With no way to identify his biological father, he embarked on a search for identity that led him far from his beginnings. An artist on the move in Europe, he came to work with Anna Freud as World War II approached. That war focused on genetic roots, raising Erikson's individual preoccupation with biological origins to a grand scale. As artist turned psychoanalyst, Erikson dropped the surname he'd acquired from his stepfather, because it was not his own. Building on the stem of his first name, he replaced his "family" name with Erikson. In the act of remaining himself, he essentially fathered himself.[4] His extended personal search became the basis for an entire identity theory—a theory that has been applied to males and females alike.

In taking the individual male's experience as his object of study and presuming the universality of what he found, Erikson carried forward a pattern set by Sigmund Freud. Freud's psychological scheme also revolved around the dynamic tension between father and son: he based his personality theory on the oedipal conflict—the quintessential male drama. Freud himself once admitted that what he was describing was the psychology of the male, whose development depends on separation from the mother.[5] The boy accomplishes independence by identifying with his father and adhering to the patriarchal rule of the culture. Although Freud garnered material for his monumental theory primarily from the accounts of female patients, he was frankly flummoxed by women—"what oh what does a woman want?"

Undeterred by his dismay, Freud abstracted female psychology from that of the male. Apparently unaware that embryologically at least human beings begin by being female, he concluded that a girl's task during the oedipal phase—a spectacular misnomer that fails to account even for her gender—is to renounce the active masculinity he thought characterized infants of both sexes. Evidently Freud considered this shift so demanding that the female could not avoid being spent in the process. Thus he conceptualized development in terms of male norms and female deficiencies—and pronounced women inferior in maturity.[6]

The single developmental outline drawn by these forefathers of psychology still holds sway in Western culture—as does its regressive portrayal of women. Freud's sense that women are by nature immature crops up often in our society, finding a myriad of manifestations that have become the just target of the feminist movement. Erikson's man striking out on his own is likewise ubiquitous in a plethora of popular images of heroic quest. In the absence of direct evidence about the experience of females, the notion that men are by themselves mature and women somehow lacking does still persist.

Although I had reason to be skeptical about the applicability to women of these peculiarly phallocentric models when I began this study, I had no alternative scheme of identity to put in their place. Erikson's diagonal chart gives the identity struggle of adolescence a continuous upward sweep that holds a certain simple appeal. Extensions of that trajectory into adulthood have suggested that identity follows a linear progression at least through middle age.[7] I perhaps unwittingly shared the assumption that identity, rudimentary and amorphous when life begins, is thrown into turmoil during adolescence, resolved via separation during youth, and accumulated in a linear manner that is expanded with age and experience. I had not formulated any contrary notion about how a self might come into being and then endure. It was only as I began to ask women about their development and heard them explain how they had "gotten" a self that I first came upon the remarkable pattern that challenges these assumptions.

The identity pattern these women trace flies in the face of psychology's simple assertions. The circular shape they give to female identity development counters the linear lockstep Erikson posits. Instead of crystallizing an identity during adolescence, women as adults reach back to girlhood to retrieve an original sense of self. Each woman's identity—the identity each felt was authentic, real, and true to who and what she was—had been present, intact, in the earliest part of her life and had in the meantime been obscured. While the details differed and the discontinuity varied among them, every woman who described the development of her identity spoke of the striking phenomenon of circling back to a self obscured and reclaimed.

As women described how they had struggled to "become the person you really are," as Willa in Chapter 6 put it, the reasons such a seemingly simple task had proved so thorny began to come to light. Some of them were no surprise: women who reached adulthood before the second wave of the feminist movement had subordinated their development to that of their husbands. Being confined to nurturant roles in the private, domestic domain had in effect (if not in intent) obscured their own identities. But beyond this obvious explanation, women's life histories contained more hidden factors to account for the eclipse of female identity. Many in the study found that tuning in early to cultural expectations of females had led them to displace the essence of who and what they were. Often it was women's subordination to impossible feminine ideals imposed by a patriarchal culture that interfered with the process of becoming themselves. While girls, many tried for prolonged periods to reshape who and what they were to suit others' expectations.[8] Some, despairing at their failure to be perfectly attuned to others, deliberately "hid" the "true self."[9]

In exposing these vicissitudes, these women informed not only the divergent course of female identity but also illuminated the double-edged character of relationships in human development. Just as crisis holds potential for growth as well as danger, these women showed how, besides imposing a threat to identity, relationships could serve as the vehicle for its restoration. Some who were damaged early by matching themselves to the images and needs of more powerful others later recovered their lost self through uncommon relationships of a particular sort: those in which they could shed compliance and express themselves as full and equal partners. The developmental gain such women made when they reclaimed the natural self of girlhood was startling indeed. Their narratives inform our view of what otherwise might appear to be "a meandering feminine process,"[10] charting female identity development according to relationships.

But relationships are strangely absent from the psychological picture that focuses on a single developmental end point: separation. The one official map we use to chart collective human progress portrays the journey of the solitary male; independence is the destination toward which he travels singly. The male bias this psychology carries exerts a continuing press on the evolution of our psychological theories—a handicap that has not only made women appear deficient but also skewed psychological concepts of human development.[11]

How is it that we have polarized the human agenda, lionizing separation and independence, leaving out, entirely, meaningful connections between people and the human capacities for intimacy, empathy, care, and compassion?

Our alignment with the "male" side of the human duality no doubt draws its power from American ideals, picking up in psychological theory a national history that hinges on independence.[12] Our country came into being through a dramatic series of defiant acts masterminded by a band of rebellious men intent on resisting collective demands. Had those men been bound to the motherland by their attachments and unwilling to cut old ties, there would have been no New World. But they galvanized a break with their homeland and succeeded in establishing themselves anew an ocean away from their native soil.

Considering that our country was given birth by violent rupture, it is not by chance that separation and independence reign supreme in our national identity. These individual values upon which our country was founded can be directly linked to our political origins. The Declaration of Independence and the Bill of Rights date our history as a nation. The body of knowledge generated by Freud, Erikson, and many other psychologists who studied males and formulated their work along the vectors of separation and autonomy resonates with the ideals this culture captures. But this consonance between American ideals and psychological theory wreaks havoc with our concept of maturity.

The trouble is that we have taken the ideals that brought this country into being beyond their use in establishing the autonomy of the nation and made them into values that define individual maturity. Setting oneself apart from others has become an end in itself rather than the pivot between the dependence of childhood and the intimate commitment of adulthood that Erikson may have intended. The psychology we have settled on holds independence paramount. A maturational bench mark, independence quickly formed the basis for a standard against which developmental progress and mental health have been and still are commonly measured—to the detriment of women. Against this monolithic standard, women appear anomalous and immature. The lack of fit between women's relatedness[13] and the stark independence this standard prescribes, when it is explained at all, is explained by women's developmental deficit or deviation from the norm.[14]

Circling back to girlhood to catch hold of an original identity raises an important question about lack of fit—one that seems to beg this negative explanation. But the particular criterion for women who were subjects in my study makes that explanation unlikely, for these women were selected specifically for psychological maturity.* And although it has been common practice in the field to consider "immature" those who do not sort out who and what they are well before

*See Chapter 12 for a description of the subjects and methodology of the study.

adulthood, implying immaturity in those who don't "succeed" at this task, that claim cannot be given to the women in my study. How is it then that their experience stands at odds with established theory?

Perhaps the root of the discrepancy lies not in women's developmental deficit or deviation from the norm but rather in the myriad cultural and historical forces that put individual autonomy at the center of the American picture and narrow its psychological definition. The events that brought our country into being—separating from the homeland, declaring independence, and staking claims to territory—continue to define our national character. This political history has given rise to individualistic values that underlie the national heritage, permeate social conventions, and pervade the social sciences. These "male" values are by no means universal goals. For instance, even the earliest training of the Japanese aims at interdependence, a functional "feminine" ideal that structures the Japanese culture, which stresses the symbolic unity of mother and child.[15] But American society is built upon "masculine" standards that prescribe a psychological ethic in which independence is the end point of maturing rather than simply one of a number of qualities that play a part in psychological development.

Psychoanalyst Jean Baker Miller recasts as strengths "feminine" aspects of development that our culture has deemed weaknesses—vulnerability, emotionality, and attachment[16]—aspects of the human agenda that, when included in our psychological concepts, are relegated to the feminine, ascribed to infancy, and swept into the background, where they are made, at best, mere points of departure. Such trivialization forces us to peer at attachment through a tiny window that can only blind us to the value of the matrix of ties that sustain us throughout life. Perhaps the mistake comes in part from associating so-called feminine traits with weaknesses that threaten true autonomy. By confusing care and dependence, by mistaking emotionality for irrationality, by coupling care and emotionality, and by fastening dependence to irrationality, we link positive human qualities with those that are taboo in American culture—and demean them.

By failing to give the lie to the culture's misconstrual of these dimensions as weak, by failing to distinguish the functions and characteristics of relationships—to say nothing of failing to examine the level of dependence or interdependence a particular relationship may reflect—we carry this bundle of misapprehensions forward to arrive at faulty standards for adulthood. Although challenges to male models of development have finally begun to come from feminist revisionists like Jean Baker Miller, and we are increasingly aware of the consequences to the planet of the devaluation of "feminine" values,[17] the male bias that permeates our developmental picture continues to distort human experience.

Contemporary experts on development are hardly immune from the cultural bias that has polarized femininity and maturity over eons. Many of them deem women's lives too unimportant to warrant serious consideration, or find women's development simply an inferior shadow of that of men. As Carol Gilligan has pointed out, Erikson's contribution to adult development consists of psychobiographies of prominent men—George Bernard Shaw, William James, Martin Luther, and Mahatma Gandhi—to which he added an analysis of the relationship between Freud and Jung.[18] Many others charting the life course have followed Erikson's lead and that of Freud by limiting their studies to males. Daniel Levinson's *Seasons of a Man's Life*, which caught attention in the 1970s, builds on Erikson's grid, fixing men's development to the coordinates of work and age. This formulation and others like it (for example, George Vaillant's *Adaptation to Life*) are taken for models of human development despite the fact that they exclude fully half of humankind. They seem to underscore the presumption that male equals human and female equals something else.[19] Their insidious implication that the female is to be understood via the male can only function to take women away from a deeper sense of who and what they really are.

A handful of scholars has concluded that adhering to present paradigms can only obscure women's sense of self as subject and put it farther out of reach. Some (Marcia Westkott, Evelyn Fox Keller, and Marilyn Steele, for instance) make the radical claim that so-called objective scientific methods themselves work against this goal because they are a hoax born of an obsolescent manner of science. They insist that retaining and reifying the artificial distinction between subject and object intensifies the problem of woman as "other," object in a culture that takes man as its subject. In a wry comment that plays on Freud's assertion about women's penis envy, Mary Brown Parlee has tartly suggested that psychology appears to suffer from "physics envy," a complex that drives the field toward "ever 'harder' data and ever 'firmer' control."[20] She contends that the field must surrender its obsession with manipulation if it is to apprehend and explain female experience, because making objectivity the goal of science defeats understanding a "new" population such as women. Even the so-called hard sciences are giving up the myth of objectivity as we broach the new age in search of a new paradigm.[21] The body of official concepts nevertheless tilts us toward separation, tracing a linear path toward the single end point of independence and suggesting clearly that independence is achieved alone.

As this study begins to show, such constructs have their parallel in how women fare in "the real world," where these constructs meet in the naive psychology of women—and put women in harm's way. Only by taking a new tack and asking women themselves how they thought about their lives did I discover how pervasive—and how damaging—the culture's dichotomy of human qualities and its devaluation of feminine aspects can be. Analyzing their narratives suggests that female development varies from that of the male in valuable and important ways. In fact, a critical analysis of the cumulative, lockstep identity path that Erikson delineated suggests that only male identity can be built in a linear manner because only the boy's development is consonant with a patriarchal culture whose institutions bolster an independent and continuous sense of self.

But discontinuity has marked the personal history of the girl, as individual identity for the female works at cross-purposes to the needs of the patriarchal culture. First a dutiful daughter, a girl has been expected to please her father in a household organized around his needs, playing at her future role as wife and mother. A well-behaved student, she has learned material in school that has had no apparent relevance to her future feminine role in the households of America. While her brother has dreamed of a future as doctor, scientist, or politician, one who will command power through the exercise of his knowledge and skills, she has long been expected to cultivate a pleasing personality, social grace, and the cultural interests that will make her a model wife and mother. Helpful in this endeavor is keeping the body trim and shapely. Yet she must bid adieu to this well-tended figure with pregnancy, when her body undergoes a radical transformation unlike any in a man.

Her experience as a mother works against articulating an adult sense of self by demanding complete selflessness. After she has practiced that selflessness by putting the other—in this case the child—first for twenty years or more, her usefulness as a mother is exhausted, and so perhaps is she. Even with the changes the women's movement has wrought, contemporary culture still provides no role for the second half of a woman's adult life; and yet it expects her somehow to do more than simply stay intact. Expendable as a mother, she becomes inconsequential to society. Later it is worse: the "older woman" in America is certainly obsolete. Having organized her life around what Jean Baker Miller calls the reproductive capacities of the womb, she is lost.[22]

Suppose we assume that this woman is a figure from the past, that she has been made an anachronism by the women's movement. What is today's woman, an exponent of contemporary culture, all about?

Now that women's roles are up for grabs, Western culture is finally beginning to ask who and what a woman might be if defined as a person in her own right. The women's movement has revealed how womanly strengths have been bent to the needs and ends of others through the traditional roles of helpmate and mother, taking women away from delineating, affirming, and expressing the self. The movement, in fact, has made self-direction and self-reliance twin goals for women, turning them at last toward autonomy, competence, and assertion. But the culture has been hard-pressed to spell out how these goals, new to women, can be won on women's own terms. These days a man can still follow in his father's footsteps to exercise such timeworn "male" prerogatives, but the "new woman" cannot count on her mother's ways to carry her through. Caught in a peculiar historic moment, she turns away from a seemingly useless past to traverse unfamiliar territory, where she must make her own way with neither a map from her forebears nor the counsel of elders to guide her.

Having abided by social conventions that keep them domestically bound, women today are responding to a new cultural imperative to make their way into "the real world." Bridling against the power-lessness of household roles and beckoned by the worldly power men have attained, women turn against the domestic sphere and charge into the work arena, determined to possess that power. Impelled to put themselves into effect in a man's world, women clearly expect to acquire an independent sense of self in this domain. Lacking a female blueprint for doing so, however, the "new woman" is turning to male models for direction. Those models demand that she push womanly concerns to the sidelines, strip down to her competence, and outfit herself in corporate drag.

Contemporary culture appears to support her goals, opening the world of achievement to the new woman's challenge. But underneath this apparent liberation from old roles, a variety of forces makes the realization of her purposes unlikely, threatening to undercut her femininity and defeat the very self-realization she seeks. Although a woman may break into the corporate world, for example, dressed in and perhaps armored with her brother's style, that world curtails her impact. Rarely in a position to initiate projects or to determine the nature of her own work, a woman is expected to harness her skills to the agendas of others.

How might today's woman pursue her quest for recognition and independence at the edge of this new territory? Absent a female blueprint, where amid the army of corporate signposts erected by men might she lodge a feminine identity? And what is she to do with the legacy of traditional female roles in this quintessentially male realm?

Woman upon woman imagines she will address these questions by freeing herself from domestic drudgery and finding a role in the marketplace. But unless she is a token woman, her position at work is likely to reproduce the homey roles she carries out in the household. Her role as nurturer is often exploited on the job: she is the one sent to fetch coffee and sandwiches. Her domestic role as hostess is borrowed here too: she ingratiates herself by arranging conferences, securing the meeting place, providing hospitality, registering participants, and attending to housekeeping details, while her male counterpart is put to use on more "important" matters. Even when she is employed at the so-called professional level, if she belongs to one of the occupations traditionally held by women—teaching, nursing, counseling—she replicates the selflessness of motherhood by focusing on the needs of pupils, patients, or clients rather than by making her own mark.[23]

Women's work, whether it is carried out in the business world or managed within the household, holds no place in the hierarchical scheme of things. In both domestic and economic spheres, such work is laid out by others and its significance belittled. And in either sphere a woman is still tethered to lesser tasks; menial, routine jobs; mundane, tedious, unmeasured chores. More often than not, this means doing the company's scut work: receiving customers and clients, answering phones, taking dictation, typing an endless stream of letters. Furthermore, a woman coming of age today cannot expect soon to advance. According to the National Academy of Sciences, reversals made during the Reagan administration will keep females ensconced in low-paying jobs—dominated by women—for the foreseeable future.[24] As secretary, bookkeeper, waitress, and phone operator, a woman routinely does the bidding of others—for a mere seven-tenths of men's pay.

While women are in the work force in great numbers, leading to the appearance that things have changed, close examination reveals that they have changed merely in content, not in form. The present demand that women work outside the home is the flip side of the injunction that used to keep them out of the work force. The new woman's coin is not freshly forged of a different metal, for the dictum issued by the patriarchal culture remains the same: attend to the baser needs of the culture, whether it is the culture of the household or that of the workplace. The lack of true change is demonstrated by persistent reluctance to provide women access to positions of leadership, and condemnatory attitudes that typify a woman's experience when she seeks to be in charge.[25] Woman's rebellion against servility at home has taken her beyond its confines only in the narrowest sense.

Thus, the patriarchy is still operating to keep women in their place—formerly barefoot and pregnant, now in pointy-toed shoes at the typewriter.[26] Today's woman appears to be no more free to carve her niche in the real world *in her own way* than she was amid the stifling restrictions that prompted Betty Friedan to write *The Feminine Mystique* over twenty-five years ago. Freedom from those restrictions appears to be a pernicious illusion—pernicious in that virile retrogressive forces that brought the movement about now lie hidden in the guise of women's freedom. Misled by the appearance that things have changed, today's woman propels herself into the real world so fast that she does not realize that the culture directs, perhaps even dictates, her place there. Virtually obliged to take up residence in the "real world," the new woman unwittingly casts her lot with the patriarchy in the name of escaping it.

Seduced by a society that chases women into the workplace, today's woman is too often blamed for not being at home. Yet our society binds her to the domestic domain even as it forces her out of it: often a working mother holds a job only on the condition that her family life hums along smoothly. If she is to be taken seriously "at work," the superwife and supermother must keep private concerns out of the public arena. The impossibility of tending to both domains is made her personal problem: she gains entry to the one realm only at the expense of the other. With less apparent right to complain, many a woman blames herself for her dissatisfaction. Few can withstand the press of a culture that drives women "forward" toward success.

Unlike a "working father," unless a working mother has extraordinary means, she is condemned to limit her commitment to her work. And unless she has unusual power within the corporation, her investment in a family is likewise curtailed. She has little choice under these circumstances but to farm her children out to others—as once the patriarchy foisted them on her. The culture dishes up an all-or-nothing proposition, disguised as the chance to have it all: a female must forfeit family attachments for a career or forgo achievements that lie beyond the walls of the household. Given this forced choice, many a woman opts for a crack at the world of work, where she can express long-suppressed needs for autonomy and competence.

Work as she will, a woman's participation in the labor force fails to relieve her of the work of hearth and home. This responsibility women routinely shoulder without the recognition that it is important work.[27] In fact, women themselves neglect to realize that they have not escaped domestic chores by working, but rather have only added to them. Study after study shows that mothers who work outside the home are saddled with dual duty, carrying not only the responsibilities of housework and child care but also those of paid work. The new consciousness has had slight impact on the burden women carry: working wives evidently spend even more time at domestic chores than their single counterparts—leading to the surprising conclusion that having a husband adds to housework rather than reducing it.

For instance, a 1985 study of 651 employees at all levels of a Boston-based corporation found that the tasks required in their jobs plus homemaking and child care consumed nearly every waking hour employed mothers had. Married mothers spent eighty-five hours a week in these combined activities, compared with seventy-five hours a week spent by single mothers. Fathers spent only about sixty-five hours a week working on these combined endeavors, a full twenty hours a week less than working mothers. Likewise, childless men spent twenty hours a week less than single mothers, a total of fifty-five hours a week. This study and others like it conclude that while all working parents are under stress, the burden falls squarely on married mothers.[28]

Many a working mother finds herself not only trying to live up to these demands, but also jogging, lighting candles at the dinner table, and shopping for a sexy negligée so that she, on top of it all, will be sexually alluring and physically fit. Contrary to the media's idealized picture of the blithe integration of family and career, the vast majority of women find it impossible to do justice to both pursuits. Hobbled in either sphere, a woman who tries to master the two more often feels cheated than gratified.

Yet women clamor for freedom, and identify freedom with paid work. And in their single-minded pursuit of freedom, they are cutting off a distinct option that only a woman can exercise: having children. As the occupations of wife and mother have fallen into disrepute, especially for women who want to "matter,"* those who might find themselves perfectly suited to family life are relinquishing its rewards because that life has been trivialized by both patriarchal and feminist cultures. A woman who stays at home these days is thought of as "doing nothing," and women too, in bondage to both authorities, have been duped into discounting their work in the family domain. So affected by the devaluation of mothering are today's pacesetting women that many are embarrassed to admit they want a family. Even married women with advanced educations claim that their pregnancies are accidental.[29] The new denigration of the feminine seriously affects women coming of age today: college students are frankly terrified of going into occupations associated with nurturance, even when such occupations match their interests and skills. They avoid teaching, social work, nursing, and even pediatrics and psychiatry because these smack of "women's work." Whereas women in previous generations forfeited autonomy, members of this generation flee care and connection.

Working women who gather the courage to have families despite the culture's dismissal of mothering find themselves subject to corporate standards even in this female process. Here again women have been coerced by "male" values, the professional overtaking the personal and all but blotting it out. Helping women to disguise their pregnancy so that it will not interfere with "business" has itself become big business. Franchised chain stores with names such as "Mothers Work" specialize in supplying pregnant women with the obligatory corporate uniform. One of many ads for stores with this intent, titled "Today's Maternity," pictures a woman dressed in a dark suit, complete with a stiff white collar, "softened" by the usual corporate tie at the neck.[30] This ensemble presumably provides her the male dress she needs to navigate in a man's world even while she

*Ironically enough, the word *matter* has the same root as the word *mother*.

manifests what Robert Seidenberg has called the irreducibles of womanhood—pregnancy and birth.[31]

Even in the quintessential female experience of birth itself, the indications are that today's woman is striving to match her behavior to patriarchal ideals instead of acting from her own authority. A redundance of articles about the "new" natural childbirth, for instance, details how women are expected to reach perfection by having a flawless labor, delivery, and recovery. According to one journalist, first-time mothers "desperately want to believe that they can learn to control this momentous event in their lives, just as they've learned to direct their personal relationships and professional careers."[32] This journalist concluded that women may well be entrapped in the mystique of the perfect birth by an old distrust of personal judgments and a continued—though hidden—reliance on the advice of experts. This reliance on authority now leads expectant mothers to adopt the same one-down relationship to the natural childbirth movement that was once held in relation to the medical establishment. The authority has changed, but women's stance remains the same.

As this book took shape, the patriarchy seemed to be absconding even with these biological female functions. With the advent of surrogate motherhood, the patriarchal contract has begun to compete with the biological tie between mother and child. And while some women have been reduced to acting as mere vessels for the offspring of men, both church and state have reverted to an archaic stance, intensifying campaigns to limit female choice in reproduction.

The church's long-standing appropriation of the feminine[33] struck home to me when a priest who heard a speech I gave about the mother-daughter relationship on the eve of Mother's Day borrowed on my material only to mangle it in his sermon the next morning, Good Shepherd Sunday. Inviting the children in the congregation to guess what was hidden beneath his priestly robes, he pulled out the curly, stuffed lamb that was his sermon prop. He then told his flock that without the shepherd there would be no baby lambs at all: it was the shepherd, he claimed, who assured the mating. He prepared the ram, shaved his belly, kept him cool in the shade, and fed him well—and then made sure he was awake for the fleeting moment during which the ewe was receptive. This priest asserted too that without the shepherd, the ewe would fail to look after the lamb at birth, and forget to feed it. In concluding this story of what appeared primarily to point to an incapacity on the part of the male's instinctual behavior, he went on to distinguish between three kinds of love:

passion, mother-love, and husbandry. He then insisted that of the three husbandry is the only conscious love. This love, he proclaimed, is what we should celebrate on Mother's Day.

Have we, as a culture, succeeded only in keeping women meek as sheep while dressing them up in wolves' clothing? While women have doubtless made important gains and I would be the first to applaud them, females are perhaps more separated now than ever before from their natural authority. Despite maintaining happy marriages, rearing healthy children, and achieving what they set out to do in their careers, many women are falling victim to "the depressive shadow of success."[34] Little do they suspect that the multitude of choices now offered to females constitutes an illusion. Most distressing, as the illusion grows stronger, women become less conscious of the split between who they appear to be and who they "really" are. The lack of real choice, and the fact that this lack is camouflaged, sends women veering around a dangerous curve on the route to the development of the authentic self.

Both historic and contemporary constructions of femininity thus thrust a woman down a path that has little to do with who and what she really is, impelling her toward a destiny that is hardly her own. Each does so by forcing a single aspect of female identity into the foreground to the exclusion of the whole—the historic by excluding all but servility and nurture, the contemporary by severing the personal from the professional and blocking out all but competence. Taken separately, either of these forces makes for a threat to the self. Taken together in a culture that pushes a woman toward one pole on a manifest level while covertly lashing her to the other, they strike a blow to identity and make it impossible to shape a meaningful life as a fully human being.

Thus the new woman lives in a man's world, where she is turned against womanly strengths that lie at the heart of her identity. Beckoned by the promise of self-development and aware of the link between the feminine and the unseemly aspects of human life, she seizes the chance to make it in a man's world. Susceptible to the lure of career success, she abandons her feminine values and adheres to patriarchal purposes. Laboring under the assumption that a woman can finally have it all, she is pressured instead to *do* it all by a corporate dictum that offers a woman but a single way to count—a way that requires her to forfeit a feminine mode. Backed into a corner where she is kept from integrating a variety of purposes by a social scheme that pits competence against care, the new woman pursues an impossible task and frequently finds herself adrift.

Is it not equally difficult for men? They too often lack access to meaningful work, and I would not want to trivialize the damage that results.[35] What's more, they are forced into roles that limit self-expression and self-knowledge. The breadwinner role, for instance, has been thrust on men and taken to such an extreme that the culture holds a man responsible for his family's financial well-being even after his death.[36] Assigning the world of work to males and deeming that world instrumental separates men just as completely from feeling as assigning the affective realm to female separates women from competence.[37]

The polarization of these common human capacities hurts members of both sexes, but men are not, as a group, disenfranchised by this opposition. Seldom expected to put aside their own purposes for the sake of others, males are encouraged to develop an independent life in what members of both sexes regard as the real world—a world that is run nearly automatically (autistically?) by what one male feminist has called a "silent coalescence of man-made and man-dominated institutions."[38] There women have been "deprived of those opportunities for self-development and accretion which men have always considered their God-given and 'natural' rights."[39] Although a man can count on his wife to fill in the social backdrop for his existence, a woman who "succeeds" often does so at the expense of having friends or family. As boss or underling, she misses out on vital aspects of the human agenda, and ends up with "a lesser life."[40] While some of a female's problems are, then, shared by her male counterpart, the subordination of women takes its toll specifically on her even as it acts to bolster the esteem of the man. The cost of operating amid patriarchal mandates is high indeed.

If she cannot confirm who and what she essentially is at home or at work, where is a woman to turn to verify her sense of self?

A woman who turns to traditional psychology—even a woman who is sophisticated, well married, decently employed in work that draws on her expertise, and well versed in the social sciences—may be put at equal risk to those who depend on the corporate world for self-affirmation. This is because of the so-called rational, objective data that buries the male bias which constitutes traditional psychology's norms. Whether she examines psychology texts or turns to the popular literature in her search for self, this woman finds the legacy of Freud and Erikson in study after study that documents the experience of men.[41] Especially if she is a woman of accomplishment, she may try to fit herself to the models she finds there, making success and achievement her only goals.* The well-defined literature on men holds many a woman's attention: like a little girl dressing paper dolls, she tacks its male garb to her female figure. Finding a poor fit, she is prone to change the shape of the doll rather than cast aside the clothes that suit her so poorly.

Hopelessly confused, such a woman may well consult a therapist. As long as women's psychology remains a cottage industry, that therapist (whether man or woman) will be steeped in the standard literature, conversant with the official models it puts forth. That literature still portrays women as less separated and less individuated than men—and thus inferior to them in development. Some of its proponents, comparing a female client with the rigid image the male-centered literature portrays, might even call her mad.[42]

Against this terrain, where men stand out as larger than life and women fall into the background, how is a woman to come fully into her own? Where is she to look for a bedrock sense of self?

The answers to these questions lie, according to the women I studied, in "the girl within," the spirited, playful, self-contained child, the independent, competent, purposeful girl that a woman carries with her in memory, a touchstone for the woman she can become. In generations past, restrictive experiences that molded us into what a female should be caused us to lose our grip on this girl. Now the opposite rendering—woman as man—threatens to derail her. Despite these destructive forces, however, some women rediscover a primary childhood identity. Those who thread their way back to this girl find in her a child to rely on and a source of womanly strength.

The women I studied clarify the image of this girl and show how important it is to rediscover her. They describe their pursuit of the authentic self and show how the female experience robs them of it.[43] They describe the struggle involved in resisting the cultural press to negate that nascent self in youth. They detail the experiences that divide a girl against herself, driving the essential girl to an inner realm where she remains hidden—even from herself. They suggest that the culture's exaltation of masculine values turns a girl against the fem-

---

*Depending on the brand of feminist writing she encounters, she may instead be directed toward relationships and told that a focus on others properly characterizes women's lives. This leaves her to wonder about her ambitions, perhaps even to question whether she is truly feminine, considering that she has goals and work of her own.

inine in herself. And they convey their shock when they discovered, long after having made adult commitments that tied them to the destinies of others, that the identities they had assumed since girlhood were bolted to a man-made foundation that was not of their own making. They detail the crisis that threw them off course and forced them to confront the "false self"[44] that stole in to take the girl's place, a crisis that, for the lucky, helped to dismantle and demolish that false self. Most important, they relate how they unearthed the girl from beneath the rubble and reconstructed an adult identity from the natural materials she had preserved. The life studies of these women and their newfound discovery of the girl within follow in these pages.

3

ADULT EQUALS MALE

atherine, age thirty-five, was a physician, wife, and mother. She lived in a big old house surrounded by woods in one of Boston's outlying suburbs. I made my way past the rhododendrons, over the stone steps to the front door, and rapped on the brass door knocker. Just back from a summer vacation, Katherine looked relaxed, tanned, and wholesome when she greeted me. Short and sturdy with straight, taffy hair, tortoiseshell glasses, and amber eyes, she gave off a feeling of practicality and carried an air of confidence.

Katherine's manner was simple, direct, and informal. She laughed as she picked up her five-year-old's Raggedy Ann doll, plunking it down in a miniature chair in the hall on our way toward a living room that was comfortably furnished with a sofa opposite the fireplace, wing chairs beside it, and a scattering of upholstered occasional chairs. In the dining room beyond, the polished mahogany table reflected a bowl of flowers that served as its centerpiece, gathering the light from the windows on the north wall. The head and foot of the table were marked by Queen Anne chairs with green brocade seats. An early American high chair stood in the corner. A long sideboard kept the table linens flat and protected the family silver. Oriental carpets covered the hardwood floors. Clad simply in a yellow blouse, a denim wrap skirt, and flats, Katherine herself seemed somehow out of place in these elegant surroundings.

Katherine began talking even before we sat down, she in a wing chair with a basket of mending beside her, I on the couch, tape recorder in hand. She was telling me that her husband was out of town at a medical convention. Given that they were both doctors, one might have assumed that Katherine and Sam would be equally involved in their careers, but Katherine's remarks made it clear that their work was weighted along typical male-female lines. Sam was a neurologist, a member of a specialty at the top of the medical ladder. Katherine, a behavioral pediatrician, occupied one of its bottom rungs. Sam taught at Harvard. Katherine, once a fellow there, now had a part-time practice counseling families whose children were afflicted with developmental disabilities.

The disparity between their positions was emphasized by Sam's association with a prestigious secular university and by Katherine's place in a Catholic one. Her daily association with the retarded—a disenfranchised group in America—made her occupation all the more mundane in medical circles. Smacking of charity, such frontline work is ignored by medical journals, whereas Sam's work, shining with heroism, put him at medicine's cutting edge.

I began to see how these weights tipped the balance of their lives when Katherine fell to talking about Sam's unhappiness with his job and spelled out its adverse effects: "He works with a bunch of really aggressive men. That's the way the Harvard system is. Everybody's out for his own skin. It's very unpleasant. Now that I've left Harvard, I can see that there are other ways to live, other ways to think—human beings out there doing things in a human way—but it isn't so at Harvard. There it is driven, terrible."

Sam had grown so discouraged and dissatisfied that he wanted to leave his position in Boston for one in Texas—a challenge to their values and to their commitment to each other, for Katherine knew she did not want to go. Katherine reached for a psychological formulation to justify her resistance to the move: "If I had been convinced that changing locations would change the things Sam wants to change in himself, I would have been all for the move despite my reluctance to leave Boston. But I honestly believe that the first thing you pack in your suitcase is the problems you're trying to run away from. They slip in before you've even opened the latch."

Clearly, there was more to it than her concern for Sam, however. Katherine explained how her attachments kept her anchored and how they reinforced her conviction that moving was not the solution: "And it would have been a major uprooting. I really am an Easterner. I love the East. I like the mountains, the ocean. I feel as though I belong here. And I have very good friends here, longtime friends from my early childhood. My best friend lives ten minutes from my house. I look upon her as my sister. I would really miss my friends. It's not that easy to make *good* friends. Moving would mean pulling up a lot of roots."

To Katherine, roots were especially important. Unlike most Americans her age, she had grown up with tremendous privilege and continuity. Her parents lived in New York City, where her father, educated as a lawyer, was a world-class businessman. Her mother, chairwoman of two music guilds, was a pianist and composer. Katherine had three brothers and a sister. She described the family as happy and close, following what she called "a traditional pattern of male-female roles." Her narrative illuminated how the particularization of these roles as well as her own experiences as a female had led her to assume the identity she had come to call her own.

"My father was a very successful lawyer. The firm he started got big-business clients right away, and then when I was about sixteen he went into the company he's now running. He's really a mover. He's been on the front page of the *New York Times* and was written up in *Newsweek*."

What she meant by "traditional . . . male-female roles" was apparent when she explained how her family revolved around this patriarch: "My mom's whole role in life was facilitator for my dad. He helped her with her life as a musician, so it was somewhat mutual, but everything they did was at the foot of my dad's career. We'd pick him up at certain corners, cater to his schedule. The concerts she gave were planned to coincide with his travel on the Continent. Everything was done for my father. It was all organized around him and his needs. They had certain basic contracts, patterns of living: the weekends belonged to the family. But those patterns were probably established by my father. He was the boss."

Almost as if to reassure me, she hastened to add: "When you meet my mother, though, you know you have met somebody. She has a real sense of self."

Much of Katherine's sense of self had its origins in a still-immediate girlhood view she'd acquired partly through her mother—and her mother's mother: "I carry the feeling from my mother that it is very important to have a sense of your self and to give your children a sense of themselves as somebody special—not just anybody. That sounds snobbish, but there were things in my life that gave me that sense of importance—things quite apart from my father. My grandmother had a musical salon every Tuesday afternoon at her house in New York. It was simple, elegant, exquisite. Always there were big bouquets of flowers, at her house and the house I grew up in. When you'd go to bed at night there would be a little tray, a few cookies, a glass of milk set out on a lace doily. That was style."

The family's style expanded her horizons: "My parents gave me the feeling that the sky was the limit—for them, for me, for my brothers, for my sister. And that sky was not the sky of everyday life. It had unbounded horizons. My parents did a lot to keep the sky wide. We were exposed to a lot of people, certainly through Dad's business but more intimately through my mother's music world. International people. When we traveled with my grandmother, we stayed with pianists and conductors, and looked into conservatories in Russia, Japan, everywhere." With a gesture of largesse, she added, "To do that took household help. While my mother worked on her committees and her music, we had a governess, a laundress, a cleaning lady—not all the time, but enough to make it possible."

Returning to the legacy handed down through the family's women,[1] she reflected, "My grandmother provided the intellectual, cultural influences that then filtered down to my mother, who worked along with my grandmother on the many things she'd initiated. She became a widow at a young age, and she remained a widow her whole life. Her husband, who was quite a bit older than she, died young. She never chose to remarry. She didn't have any man. That left her a widow for thirty-five years. My mother got her role and her satisfaction in life from her mother's interests and through my dad."

Because I was curious about what Katherine made of this contradictory heritage—a grandmother who found culture enough and did not need a man, against a mother whose life included that culture but who set her course according to her man—I asked Katherine what image she'd had of herself as a woman while she was a girl. In a response that not only addressed my inner question about reconciling that contradiction but also spoke to the outer conflict between her identifications with her mother and with her father, she said, "It wasn't a picture of being a doctor. I had wanted to do something more like my dad. He and I are most alike. We even look alike. My baby brother and I both look like him. The others all look like my mother. And in personality, I think we are similar too. At one point my dad was a special representative to the UN to inform them on introducing industrial materials to underdeveloped countries. My brothers went abroad with him then and lived there for a while. So I can remember thinking about that kind of existence.

"But then I thought, You know, that kind of existence isn't going to suit me because there's a lot of traveling and I'm going to want to have a family. I always knew I would have a family, I never thought I would not have a family. And, I thought, How am I going to organize doing something that involves traveling and still have a family? So I can remember thinking early on that this is not going to fit.

"By the time I got to college, I was fluent in Spanish and French and had taken college-level literature courses in those languages. I had traveled a lot with my mother and grandmother, and studied history, and my dad had always been peripherally involved in politics. I had thought that I would study linguistics or political science."

As I began to wonder where medicine had come in, she added, "And then I decided to get my science requirement out of the way, freshman year. I took nat. sci. and really liked it. I switched right away from history and literature to biology. I suppose when I did that, I opened the door to medical school."

That Katherine used the word *suppose* in connection with such a compelling career decision seemed odd to me. It did not fit the heroic quest associated with becoming a doctor. Katherine appeared, in fact, to have drifted into medicine, not drawn into it by the usual promise of becoming one of society's demigods but inspired instead by a particular teacher—and by the glimpse he gave her of the inner workings of the human body.[2] Her focus in his class, unlike that of her premed classmates, was organic and personal. For her, the course was an end in itself, one that "happened" to lead to medical school: "It was really that first science course that did it. The professor was a magnificent teacher. He really got me interested in biology and biochemistry. I loved finding out how the body works, how all the blood goes through the heart and the heart pumps it, that the entire nervous system is regulated, connected to the brain. That came as a revelation to me. And I met Sam in that class."

When I asked how she had decided to marry him, she spoke for legions of women of her generation: "I just sort of knew that I'd get married, and I liked Sam so I married him. It just seemed like the next step. In those days, people did that, you know. They went to college and then they got married. We got married maybe two weeks after my graduation. Sam finished his first-year med school exams on a Friday and we got married the next Tuesday."

Instead of fixing her career to an abstract "Dream" and plotting her progress along the coordinates of career success and chronological age as the literature on men would suggest,[3] Katherine had followed particular people in making career choices. Crisis and ambition also played a part: "At the end of my first year of medical school, Sam became seriously ill with endocarditis—an inflammation of the lining of the heart. He couldn't even breathe comfortably, but he wouldn't do anything about it. I felt like a child in the face of it. I needed somebody else to intercede. I had gotten close to one of my professors in medical school. I call him my sponsor for lack of a better term. So I went to Martin, and he took me in his car to where Sam was working, leaving his own work behind, and we took him to the hospital. After he was discharged, we stayed the summer at Martin's while Sam was on bed rest. Martin himself had had two heart attacks, so he and Sam sat around and talked all day while his wife and I rode horses, played tennis, and had a wonderful time. We became close friends.

"Martin was one of the bigwigs in an area I was interested in, so I went to work for him. My experience with him moved me closer to 'hard' science and a little away from working with people for a couple of years. I really liked being with people, helping people. But I wanted to do something significant in my professional life beyond the one-to-one level I work on now, something academic that would be significant in the larger scheme of things. It was my Dream."

Katherine's "Dream," merely a wish to do "something significant," held virtually no content. In its formless state, it could easily be molded by chance relationships: "Martin continued 'the Dream' for me. He told me, 'You are smart, you are special.' Here he was, the most famous person at Yale—and he picked me. He fostered me. But he always said, 'I'm going to lose you, I'm going to lose you to psychiatry.' I would have stayed in his field, but when he died I really couldn't continue my work in that area because I had been so close to him and had loved him so much."

The loss of this important person devitalized the particular Dream he had carried for her: "After he died, I did a year of psy-

chiatry, and now I'm in pseudopsychiatry. I went to New York to do
the psych residency because I so hated Yale after Martin was gone.
That year I had a child."

Her compelling interest in family made medicine, which ordi-
narily requires the abandonment of any semblance of a personal life,
a tough choice for Katherine. The near-total absence of women in the
field intensified her conflict. The few women who were on the scene
engaged their careers with a single-minded pursuit she knew she
could not abide: "I always knew I would have a family—I never
thought I would not. But there were no models for me, no women
in medicine who had families. There was one woman on the faculty
who I admired a great deal, but she wasn't married and she didn't
have children. The only other staff woman had some piddly position
there. One woman resident had a baby during her second year, and
boy did she suffer. On some rotations, she had to stay over at the
hospital every other night. Nobody would switch with her. If her kid
got sick, no one would cover for her. She was destroyed by that year.
I decided to wait even before I saw what happened to that resident.
I knew it would be too hard on me. Without any idea of how to put
it all together, I just delayed having a family until I finished my
residency. It was impossible to figure out how a woman might be a
physician, marry a guy, and have kids."[4]

In addition to this dilemma, Katherine faced another: she knew
that having a baby could weaken her scholastic standing. Then as
now, to succeed in a so-called man's profession, particularly this
profession, Katherine had to do outstandingly well—and to make
sure her qualifications were beyond reproach: "I had to collect excellent credentials. To go where Sam goes, I've got to have better
credentials than he does because I'm a woman. I was top of my class,
a really good intern, and a good resident. I knew that if I had a kid,
I was liable to lose that standing. We were married when I was twenty-
one, and I did not have our first baby until I was twenty-eight."

Becoming a mother gave Katherine everything she expected,
and more: "Having a baby made a real difference for me. This baby
filled the walls of the house with life. It was like a shell without any
baby there, and she made it very exciting. And I really liked being
a mother, nursing her and changing her. I liked the identity I had
with her, that she was flesh of my flesh, and that everything in her
was part of Sam and me. Even her poop was digested breast milk
from my body! I didn't think about the Dream that first year of
motherhood."

The allure of motherhood did not permanently blot out her professional aspirations, however. Just as before, a prominent man reinspired Katherine's ideals. But the shock of seeing the effects of ambition on him caused her to drop "the Dream" again: "And then I did a fellowship with a man I hoped would continue the Dream, a man who held out promise. But I began to see what the Dream had done to him, as a person, his family life, his children, his intrapsychic life. That's what happens if you dedicate yourself to a dream that is not beyond your ego, not outside your self. And I didn't want any part of it. So I have given up the Dream."

When she relinquished "the Dream," Katherine began to resent Sam's commitment to his profession because it competed with time for the family. But ultimately Katherine came to respect him for holding on to his goals, and to appreciate him for carrying "the Dream" for the two of them: "My husband hasn't given up the dream of really doing something significant and important. I fought against his Dream for a long time. I wanted him home, I wanted help with bringing up the kids; they want him here, they love him. It's lonely when he's out there pursuing his Dream. But recently I saw two people I respected in medical school—two brilliant men—who are now leading perfectly pedestrian lives. That's what happens when you give up the Dream. So now I respect Sam for fighting against closing in his horizons."

Ideals of femininity, especially the feminine imperative not to be selfish, limited her horizons: "I see the Dream as selfish. I wouldn't want to dedicate myself to it because it's selfish. I don't like being selfish. So now I have probably given up the Dream. I have closed in my horizons and said, 'OK, this is what I can handle and that's it.' The sky is no longer my limit."[5]

The very appeal of work of her own drives her away from seeking it: "I am devoting myself solely to clinical work because it's easy and comfortable with a family at home. It means giving something up, though: My Dream is in abeyance and my career is blockaded because I have not published my research."

In a clear indictment of a system that pits competence against care, to the immense detriment of the system itself by making it impossible for women who tend to others to contribute to medical research and training, she commented: "Clinical work is much easier to limit. There are so few women with children in any other kind of work in medicine. It's a shame because clinical work is the absolute underdog. It's low prestige. Catholic hospitals are full of women like me; it's where they go. They're all doing clinical work in your second-level places. They're not at the big academic centers. They're where I am. And they're smart. The women I work with are smart."

The sacrifice Katherine has made—a sacrifice of "the Dream"—is no small one, and it would not have to be made at all were her family responsibilities in the hands of a wife, as they typically are for a doctor: "It's awfully narrow in this practice, but any other job would tie me down too much, make me too dependent on household help. If you're tied down by your job, you really need a wife at home. And I don't have a wife at home."

Simply delegating the family's well-being to household help was implausible because of the value she placed on emotional function: "Recently my housekeeper got depressed. I talked to her, let her know. She said she was doing everything she was supposed to be doing, and I said, 'You are, but you are too remote. And either you pull yourself together or you leave.' Because I can't have that kind of depression in my household, that tension of feelings."

Threading her way back to her mother's "career," Katherine identified the invisible support commonly provided by women, support that makes it possible for society at large to maintain the illusion that men who succeed do so on their own: "My mother thinks that since the men work hard all week, it's up to women to do for them. But in fact the person who's the most hardworking in my family is my mother—by far. I've seen what it's like out there in the men's world. You work there, but you sit around, talk to your associates, have lunch with your buddies, get the secretary to protect you from interruptions, and let your staff do your bidding. In the women's world, you *really* work. You are physically working all the time. My mother wouldn't dream that any of my brothers would come back home and not have flowers set in their rooms. She still does their laundry when they're there, and one of them is thirty years old.[6] And I have acquired that legacy. I feel very badly if I don't have the household running smoothly for my husband. I feel guilty making demands on him. I can't think of any demands my mother made on my father."

Following her mother's and grandmother's lead precludes expressing the ambition that characterized her father, countering her identification with him: "If I did not have children, I would have much bigger professional aspirations, more motivation. I would be tough and driving in my career, like my dad. My dad is tough. In order to be good in the business world, you've got to be tough—and direct and straight. And he is all those things. He doesn't have any hang-ups about it. He's very powerful. Had I not been a woman, I would be out there battling the world, too, right in the fray."

Returning to the conflict between family and ambition, she suggested that being a woman itself nullified her inclination to adopt her father's competitive attitude: "Being a woman changed that because I was committed to having children and a family. I don't allow myself to be tough and driving in my career. I like to work and leave. I have to keep the lid on my work because there is so much I could do and am interested in doing, lots of things I'd love to do. But I just don't want to spend that kind of time, energy, and 'money' out of my emotional bank right now. The kids are the ones that pay me high dividends. They're a good investment in terms of my happiness. They are a great source of happiness to me, and I really have a good time watching them grow up. I am much more fulfilled for having become a mother. I'm sure that I could get more out of my work, but I'd have to make a much larger capital investment in order to get more back."

The dynamic tension between love and work that structured Katherine's life and curtailed her ambitions was bound into a value system particular to women, one that provides a relational criterion rather than an occupational one for success: "Sam's job is his life. He measures his life by his work. I don't measure my life by my work, I measure my life by my family. I measure my level of success by whether I feel relaxed about what's happening at home. I always feel unsuccessful when things don't go right at home. I don't feel unsuccessful when things don't go right at work."

Katherine drew on values established in childhood to assign priorities as wife, mother, and pediatrician: "My family is first. I made that decision way back in my childhood. That's the way my mother was, and my grandmother too. It was a pattern. I am giving the time and energy and effort it would take to pull off a career to my family. I never really questioned it."

Given her concentration on family, I questioned why Katherine worked at all. In a comment that put me in mind of Freud's view that work ties a person to the reality principle,[7] she clarified how work itself kept her connected to the world beyond the walls of the household, in a most organic way: "Work brings me in touch with the realities of existence. I like to feel the pulse of the world, I don't like to feel that I am planets away. Work makes me feel as if I'm not totally withdrawn from the world. Family is so important to me that I could be, you know."

But there was a special aspect to work, a way in which it functioned to enhance her family life as well as to balance it, imbuing home with a meaning specific to Katherine: "And I like to come home. If I were home all the time, I couldn't come home. One of the things that makes home special is leaving home and then coming back. Work justifies leaving home so I can come back. I love coming back. I have always liked to come *home*." She explained what this meant to her daily life: "It comes back to family. Now I drive home from work, the kids hear me coming up the driveway, and all three little girls are down at the bottom stair in the garage to greet me. There it is. I really like it. I really feel good when I get home."

This contemporary image transported Katherine to a lush girlhood memory, taking her back to a primary identity that galvanized her life as a woman. I suddenly understood the meaning of our lavish surroundings when she recounted this sweet remembrance: "And when I was a girl, it was very nice when I came home. My mother would usually be practicing the piano, Brahms or Schubert, and it sounded wonderful. I'd walk in the door and go down this wonderful, long, beautiful hallway past that beautiful chair that now sits here in my living room, and it was visually very pretty, idyllic. The doors into the drawing room were always open, and I used to go in and kiss Mama, and she'd go on playing. I'd go back to the kitchen to this wonderful black cook, a black earth mother who stayed with us for thirty years. I had all these wonderful mothers, you understand, my own mother, my grandmother, and this earth mother, who would give me a bowl of junket with freshly grated chocolate on top. And I'd sit down and have that and chat with her. It was nice at home. And it still is nice at home."

Expanding on the profound impact of her childhood on the contours of her adult life, she continued: "When I was a child, I went away to the country with my family on the weekends. Other kids did things together on Saturdays and Sundays. I didn't because I had my own life—my family life. We had a farm sixty miles north of New York City. We loved the weekends and the summers at that retreat. We had an old house built in the seventeen hundreds. We put in the wiring, the plumbing, the roof, as a family. We made a vegetable garden and built an orchard, made a lake out of a horrible bog loaded with mosquitoes. We took care of horses, tended the plants, ate lunch out of the vegetable patch, played football. We had a good time.

"We had a lot of help at the farm. My mother was the lady of the house, a lady of leisure. She played the piano, read, did some gardening because she likes to garden. We could do anything we wanted to, nobody bugged you. My brother ran a riding camp. My sister never left the porch. All she did for four months was read. I was more active. Sometimes a close friend would come up."

This family pattern was a compelling one, overriding even the usual adolescent strivings for independence: "Towards the end of high school, I was allowed to stay in the city if I wanted to, but there was no encouragement for that. If you stayed, you stayed by yourself. It was tough to come home to an empty apartment when you were used to five kids and the cook and the governess and tons of people who all loved you. If you stayed, you had to really want to do it. It wasn't a casual event. Everybody that mattered was at the Country."

Family life displaced school routines as well: "And we left for there on Friday mornings. I did not go to school on Fridays, except occasionally when it suited my father's schedule, which was not very often because we had to beat the traffic out of the city. And sometimes I did not go to school on Monday mornings. If my grandmother wanted to take me to Europe with her during the school year, I went. School schedules did not dictate our lives. What dictated our lives was family, and my dad's work."

Katherine carried forward her father's freedom from institutional schedules—as well as his arrogance about them—through college, and beyond. "I skipped freshman orientation at Radcliffe to stay on at the Country one summer. My dad said, 'You don't need to go to orientation. You're too smart to do that kind of thing.' I got a call from the college, and I said, 'I'm coming when I am ready.' That was condoned by my family. Never would they do something because an institution thought you should if it seemed unnecessary for you to do it. It was summer, and we went away all summer. We didn't do things that everybody else did."

She shared a funny vignette to show how Sam had discovered her reliance on her family: "After I started college, I still spent summers with my family and the family remained important to me. I remember I came up here once to go to a summer dance with Sam. As soon as I got here, he and his roommates confronted me with raw steak and green beans—that I was supposed to cook! I had never cooked a meal, not in my entire life. I had no idea what to do, so I took their phone into the closet and called my mother. 'What do I do?' I asked her. My mother had never been in a kitchen either, but she knew how to do steak and green beans. She told me what to do, but when I turned to look at that food, I still didn't feel that I had it down right. I finally told these guys that I didn't know how to cook. It was really funny because they just assumed that I would cook. They expected me to step right into it because I was the female—even though one of those three rowdy guys was working as a chef that year! That was Sam's first real introduction to how close I was to my family, and how different we were from other people."

The predominance of home, rooted in the garden of girlhood, paradoxically permitted Katherine a certain adult autonomy, allowing her to be true to herself even in a situation that by its basic demands obliterates individual qualities—medical training: "Even as a medical resident, I set up barriers and limits so I could be home. I am a very organized person, so I could get my work done and go home for lunch. I did that as an intern too. I protected my chance to do my own thing by getting excellent grades and staying at the top of my class. It gave me the freedom not to kowtow to other people. I even refused to live in the medical compound. We had a small apartment in a row house out in the ghetto, with a little garden in back. I'd fix myself a sandwich and sit in the sun in the garden."

As with any move toward individuation, the fruits of this garden were not entirely sweet: "It drove them crazy, but they couldn't complain because I was the only intern whose charts were meticulous and up-to-date. I've always had my own life. That alone has given me distance from the people I work with, and made it difficult."

Ever a dutiful daughter, Katherine still spends vacations at the family compound. "Part of my adulthood is being controlled by a father who's still the boss. It is he, now, who expects me to bring the children, he who seems to need that contact with them for his mental health."

Easily seduced by the rhapsodic country idyll, she slips into a womanly mode with her mother, recapturing girlhood pleasures: "When I visit there summers now, I do household caretaking because I'm comfortable with it and I like to free my mother up to do the things she loves to do. And I still love to sit on the screened-in porch on these little green chaise lounges, and it's very beautiful. And I used to rest there, after lunch, on this particular chaise, with my mother and my grandmother. It was a womanly thing to do, to take a rest after lunch. You look out from this one chair and there are oak trees and maple trees and Japanese maples and some evergreen trees—all different shades of green. I want to sit there, just sit there. I don't want to hear anything, talk to anybody, do anything. I just want to sit there and look, day after day, really let all the tensions go, just look at these different shades of green which I've loved."

In the country, she also acts as a pivot to facilitate the transfer of family gifts between the generations: "One of the things I free my mother up to do when I go there now is to teach my daughters piano. My mother's a brilliant musician. Here's a wonderful opportunity for my kids to be exposed to music. I love them to have that time with her every day while I'm there. My greatest pleasures come from that, and from seeing my brother teaching one of them to ride a two-wheeler, my father playing tennis with my three-year-old."

Has Katherine left the dutiful daughter role and truly become an adult? Her adulthood virtually duplicates her childhood. Still very attached to her family of origin, she herself is not sure she is adult—as I learned when I asked my research question. I did not even begin to understand her uncertainty until I heard a good part of her story. She had been doing some handwork to ready a dress for the annual ball that would herald the turn of the medical year. I practically had to interrupt her prattle about the dance to formally begin the interview. When I did, her response to my question threw into sharp relief the very ways in which the expression of attachment that so characterized her life could function to jeopardize a woman's adult identity. Her responses reveal how important it is to examine the term *adult* and to ask what that term means.

"My question is, If we were writing your biography, how would you describe your adult life?" I had asked.

She instantly replied: "That question is too hard for me. 'If I were writing my biography, how would I describe my adult life?' I can see that I'm not going to get any stitching done while we talk. Your questions are too complicated." She put down the bit of lace she was fastening to the bodice of her grandmother's dress. "First, I would say that I spend a lot of time and energy avoiding that concept, of actually being an adult. I often see myself as very similar to a photograph taken of me when I applied to college. When I look in the mirror, I see that I look like that person even though it was nearly twenty years ago."

Taken aback by her response, I thought to myself, How could this be? Surrounded by the accoutrements of adulthood, Katherine seemed fully adult to me. Wife and mother are certainly adult roles, and her profession as a physician would have seemed to put her adulthood beyond question. Yet she avoided identifying herself with that term; her inner image was of a girl half her age. That picture had to be at odds with the way her children, husband, friends, associates, and patients viewed her. What could account for the discrepancy?

Unhampered by my surprise, Katherine quickly discarded the word *adult* as she went on, using instead *grown-up*—a child's label for adult. Making the usual associations between age, parenthood, and maturity, she mused, "When I was a kid, I used to look at my parents and say, 'They're grown up.' I used to think to myself, 'When will I be grown up?' And in a way I am never sure. Somehow I can remember thinking that thirty-five was pretty old when I was a kid and my parents were thirty-five. And now *I* am thirty-five. I don't feel that I am as grown-up as I viewed them. But maybe I really am as grown-up as they actually were. Because in fact my mother had her mother right there. And it was unclear to me who was taking care of whom—but certainly it was very mutual."

This was the first real clue I had about what put Katherine at odds with herself as an adult: the exchange of care she saw between her mother and her grandmother did not fit her concept of adulthood. When she was a child, in fact, adulthood had looked simpler to Katherine than it did now at age thirty-five. On reflection, she was not at all sure that those she'd then viewed as grown-up should qualify. Her question about her adult status seemed to revolve around the women in her family—her mother and her grandmother. In focusing on their closeness, she was putting her finger on a latent conflict that extended well beyond the particulars of her family history. Her comment suggested that the caring ties between these women were incompatible with adulthood.

Such a conflict bodes ill for a woman coming into her own: If she had to choose between womanly ties and her adulthood, how could she be both attached and grown-up? If Katherine's mother and her grandmother seemed properly cast in limbo, kept apart from the province of adulthood by virtue of their connection with each other, what about Katherine? And if adulthood could not belong to them—or to her—to whom might it belong? What attributes would an adult have?

As if reading my mind, Katherine volunteered: "I view my dad as much more adult than my mom. He was independent, and he was doing his own thing. He didn't rely on anybody other than himself. He was born when his parents were quite old. And he had a really unusual upbringing because he lived in the backwoods of Oregon, where his father had a lumber farm. They were totally isolated. He didn't go to school until he went to college; he was tutored at home.

"His parents didn't want him to go to law school, but he went. He did things they didn't approve of at all, just made up his own mind and went about his own business. Nobody else influenced his decisions. His father and his mother died when he was young, and he was on his own. I see my dad as an adult because he didn't really have any parents. My father is the only person I can think of who is really, really adult."

The mystery was here unraveled. Katherine's father was the only person she thought of as "really, really adult" because he was radically separated from his parents. His self-sufficiency, independence, and rationality made for adult qualifications that conflicted with her womanly focus on care and connection—a focus that not only organized Katherine's personal relationships but also structured her work in a helping profession. To her, adulthood spelled the antithesis of care, yielding a set of associations that resulted in an unwillingness to define herself, her mother, her grandmother, or any other woman in her family as adult.

Faced with the apparent impossibility of being both caring and adult, Katherine determined that she and the women in her family were, at best, pseudoadults. "I still don't think of my mother as adult. Her mother died and left her, but now I've taken over parenting her." Perhaps Katherine's image of her mother as adult manqué persisted because she had reinforced the tie between them with care— almost as if to save her mother from adulthood.

Clearly then, to Katherine at least, care and maturity were cast in a dichotomy, the one aligned with childhood and femininity, the other aligned with adulthood and masculinity. To her, womanly connection was juxtaposed against manly self-reliance. Compelled to choose *either* adulthood *or* femininity, she opted for femininity.

Katherine elucidated the opposition between care and self-reliance, exposing the detachment associated with adulthood and showing how it goes against the female grain: "If you say you're adult, that means certain kinds of separation—as opposed to letting relationships change gradually." When she said that, I could see that, for her at least, adulthood not only represented the antithesis of care but also posed a threat to sustaining relationships.

In their reverence for autonomy and separation, traditional analysts might well interpret Katherine's orientation to care and connection as a resistance to adulthood or even see her stance as
pathologically dependent. Followers of Freud and Erikson, for example, would likely assert that her emphasis on family attachments
provides ample evidence of a lingering immaturity, reason enough
to dismiss her narrative or to discount it as childish. But others would
see in her alienation from adulthood an unwitting submission to
deeply rooted cultural values that social scientists are finally beginning
to pinpoint and to question.

The now classic Broverman report about sex-role stereotypes
attests to the discrepancy between adulthood and femininity that
Katherine's personal conflict reflects.[8] These investigators found that
sharply drawn stereotypes of masculinity and femininity delimited
concepts of adulthood held by a variety of subject groups. Regardless
of their level of education and professional sophistication, men and
women in the study attributed a specific cluster of traits—independence, rationality, and self-direction—to the ideal man while assigning a different cluster—namely warmth, emotional expressiveness,
and relatedness—to the ideal woman.

The problem with this apparently benign distinction became
clear when subjects were asked to designate the traits desirable in
"an adult," sex unspecified. Seasoned professionals as well as college
sophomores consistently chose only those traits associated with masculinity. Furthermore, whereas a "healthy male" was seen to possess
some positive feminine traits, a "healthy female" included none that
were masculine. Relative to men, whose characteristics were considered positive and healthy, women were judged dependent, subjective, passive, and illogical—qualities that both men and women of
all levels of sophistication considered undesirable in mentally healthy
adults of either sex.

The authors of the study concluded that an adult woman is a
contradiction in terms, and their finding bears directly on how women
themselves interpret their lives. The study specifies how "women are
clearly put in a double bind by the fact that different standards exist
for women than for adults. If women adopt the behaviors specified
as desirable for adults, they risk censure for their failure to be appropriately feminine; but if they adopt the behaviors that are desig-
nated as feminine, they are necessarily deficient with respect to the
general standards for adult behavior."[9]

Thus a woman is caught in a contradiction. Either she can be

DONATION BOOKS
PLEASE INDICATE YOUR PREFERENCE
<u>"A"</u> ADDED TO COLLECTION
<u>"D"</u> FOR BOOK SALE

Q. CARTER_____

E. DUANE _____

R. FULLER_____

S. ROTENBERG _____

feminine or she can be adult. Although it may be true that the wedge we force between adulthood and femininity derives from a problem with fundamentally distorted concepts rather than from women's developmental deficit,[10] what Katherine so clearly shows is that competent, mature women bend the contradiction back against themselves, undermining the very foundations of the self. Unable single-handedly to effect a social redefinition of adult that includes feminine qualities, a woman eliminates herself from the category and negates her adult identity.

When I pressed her about when her adult life would begin, Katherine pointed not to separation but to the quintessential experience of connection, marriage: "I would say, if I had to pick a particular time in my life when I felt I was probably becoming an adult, it would be getting married. It was a *rite de passage*. We went off, we had a honeymoon. It was nice. After that I could stay in the same bedroom with my husband at my folks' house. That was a big difference. And when I was married, I moved into my first apartment that wasn't part of the university and paid for by my parents. I took care of myself and my husband. Before that I didn't have anything to be responsible for. Responsibility has a lot to do with being an adult. And being on your own."

When she named marriage as the *rite de passage* that approximates adulthood, Katherine identified the social prescription for womanhood. While this prescription contained an element of independence, as does the standard "male" definition of adulthood, Katherine meant something different by it than what she saw as the independence her father personified. Her way of being on her own had nothing to do with isolation from others, or disregard for parents, as being on one's own had for him. Marriage instead functioned to put her at the center of a web of relationships woven together by ties of affection.[11] The irony was that securing a lifelong attachment was what led Katherine to feel that she was on her own.

As a point of demarcation at the far edge of childhood, marriage seemed to offer Katherine a link to adulthood. But there was something amiss. In affirming womanhood, marriage appeared to cancel out rather than to confirm adulthood. Katherine's account seemed to confirm a contradiction between the terms *woman* and *adult*.

By associating marriage with adulthood but not quite defining herself as adult, Katherine explained why putting women into the standard adult equation did not add up. If adulthood spells solitary self-sufficiency, and a female's *rite de passage* out of childhood is an act of attachment, there is no way for a female to become adult. Equating the feminine with connection and the masculine with separation, and making separation the bench mark of adulthood, is what led Katherine to disqualify herself as an adult. Given these factors, adulthood and womanhood simply do not compute.

Katherine established whatever maturity she has through her marriage to Sam rather than apart from it: "Part of my maturity has been having a coupleness with Sam that doesn't include anybody else. He has insisted on it. And that means you have joys, anguishes, that belong to the two of you and not to anybody else. My husband has insisted that we make important decisions together. He set it up that we both direct our course together. In my family, it wasn't that way. My dad made the decisions and everybody else went along with them. In my childhood there was a tyranny of the group schedule. Sam and I don't do that. We make joint decisions."

She had come to realize that she could not follow in her mother's footsteps to get what she wanted: "For me that has meant saying that my mom gets a lot of fulfillment through my dad and saying to myself, 'That really isn't going to be the pattern for me,' because Sam is not the star success my dad was. I can't hide behind him because he is not going to provide it for me."

Dealing with this disappointment has forced her into a feminine independence: "I'd assumed that my marriage would be like my mother's and father's. I realized it couldn't be when Sam got depressed by the Harvard situation. I am scared of his depression. It puts a distance between us that frightens me.[12] It disconnects me from him. I have gotten more independent since Sam's depression. I have had to be more responsible for myself, to say 'I am me.' I can't reach him. But I am still me. I don't think I would have moved into so much independence had I not been forced to by his depression. There's been no model for me being more independent in the relationship. My mother and father were twined around each other like trees."

Sam's unwelcome distance from her has forced Katherine again to confront selfishness: "What I am struggling with now is coming to terms with what I have to do for myself. In a sense it is selfish to ask for what you need. But I am being pushed into it by the realization that Sam cannot provide for me everything I need and want. It may have always been true, but I didn't accept it before."

This acceptance has prompted her to a new level of independence: "I am increasingly and more appropriately independent from

Sam. I used to always think that if he died I would kill myself. I was very sure of that. Then I had kids and I'd think, I can't kill myself if he dies. I have to have something more for me. I can't have that kind of total dependence on another person. I'm moving into a more independent phase of existence than I've ever had in my life, basically, trying to prepare myself to function more independently and still operate within the confines of marriage, wife and mother, daughter, all of those things, but more independently."

The independence Katherine subscribes to—functioning more independently, still within the confines of the feminine roles of wife, mother, and daughter—is certainly different from the stark independence the male-centered psychological literature conveys. The independence she describes is struck in conjunction with others—a kind of in vivo independence that contradicts conventional meanings of the term.

By grounding independence and maturity in their living, social context, Katherine makes them personal and relative instead of permitting them to stand as abstract and absolute. Her account reveals the extent to which others figure into the process of becoming one's own person, drawing to the foreground the social nature of human life that only men have been able to push into the background and deny. Like "joint decisions," her independence is a kind of joint independence that emanates from a self-in-relation.[13]

When I asked her how she would now describe herself, she returned to the images of girlhood and their continuity in her identity: "If I had to describe myself, I'd say I am a person who's family oriented; I'm interested in how people work inside, and in relationships. I'm not into social things. I am a pretty definitive kind of person. I have my work and my profession. I like peace, I like music. And I am told that I've always had a sunny disposition. My mom kept little books about each of us. It's just amazing. She writes in those books every year. And it's like a snapshot, the same snapshot again and again. You just see the same person, growing bigger, year after year. She did a lot to keep that snapshot just the way she saw it.

"I think there are certain things in my personality, like temperament, and certain things that have been fostered that make me who I am. It's like a garden. You've got flowers and you've got weeds. What I see as my job as a parent is trying to get the flowers to grow in the child's personality. Not that one child is like one flower. The whole personality is like a garden. And you want to nourish and make beautiful the potential that you find there." The metaphor is a generative one, completely unlike the standard monolithic image of the man standing alone.

She came back to the theme of care, the thread that weaves through the fabric of her personal and professional life: "I think my special thing is being able to be involved emotionally with family and a few close friends. It is a strength to really be able to care. I care in a warm and communicative way."

In a tacit acknowledgment of the depth of our discussions, Katherine quietly reflected: "Not many people know what I really care about or where I am coming from or where I am going. Most social time is not at that level. Who I really am, people don't understand—the unique aspects: growing up in a family in a way that other people didn't; not doing things the way other children did; and very little peer contact outside of going to school. The uniqueness is the tightness of my family, the exclusive relationships I had with my brothers and my sister and my grandmother and my parents. And the sense that you are not subject to rules and regulations, and bureaucracy. Like never going to school Friday afternoons in my whole life. You know, now I get little notes from Elizabeth's school saying, 'We are reminding you that your children should not miss school because of family vacations.' That was the kind of thing that just used to make my father say, 'Ha-ha, ha-ha.' He used to scoff at ridiculous laws even though he's a lawyer."

She had something pressing to say before we stopped, something about exactly how she had become herself. In addition to melancholy, there was quiet, sustained anger in her voice as she reflected, "Part of who I am has to do with my grandmother dying four years ago. It was the first time anybody close to me died, and I was *really* close to my grandmother. I really got in touch with my mortality then. I had no sense of being mortal before, even though I was the doctor and all these people were dying around me and I was resuscitating them. It never touched me until my grandmother died. My husband sees it all the time too. But he doesn't know about his own mortality. His denial makes me angry. That's when I said, 'OK, we're all mortal. We are all going to die and we might die at any time. So stop pretending and living for what might happen down the road and really live for now. Stop delaying. This is your life, you are living it. *Now*. Do now what you want to do, because you might be dead next week.' "

Coming to terms with the less idyllic aspects of her life led Katherine to claim her maturity and to define her identity. "I have a lot more sense that *this is our life now.* Sam's been pretty depressed for quite a while. And I am impatient with his depression. How can he live that way? How can you be depressed? I really got in touch with that very soon after my grandmother died, feeling very angry. It's the reason I've become me."[14]

Her distance from Sam through depression, her loss of her grandmother through death brought Katherine to focus on who she is, texturing the sunny girlhood picture with a dark adult reality. Only when she had revealed her hidden, darker side could Katherine conclude: "And now you know my true self."

Katherine's sense of connection is her motif. Her narrative reveals how important it is to examine what the term *adult* means. She, like other women, locates the process of growing up in the context of relationships. Embedded in her account is a concept of the adult self that shows the social nature of human experience rather than ignoring it. Her voice speaks of a fuller definition of adulthood than does the standard definition. It speaks to a connection between attachment, care, and commitment that encompasses feminine values. The personal, familiar elements Katherine's narrative connects together provide a foundation for a new definition of adulthood. Against this "feminine" definition, the abstract patriarchal definition pales. Were we to take women's life experience as it stands, the whole of it, as a foundation for defining development, we might be able to take adulthood off a dichotomized grid and view identity as it really develops—in the round.[15]

4

MARRIAGE: WOMEN'S CRUCIBLE FOR GROWING UP

omen I talked with almost invariably framed their accounts with marriage. Like Katherine, they made the break from childhood by way of attachments and commitments. "I became an adult the minute I walked out of my parents' house: when I got married," said Miriam, an educational consultant in her middle fifties. Whereas men point to striking out alone in order to become their own person,[1] women hold that joining forces with a mate is the significant event. "I felt then that I could manage my way in the world," Miriam explained. "I didn't think I could do it myself, but with my husband, we could, *we* could manage our way in the world. I was very confident and very secure about that. Together we could do anything we wanted. And we did!"

Whereas the subject of the male statement is apparently *I*, that of the female narrative is consistently *we*. Whereas men emphasize separation, women focus on connection. This condition of connection formed the centerpiece of women's accounts in my study. They echoed Miriam's assumption that being an adult means "manag[ing] my way in the world"—in tandem with a husband. In undertaking marriage, they did not aspire to solitary independence but to the sort of "joint independence" Katherine had described.

It hardly ever occurred to women in this study that they might end up single—by accident or design. "Getting married is what you were supposed to do," they said. "It's what you did." This social pattern, laid down over centuries of civilization, insinuates itself into their assumptions long before girls are old enough to act on it. When they became brides, women felt they'd been carried over an invisible threshold between childhood and adulthood.

Those who did not marry remained in limbo because of their unmarried status. A friend I visited when I began these interviews, for example, disqualified herself from adulthood. Forty-seven years old, she headed her own nonprofit agency in New York City and had a country house, yet she claimed: "I could not possibly have been a subject in research like yours. I do not qualify as an adult: I never learned to drive a car, and I never married." By way of this comment, she named our culture's symbols for attachment and autonomy— requisite components of adulthood. She suggested that when a woman remains single she—unlike her male counterpart—feels somehow less than adult.

The symbolic value marriage holds as the emblem of adult woman-hood is so great that some women in this study undertook marriage in a deliberate effort to grow up. Wendy, a thirty-nine-year-old house-wife who studied music, recognized as a college freshman that she needed to free herself from childhood. Faced with a dilemma about how she might become adult, she reached for the typical female solution: "I'd begin my adult life with my marriage, my first marriage," she said after she'd settled herself on my living-room couch. "It was motivated in part as an effort to grow up. I saw that very consciously. It was intended to finish some growing-up process that I hadn't done. I saw myself as choosing another family, his values and so on. In a sense who I lived with decided what kind of an adult person I was going to be. I really wanted to get away from home, and going to college wasn't enough."

Wendy seemed a gentle, reasoned sort of woman, not the type to rebel against her parents. Just a few years older than Katherine, she had grown up in a typical middle-class family, one that was as anonymous as Katherine's was distinct. She lacked the arrogance bred of privilege; she possessed no particular worldly ambition. She lived with her second husband and their children in an older house not far from mine. She'd pedaled her bicycle over to my house and brought it just inside the gate to deliver a questionnaire from the straw basket before we started. I knew from what she'd put down on it that she was the oldest of four children, the only daughter in a New England family by whom a proper social marriage would be entirely expected. She had written about that family, "Cleverness and cheerfulness were prized; conformity was a close third." Apparently Wendy wanted out: her story seemed to reflect a need to shed her family's conventionality. But she was bound by the limited forms of socially sanctioned attachment in our culture: parent-child bonds and those between husband and wife. Like thousands of other women, she used the one to break the other. But she did not wait till after college, as one might expect, to make the trade and thus enjoy her parents' blessing. She decided as a college sophomore to elope.

Wendy realized, even at age nineteen, that what she sought in marriage was an antidote to childhood. And even though the marriage was secret, she achieved her goal: "When I got married the first time, secretly, I knew inside that it was different; I knew I'd been let out of childhood."

Wendy's marriage is remarkable for its lack of public recognition. Despite the fact that it failed to change her daily life in a single respect—she continued to attend classes, to live in a dorm with a roommate, and to spend vacations with her parents—Wendy saw this marriage as "getting away from home." Since she delayed a formal wedding for a year and a half, Wendy was let out of childhood only in her mind's eye. The uniqueness of her situation is that there were no social consequences whatever to the marriage; others' perceptions of her remained entirely unchanged. What did change, however, was Wendy's perception of herself. So powerful was her decision to marry that she described it as "the action that got me out of the house."

Nearly twenty years later, she still viewed this choice as the act that defined her as something other than a child: "I keep coming back to that first decision really, of what I see as a kind of radical, though underground, act to elope. It was a declaration of purpose, a promise I whispered to myself, 'Yes, you can make this decision yourself, nobody else is part of it, it is really your own.' "

Although Wendy spoke of the choice upon which she predicated her adult life as one that "nobody else is part of," it was one of relationship and commitment. Her decision to marry, like anyone's, was hardly made alone. The act she spoke of as radical and independent entailed the most intimate connection with another. "My marriage was a chance to make indelible an adult identity. It's almost as if you're bringing yourself up. I think marriage is a re-creation of a cocoon at the same time that you're also a fully grown butterfly. That metaphor isn't quite right, but that seems like a good characterization anyway."

Marrying also served the critical function of helping her to escape from the dutiful daughter role. For Wendy, this role carried a painful duplicity: "Before I got married, I had two simultaneous selves. One was the dutiful daughter who would write home. And then there was the other one, who led an intense life with Philip, a man I met in freshman year and fell in love with."

Just as Katherine had not been permitted to sleep in the same room with Sam until they married—even though her brothers routinely took their girlfriends upstairs overnight—so Wendy had somehow to deal with the double standard long imposed on females and find a way to establish herself as sexual. Only marriage permitted such legitimation while she was coming of age. Without this vessel to the promised land, women have faced and perhaps still face a condition of permanent asexuality. Confronted with the danger of immutable immaturity in a culture that only recently has begun to come to grips with females as having sexual needs independent of the role of wife, females eager for confirmation of their womanhood have typically reached out for the golden ring on the carousel—marriage.

"That first marriage was an effort to bring the two selves together and not to have to be so split. One aspect of the conflict had to do with guilt over having a sexual relationship while not being married. And the other was that I knew that one of the selves was a very childish self, and I wanted to get beyond that. Marriage was a promise to move ahead. So I began to close the gap with it.

"It had been intolerable to me because the two roles had seemed mutually exclusive, the one as dutiful daughter, the other as adult woman. And the tug back to the dutiful daughter was strong enough to make me uncomfortable. It seemed to me that I couldn't play two characters at once. The marriage was a way of choosing one self over the other—not bringing the two together but having one."

Oddly enough, settling the issue privately appeared to be sufficient: "By being secret, I settled it for myself even though for my family, I still had to go on being naive, being their daughter, doing whatever was expected of me. The formal wedding, nearly two years later, really secured an end to the outrageous aspects of the dutiful daughter. Then I quite literally moved out of their house, had a place of my own, and could contain and limit the dutiful daughter role."

The urge to wipe out a childhood identity proved so overriding that it compelled Wendy even beyond her public wedding. "Even after we were 'publicly' married, I remember wanting to wipe out that identity, those first two decades. I remember filling out the form for college graduation. You were to write down how you wanted your name to appear on the program. And I saw it as a choice, a major choice, whether to put my maiden name down for my middle name. I knew that you were supposed to, but I didn't want to do it. I wanted to eliminate it—as if with a stroke of the pen you could say: 'This is your adult identity,' and erase that childhood identity."

One reason for erasing this vestige of childhood was her sense that being a young unmarried girl was somehow incompatible with her need for independence. In addition to displacing the dutiful daughter role, marriage affirmed that need for independence by marking her new status as an adult. Establishing independence seemed impossible as a female on her own; the mere passage of time, she knew, would not bring it about. To permit her independence and stamp her life with her own signature, she had to make herself adult. And making herself adult required marriage. As she explained it, "There was some instinct for independence that I always felt awful about until I was married. I wanted to grow up fast. I felt it had to be sudden, a cataclysm. I was trying to *make* myself adult. Marriage was the first act of what I still think of as adult decision making."

Making any other decision was something Wendy seemed peculiarly unable to do in the context of her childhood family. She needed to create a separate context in order to decide things for herself. Her account, like Katherine's, shows how attachment and commitment can facilitate independence rather than interfere with it: "I didn't see how I could make my own decisions about what kind of life to lead, what kind of work to do, all those things in the context of the expectations of my family. As it happened, the work was far less a troublesome decision. But this relationship with a really new person—independent, nonfamily—was the major act of independence. It was the first really independent action I took. So many other things followed from that one." Through marriage—an act of attachment—she won her independence by cutting herself off from the influence of her family. Paradoxically, when other decisions were made in the context of marriage, they seemed to be her own. But acting on her own at all, apart from that original family, seemed radical in itself: "I needed to do a radical act like that. I suppose it would have been more radical not to have married at all. That would have been the most radical thing, but that was never an option for me. I never thought of myself as a person who would not be married. It was a given."

Although marriage itself may have been "a given," Wendy had observed early that it would not be enough for her. She remembered sitting on a curbstone at the age of ten, having a conversation with a friend about being glad she lived in that town and had the parents she had. She said she wanted it to be just the same way when she grew up. But this view was to change. The origins of her womanly independence lay in a revision of that stance: "Once I was an adolescent, I knew there were many features of my parents' life I didn't want. I imagined that I would live in an interesting place, a stimulating place. I was keen on moving away from the town I lived in."

She determined, then, not to follow in her mother's domestic footsteps. Like Katherine, she saw excitement in the man's world, in part because it went so far beyond the confines of traditional womanhood. "I didn't want to be as parochial as my mother was. She was a housewife with a narrow world. She didn't use her education or her musical ability. I wanted a more productive, cosmopolitan life, like my father's."

Her adolescent reflections were specific to womanhood: "In my family, the women generally didn't work; they stayed home, did volunteer work, and had children. During adolescence, I was critical of that. I remember quite vividly talking with friends about styles of living and how we imagined ourselves when we would be adults. And I know that I imagined myself to be different from those family women. I'd be married, have children, but I knew I would work, probably teach."

These contemplations, many of which revolved around female models, were entirely internal: "I never had talks with my parents about this, but I do remember once my mother asked, 'What women do you admire?' There was one, a cousin four years older than I was. When my mother asked that question, this cousin had done, in her way, what I was to do in mine. She married, also while she was in college, and then went on to graduate school.

"The other was my mother's sister, my aunt, whose marriage was disapproved of by her family because she had married her first cousin. I saw how upsetting this marriage was—and I saw it as a really heightened crisis, *whom one chose.* It sounds like eighteenth- or nineteenth-century business as I look back on it, but I didn't have that perspective then. I saw these two women as radical for making up their own minds."

Wendy borrowed on her girlhood identification with the unconventional aunt to break with female, family tradition. "I had a very close relationship with this aunt. She lived nearby while I was in elementary school. I would almost always have lunch at her house. To a large degree that home was another home for me. She was a delightful person, witty and understanding. She was sort of arch, outwardly, but really sweet and dear on the inside. The identification between us was a strong one. She was an important, alternative model. She seemed to make decisions quite independent of her family. Certainly to marry this cousin, to have a child with him, was a courageous decision for both of them. She provided a pattern for how to buck a certain oppressive intrusion in a young woman's life."

Wendy underscored the importance of full womanly independence and related it to a departure from the dutiful daughter role: "Making my own decisions as that aunt had came to me first by grabbing the chance that way and declaring that I just wasn't going to be the dutiful daughter any longer. I saw this as the real beginning of an independent life. It took a number of years after that to secure a more solid independence, having acted and made this marriage. That was something else."

A truly independent identity required something more than marriage: "I know I would have been swallowed up and had just the same kind of dependent relationship to my husband that I'd had as a child to my parents if I neglected to establish a separate identity. I remember early on finding it easy to slip into—a talk on the sofa, depending on him to decide, and then being happy with the decision. I could have just traded one outside identity for another. I still needed to make solid my own."

A sense of purpose outside the marriage, an independent tie to the world beyond the marital couch, was essential to a real, adult identity: "I made solid my own identity by going to graduate school and becoming a teacher, earning a salary, at times being the ultimate authority over a decision my husband and I made." In a remark reminiscent of Katherine's comment about making joint decisions, Wendy added, "Certain decisions were made in tandem, but I wouldn't give up my part in them. Those are the things I accomplished in the five years before we had our first child. . . . It would have been difficult for me to come into true independence without having first had the job. There's something very nurturing about the incremental growth of work. It's the easiest way of growing and there's satisfaction in addressing certain tasks."

But just any work likely would not have led to an identity of her own. Wendy's particular work context, a veritable incubator for individual development, was unique: "The school where I taught provided a great deal of freedom. There were some courses that had to be taught, but otherwise there was a lot you could devise on your own. And if you tired of something, you could reperiodize the material and get another perspective, or dream up a new course."

As for Katherine, much of what Wendy did depended on particular people: "The headmaster was terrific to work under. He had some unique ideas, but essentially he really had the children's interests in mind. He would spend a lot of time with kids. They'd spend a whole period in his office, and he'd mostly do the talking. It sounded like ordinary conversation, but he was really outlining things for them.

"He would do things I would not understand until much later. Once he took a weak student and focused the whole school's attention on him. At faculty meeting and morning assembly, he explained to everyone that this young man was from an undeveloped nation, a primitive country, and said that because he was tall, he would probably be made a national leader, so we'd better educate him somehow to take on that responsibility, pay some special attention to him, help him in certain ways. I'd never heard *anything* talked about that way. He really helped that kid, and indeed he did become a leader of his people. Maybe it would have happened by itself, I don't know. But the lesson to me was that *this headmaster intervened.* When he saw a kid foundering, making a fool of himself, he *did* something about it."

The headmaster's active stance, his independent and unconventional views, also counted heavily in helping Wendy weave together family and work: "He helped me too. When I became pregnant, he said, 'Well, you're not thinking of stopping are you?' I said no, I wanted just to work something out that was good for everybody. He said, 'I think it's great if you just work up to the last—as long as you can. It's good for you and it's good for the students. And I think it's especially good for the girls to see a very pregnant woman going about her business without being confined.' Certainly I thought that too, but he was quite open and direct about it."

The headmaster's encouragement was an integral part of a broader philosophy he backed up with action: "There was a young transitional faculty member there too at the time, who had some sheep. He just had them around, they were mowing the lawn, and he liked that. This headmaster would light his pipe at the office window and say, 'You know, you should be able to look out of your classroom and see sheep as part of the landscape. And you should see a very gravid woman there too.' The last month I taught just half my course load, and that was fine, we devised a way to make it work. I did have that child, and it did work out as he said it would. Then I started teaching half-time, in the mornings, which worked out as well."

Her work with that particular headmaster had much to do with Wendy's self-definition: "My job had satisfactions to me in defining my ego. I would have been hard put to stand up for myself without it. That work really was a matrix—a very feminine word, for it derives from *womb* and stems from *mater*, which means 'mother'—for growing up." Indeed the school, under that headmaster, proved to be a womb in which her development flourished.

The gentle progress of Wendy's adulthood came to an abrupt half when her journalist husband was killed in a freak accident while covering the civil war between Nigeria and Biafra. His assignment there was nearly up when his jeep missed a bridge and overturned. Wendy, young and tender, lost her grip on her sense of self. She was literally dumbstruck by this wrenching shock: "The first part of life after that loss was getting a hold back on myself. I remember almost nothing about the first six weeks, but I remember my muteness. I was just barely responding, I could hardly talk. I'm sure I took care of the baby and did whatever, but I don't remember much. Nothing stands out. I had come to an end."

Coming to terms with this loss helped Wendy pierce through a childhood veil of protection. Like the death of Katherine's grandmother, Wendy's husband's death shook her out of an illusion into a new reality: "My husband's death led to my first realization that things didn't work out the way they ought to. He could have chosen a tame, complacent situation, a small-town all-American subject to write about. But we were very idealistic. Covering the war in Africa was our decision together, a mixture of ethical and humanitarian reasoning which I shared. I suppose the ultimate thing I shared was the illusion he had, you know, young men really don't think that they are going to die. They feel invulnerable. So he went, and two days before he was due to come back, he was killed in that accident. It was a shock to me. I was angry; I felt abandoned and tricked.

"After he died, I faced a myriad of choices. I determined I'd better go back to work, I needed that ego support. I wanted my old job back. I got a job teaching civics, but it wasn't even my subject. At the same time, I had this child, an important continuity, and I realized he had to be raised properly. I was glad to be able to make some decisions, but it was just so hard I can hardly believe it."

In addition to being grief stricken, Wendy was thrown into doubt about her status as an adult when she lost the role of wife. Her life study reveals just how shaky a foundation marriage can be for a woman's adult identity, for if marriage confers adulthood, its loss, by simple corollary, nullifies it. Reverting to a preadult condition at age twenty-six with a two-year-old son was an unwelcome change on top of trying to deal with the painful loss of the man she loved—and the blow to her sense of self: "I felt thrust back into adolescence when my husband died. I remember feeling like a college kid again. My parents expected me to come back to live with them. After he died, it would have been natural in a way to go back and start all over again, picking up where I'd left off. But I really wasn't sure who I was at that point. I mean, I could always look to my child and the job I had held and was trying to get back to. But some bedrock sense of myself I really had to find."

To find the sense of self she sought, Wendy needed to escape, again, the dutiful daughter role and to depart home. Her parents' benevolent gesture threatened to undercut her effort to maintain her adulthood and reclaim herself. She could not abide living "at home" with them, no matter how benign their intent. Old patterns rankled even during the few short weeks she tried it. "I was certain I could not maintain any sense of myself if I had to live too close to parental criticisms and interventions. I needed some distance."

For Wendy, marriage had offered the wedge she needed to distance herself from her daughterly role and had provided the leverage she needed to become the woman she'd promised herself she could become. The loss of marriage threatened to revoke her hard-won individuation. Returning to a daughterly state drew her backward toward immaturity. To defeat the dutiful daughter stance, she had to confront her mother directly—without the protection marriage in and of itself had afforded: "I mean, my mother would want to introduce me to new men, tell me how to comb my hair, what lipstick to wear, and all that. I knew that at some point I just had to tell her she couldn't make petty demands on me anymore. I had to confront my mother and say to her, 'You've got to stop this! Look how old I am! I'm not thirteen any longer!' "

Although it was precipitated by trivial requests, the confrontation between her and her mother was a critical battle in Wendy's second effort to grow up. She acknowledged how difficult—and how significant—the encounter had been: "That was harder to do and took me longer to do than to make a proper marriage, or to have a child. That confrontation effected some final growing up. It was a major turning point. That was when I felt, 'You've found and come to know yourself.' " Self-reflection and inner knowledge represented not only a breakthrough with her mother but a break with her own unenlightened past. "I hadn't had the kind of upbringing that leads to that."

In pinpointing her maturity in this incident, Wendy linked the death of her husband to the shift in her relationship with her mother: "The death of my first husband was a major watershed. I realized then that I had had this momentous experience with death, one my mother didn't understand because she was too fearful of it. I felt older, more experienced, and somehow wiser than she. Suddenly I knew that I had had all kinds of experience that was beyond my parents' ken."

In a conscious effort to start anew and reconstruct her life, she married again: "My second marriage has provided me a second chance. I really wanted more of a family. It was part of my putting myself back together. We wanted to have two children, to win over the past. The second marriage has been more of a realization of potential than the first one, when I had no perspective. It is doing these things with a self-consciousness that comes after scrambling that helps you realize potential. You shape it in a clearer way, like a sculpture."

She sculpted a metaphor for her development, starting out with formless matter: "If I had to choose an analogy for my development, it would be a three-dimensional sculpture. You start with an enormous amount of material and it's not clear what shape it's going to be, exactly. It's evolutionary, but it's also a matter of simply working the stuff, to find the hard parts. And it is adding on here and there when that becomes necessary. As I imagine it now, it has a natural female form. It isn't just a replica of myself. There's something more generic about it. That's the visual sense I have of it, a combination of my mother, my aunt, a friend. All the important other figures are somehow melded into the thing. Not only female figures, also my children, my father, husbands, mothers-in-law, anybody who has meant anything to me."

She mused on what maturity is all about: "As I see this process of maturing, I think that it is some combination of learning how much and what sorts of things you do yourself, and how much of other things are really quite shared." And, like Katherine, she defined independence in a "feminine" manner: "I imagined earlier that independence was black and white. It's clear to me now that it's a much more mottled creature. And independence no longer seems so clearly delimited as a stark, geometric figure. It seems much more painterly."

In searching out the elements of her identity, Wendy reflected on childhood and adult roles: "I've become the person I am by realizing certain roles, realizing the role of wife, the role of mother, the role of professional—all of which supplanted more transitional roles: student, daughter, girlfriend."

Tracing the pattern those elements made over time, she pointed to her father's role in their girlhood roots: "Part of me has not been all that varied—the playful part. My father was a blessing in developing that part. I remember playing with him when I was a girl, how he elicited my competence. He taught me tennis, taught me how to throw a ball. He introduced me to skiing. Our relationship was natural, uncomplicated. That was a lighthearted, game-playing time, not just with him but with large numbers of people. There's a lot to be said for the resiliency that sort of thing provides: through those games you learn various roles, and find you have to abide by the rules. Grabbing hold of life, taking it in your grasp and riding on a sense of invention gives a person initiative. It gave me something to rely on in a time of crisis."

Not all women expand their identities by making an amalgam of relationships, sculpting a womanly figure from the stuff of their lives when a marriage ends. Helen, age forty-nine, had been crippled at age thirty-five by her husband's decision to divorce her. Because she had been unable to "gather the wherewithal" to act on her own behalf when the marriage fell apart, her life had been at a standstill during the nearly fifteen years since it collapsed. Completely unlike Wendy, Helen saw herself as a victim of circumstance, one who lacked the initiative Wendy had identified as key—perhaps because she recalled in herself not a self-reflective girl who sized things up and seized life in her grasp but rather a child who felt unwanted. Her story provides a chilling illustration of the costs of founding an identity on marriage without maintaining a commitment to the self as an individual. Her history raises a host of questions about the void created by an absence of self-possession during girlhood.

An editor, Helen had the stark gray hair, aquiline features, and sharp blue eyes that were exactly what one might expect. Her ruthless treatment of manuscripts had given her a formidable reputation; her sardonic wit caused many to beware. Impatient with embellishment of any sort, she'd transferred her editorial bent for the concise to an entire way of life. That critical attitude colored her everyday give-and-take, and provided her a powerful facade. Yet there was something endearing beneath the surface. And she herself had made a vulnerable plea in relation to this study—although she later tried to mask and negate it: In replying to a questionnaire that asked her to describe her present life situation, she'd typed in and then x-ed out: "I cope, on a practical level at best, but if it weren't for my child and probably my own cowardess [sic], probably wouldn't bother. That sounds melodramatic but it's not meant to be." Then she'd let stand "I guess I'd rather not contemplate it." Although other women in the study may have been depressed, this ambivalent message, combined with Helen's demeanor, gave her outlook a particularly ominous tone.

Helen parsed her life as though it were a sentence. From across a glass and chrome table in her office, she outlined her experience. Marriage and divorce bracketed the single period during which she had possessed vitality. "Two watersheds mark my life"—she said. "One was when I was about seventeen or eighteen and I entered the society in which I remained after I married. And the other came at thirty-five when my husband left me."

A person who "lacked self-confidence to a pathological degree" while she was growing up, Helen began to feel that she had something to contribute only when she tapped her intellectual resources in college. Happy among like-minded others, she was relieved when she secured her place in a scholarly group by marrying a professor. "He was something of a boy genius and attracted all sorts of attention in the academic world. Being caught up in a glamorous academic life made it easy to swallow up the child I then was."

Even though Helen perceived her distaff role as ancillary rather than fundamental, she came to depend for her sense of competence on the structure her husband's intellectual group provided. When she described how her self-esteem remained contingent on his world, she compared it to "an edifice." A metaphor quite unlike the fluid, organic form Wendy had shaped with her own hands, this was a rigid, stationary framework built by others, one Helen simply occupied as a tenant: "The construction of my adequacy was not mine. It was my husband's. He gathered extraordinary people. By the age of twenty-five, I knew all the dazzling people there were to know. As time went on, I was addicted to that kind of life, that edifice, which depended on my marriage. It was an edifice I could never have built myself. I could only keep it in repair."

She came to see the edifice as essential to her identity, and felt markedly incomplete when it disintegrated with the breakdown of her marriage: "Within that framework I was functioning perfectly well. But I was aware that I was not a whole person and that I would never be. I was half a person and I needed the other half, the edifice, just to keep me going."

Helen and her professor husband were living in university housing when he decided to divorce her. Since he had a faculty position and she was "merely a faculty wife," she was the one who had to leave—marriage, house, community, everything. Although she moved just four or five blocks away, the dazzling academic world for the most part simply deserted her; the edifice that had housed her vitality stood at an impossible distance.

"I went off to the country for a few days with my daughter—the one bright spot I have. She was only three, and I wanted to avoid too much trauma while our stuff was being moved. When we came back, we were greeted with a living room filled with flowers. A few loyal pals had put them there to welcome us to our new home." Although the flowers were obviously given to her as a well-meant gesture, Helen took their display as a memorial to the collapse of the marriage that had sounded the death knell to her expectations: "The vision of those flowers almost did me in. I saw the corpse of my life laid out in all those lilies. I felt like I was attending my own funeral."

She was immediately "plowed under" by a hoard of practical problems, not the least of which was an absence of income. Her parents did not invite her home or offer her solace, as Wendy's parents had. Loneliness and desperate circumstances overwhelmed her. "And I broke my arm the first week out. I couldn't open a can of food to feed the dog, or get my daughter's shoes tied in the morning. The littlest things loomed so large that I could hardly get through the day."

When she started to get things under control, Helen considered picking up an academic career, for unlike Wendy she did not seek another marriage but rather assumed that she would remain alone.

She'd studied the classics, and had nearly completed a Ph.D. All she lacked was the dissertation. But she decided that fifteen years away from her studies was too long a time to revive the bent for independent research required to finish. She considered starting in another field, "but that seemed like pure folly at my age." Later on she moved to Boston, but she still was stalled by the bureaucracy. Between the time she'd quit graduate school and the time she had to look for a way to earn a decent living, the doctorate had gone from being a teaching degree to being a meal ticket. Without it, she was stuck, at least in academe, in "female jobs."

Helen had no family example of womanly toughness to inspire her toward goals of her own: her mother had married to escape from having to work. "Not until she turned sixty-five did she let on that she'd always wanted to be a sanitary engineer. It turned out she'd been reading books for years on irrigation and dam building." But this goal did not fit the times. She trained Helen in the tasks of domesticity: "When I was five I learned how to iron handkerchiefs, and at six I started washing dishes. These were the tasks of a domestic adulthood."

Her academic father, too, had failed to inspire her. "You're going to be half-baked like your mother," he'd said to her when she had married without "finishing." "He'd decided he was a failure for never having gotten his magic letters, so I was to do it instead. He was determined that I'd be Phi Beta Kappa. I was a dutiful child and got my key in junior year."

Perhaps because she'd been regarded as a carrier for her parents' unrealized goals rather than a person in her own right, Helen had felt in the way as a child. She lacked a sustaining interest of her own. "I used grammar school as a refuge. I would crawl to school even with a fever and spots, sneak out of the house before my mother woke up so she wouldn't know I was sick." But school could not compensate for an identity that languished at home. Worn flat between the household tasks that took the place of her mother's own strivings and the burden of fulfilling her father's promise, she simply had no image of herself—either present or future. "I never knew what to say when people asked me what I wanted to be when I grew up."

That same absence manifested itself after she lost "the edifice." Unable to construct a viable image of herself, she held a series of menial jobs that put her further and further behind the scenes. Having failed at both her father's and her mother's assignments, she saw the world as an unyielding place that constantly reminded her that she was incomplete without her marriage and the way it had defined her.

She pointed to her own passivity as what prevented her from regaining her vitality: "Somehow security means being surrounded by warm bodies all the time, or at least knowing that those warm bodies are available. I crave that kind of structure, but I am totally incapable of building one myself. I can't collect my own warm bodies. I'm just incredibly passive about it." The rupture in her marriage returned her to the sense of futility about "the relentlessness of fate" that had devitalized her childhood.

With her fiftieth birthday fast approaching, Helen concluded: "You ask me what my adult life has been? A vacuum, that's what it's been. By the age of thirty-five, I was a corpse. And now I am almost fifty and I can't even account for the intervening fifteen years. I've brought up my child, but my sense of time has disappeared." Indeed, there was little narrative sense to her description of her life since the divorce. Time had stood still for her, as it does after death. The vitality associated with "the edifice" had been buried with its demise.

Helen's experience followed a pattern much like a sine curve, "the summit at seventeen or eighteen when I fell into a group of people who became the core of my edifice until I was thirty-five. Before then I was a very solitary child, and since then I've been a very solitary adult." The collapse of Helen's edifice confirmed an archaic conviction that had lurked around the edges of her life while she was a girl. The return of her childhood self was the return of a defeated girl. Perhaps because that child had never been encouraged, perhaps because Helen had not reflected on the links between her girlhood and her adult life, she redeemed only isolation.

Helen felt mired in a life that seemed "empty and arid." She had carried over the dependent style she'd developed in relation to "the edifice" into what could not quite be called a social life. She had few friends, and feared that no one would notice if she fell ill or even died. Her adequacy and optimism had been circumscribed by the years during which she maintained the edifice; initiative eluded her. Rather than shaping a life of her own, she had continued "to drift toward infinity." "Forced" into a drab existence, her brainpower had been concentrated on cutting others down to size. She had become neither the subject of her own experience nor the object of her own care.

Given the importance of relationships and commitments to the formation of women's identity, it is not surprising that Helen lost her self-definition when she lost her marriage. The logical consequence

of formulating a sense of self by means of relationships is a radical
threat to the self when an intimate relationship is jeopardized or
destroyed. But Helen's despair was jarring. It called into question
the entire issue of marriage. What, I wondered, might enable a
woman who was married to enhance a sense of self? I would find that
answer as I met with other women: it lay in the choice made by the
girl within.

5

A CHOICE OF
ONE'S OWN

Megan lived in an unassuming second-story flat in a three-decker house north of Cambridge. When she came down the stairs to let me in on a chill February morning, I was struck by how Irish she looked. Her black hair, alabaster skin, small dark eyes, and sharp features gave her an intensity that was also conveyed in her wiry build and quick movements. Dressed for the cold in a woolen vest, corduroy pants, knee socks, and clogs, she led me up to the front room, furnished in early Salvation Army, where she sat in a spindle-backed rocking chair and gave me the couch. Divorced, Megan was living "alone" with her six-year-old son, whose father had custody of him half the time. Since separating from her husband three years before, she told me, she had been "consolidating, refining, and acting upon my self-definition, becoming more myself."

Becoming herself was indeed what Megan's story centered on. What interested me was how she had managed just that—pulling flowers out of the ashes when her marriage went awry—instead of being derailed by divorce as Helen had been. As Megan described her experience, it began to look as though carving out a sense of self in the midst of confusion and vulnerability had hinged on making choices—not the knee-jerk choices of adolescence, but the conscious, deliberate choices of adulthood. Making choices of her own seemed, in fact, as important to Megan's adult identity as securing a room of one's own had been to Virginia Woolf—and every bit as difficult.

By thinking aloud, Megan revealed how the female experience itself can impinge on making choices based on personal convictions. She also showed how crisis can bring forth an inner authority that prompts decisive, purposeful action. Most important, she quite inadvertently turned up the root of such natural authority: the girl within. It was she who helped me see how even contemporary women, women who seem to be in a position to make whatever choices they please, are subject to hidden forces of a particularly female sort that displace this authority—forces we have ceased to acknowledge in our fervor to make our own way. A graduate student at Harvard, Megan was and always had been the picture of independence, competence, and assertion. But at age thirty-one she was no more free from what she called "patterns of womanhood" than her homebound sister of an earlier era.

For instance, while Megan was growing up, she always knew that she'd be married. She had no specific idea beyond that about who and what she might be as an individual. While she hardly saw marriage as a be-all or end-all, she did expect it to form the backdrop for her experience, and she assumed that choosing a husband would secure her future. Once this was accomplished, she figured, everything else would fall into place. This much she knew while she was a schoolgirl. What came as a surprise much later—when the tie between herself and her husband was jeopardized—was that she'd also looked to marriage itself to settle a host of questions about who she was and where she belonged in the world. In other words, like many another woman before and beside her, she expected marriage to provide her an identity: "As an adolescent, I had preconceptions, images of my life," she said. "I thought that things would be smooth, that you would inevitably make choices, but they would be fixed choices. I assumed that I would be married," she said. "I'd choose who I'd get married to, perhaps, but that was an assumption, a fixed choice."

She decided to marry at age twenty-five—expecting marriage

itself to vitalize her adolescent image of adult life as "a smooth un-folding." Hinting at a simplistic view of choice that was destined to change, she hurried on, "Certainly I wasn't aware at that point that things were as difficult or as painful, that choices were as hard as they turned out to be."

Little in her background prepared Megan for the complicated choices that came her way. An unusually intelligent and attractive young woman, she had grown up in New York City and its surround-ings in a family she described as close-knit and loving. Her mother's interests went well beyond the walls of the household: she finished college before she married, and went back for a master's degree after Megan and her younger brother and sister were in school. Her father, a graduate of Annapolis, held an advanced degree in political science.

Megan herself did not intend to follow a purely conventional course. She obtained a measure of independence after graduating from college by spending a few years in New York, dabbling at singing and acting. But she had not pursued any particular goal. Eventually fed up with her own aimlessness, she followed a lover to California, "looking to him for the answers," but she soon regretted this typical female maneuver. Irritated with herself for "letting a man define my life," she came back East. "To leave and come back meant I took my life into my own hands and made an autonomous decision. I felt then that I had to define my life for myself. And I left and came back and was just getting into the process of trying to do just that—when I met Mark and got married. Instead of defining my own life—apart from the prescribed course—I reneged."

By marrying, she ducked the challenge of self-definition, blunt-ing her impulse toward autonomy with the standard female option. Ruefully, she confronted the truth: "My marriage was due to an unarticulated feeling of not having defined myself. It's as if I said, 'Well, this is too hard, I think I'll bypass it.' "

When she married Mark, Megan simply confirmed what she had long taken for granted: that she would marry well, bear and raise children who would thrive, and make central the tasks of marriage and motherhood—following "Woman's Life Plan."[1] She had no reason to think that marrying would limit her opportunities for self-expan-sion, and in fact her marriage did not in and of itself impede her development. Her experiences as a wife and mother had everything to do, in the end, with realizing her true identity. The trouble was that by assuming that marriage itself would supplant her childhood identity, she initially abandoned her own sense of self. As she stepped over the marital threshold, she avoided a host of individual choices by making this single, socially programmed one.

The first catch in Woman's Life Plan was Megan's pregnancy. She saw quite suddenly that with this choice, unlike others, there was no turning back. Her gravid state would not be reversed by second thoughts or a passing mood. The coterminus tie between herself and the fetus meant life itself to the child to come, and carried enduring implications for her too. The fact that gestation would progress in a highly visible and measurable manner although her emotional commitment to it might waver made this decision different from the relatively free choices of adolescence—even the apparently fixed choice of a mate. Pregnancy complicated the simplicity she had accorded to the "Plan" and to the orderly sequence of life events simply because it was neither pliable nor reversible.

Megan explained how childbearing permanently changes the course of a woman's life: "While I was pregnant I became aware that it is something you can't stop. There's an inevitability to it. I don't think that men have the same experience, ever, the sense that once they've started something there's no way to stop it. I mean, you can have an abortion up to a certain time. But if you decide you want to have a child and you get to be six months pregnant, you can't stop it and you don't know what's going to happen. Suddenly it dawns on you that it might not work out, you know, physically you could be seriously compromised, even die."

Indeed, for Megan, this life-giving experience became life threatening—a real jolt to her persistent adolescent expectation that things would stream along naturally. "My son's birth was a difficult one," she explained. "I was in labor for about forty-eight hours and I finally had a caesarean. Nobody could figure out exactly what was wrong. It was unexpected." This last comment seemed to deliver a silence between us as she considered the extreme situation she'd been in— a woman still expecting to follow a simple blueprint yet unable to extricate herself from danger. With the consequences of pregnancy, she'd found that choices are double-edged: the same course of action could appear to ensure her future while actually threatening it.

Imperiled by this biological process, Megan reinvoked her adolescent certainty, saying, "I don't remember feeling frightened because I still thought that 'somebody will take care of it.' " She conveyed how much reassurance such an assumption could offer— and how much anxiety its loss entails—when she explained, "I still held the hypothesis that things would work out, that everything would be fine, that this was the way life was supposed to be." Her dismay was disarming as she recalled how coming face to face with death in the process of giving birth had dislodged that assumption: "But when the process didn't unfold smoothly, I was taken aback. I realized then that I had no real control over what happened."

Her confidence in her assumptions badly shaken, Megan was also physically debilitated by the surgery—a real double-whammy. As if all this were not enough, she and her husband were in a transitory situation. They had recently moved; Mark worked at quite a distance from home. They were isolated within the broader community, and disconnected from each other. The idealization of new motherhood was abruptly crushed under the enormity of Megan's solitary responsibility. Like those of all newborns, her baby's needs were immediate and compelling. Megan had no choice but to respond to his incessant demands: "I couldn't stop doing it when I got tired of it, I couldn't walk away from this choice. You can get away from your spouse, but you can't leave a baby. You have to pay attention to it just for it to survive. It's pretty elemental: the child is there."

The obligatory altruism of motherhood obliterated any remaining vestige of the selfish omnipotence that characterizes conventional adolescence. "Having to take somebody else into account at that level means not being able to be selfish. I couldn't choose not to be whatever this baby needed me to be, whether I was tired or sick or lonely. I would sacrifice other things, pay attention to this. Life's ordered priorities dictated that I consider his well-being above all else."

The paradox of choice in a mother's life, where choice is tied to lack of choice by a cord of responsibility for another's very survival, became evident, too, as the sudden absence of freedom that this "free" choice entailed hit Megan like the proverbial ton of bricks. The enormity of the responsibility shifted not only her daily orientation but also her self-image in a profound way, catapulting her into adulthood: "The experience of having this child to care for was a conscious 'I am an adult.' I had never before said that to myself, consciously. It was the responsibility of having to care for him. The overwhelming feeling was that a sense of responsibility is connected with adulthood, a sense of not being able to escape it."

The consequences of this choice were permanent. "A child is a reality you can't undo. I had a responsibility of my own choosing. I was forced to say to myself, 'This is all yours, you chose it, it will never go away.' " The realization that she herself had chosen motherhood made its utter inescapability all the more grating, as the adolescent urge to divide the world according to "us and them" gave way to adult experience: "I had to own up to having this baby. I could not go to 'them' and say, 'Things are terrible—I hate this kid. I just wish it would go away.' "

Beyond the normal all-consuming impact of motherhood, Megan had particular reasons for resenting her baby's birth. She explained how "having a child exacerbated the problems of the marriage," touching off a serious crisis between herself and her husband. This crisis evoked a pivotal confrontation that led, ultimately, to a long-stalled and badly needed process of self-definition. The confrontation that mattered, however, was not with her husband. It was with herself.

"I guess the really crucial thing in acquiring an identity of my own was the whole marital conflict precipitated by Jonah's birth. My husband's reaction to it was very disorienting. He was jealous, and he was immature too. I remember him saying, very forcefully, 'You're paying more attention to my son than you are to me, and I don't like that.' And my feeling at the time was, 'Well, I have no other choice. Don't you see that? I'm barely surviving, I'm just hanging on by the skin of my teeth.' "

The isolation of new motherhood, the fatigue from pregnancy, labor, and the caesarean, the sleep deprivation of the first months of her baby's life, and the desperation of her straitened circumstances collected in Megan's voice as she described the crisis that nearly made for her undoing, one that initiated the important developmental process of first abandoning her adolescent assumptions and then articulating a sense of self. She looked suddenly vulnerable as she confided the details: "When Jonah was about six months old, Mark had an affair, very brief, and he told me about it. It really shattered my image of how life would be. My assumption had been that my husband would never hurt me and would always help me and be good. And after that, it wasn't true. It just didn't hold. My hypothesis about life was no longer valid."

"My husband would never hurt me and would always help me and be good"—a simple, childlike lament embedded in a sophisticated adult thought held the tension between the little girl in Megan and the woman she would become. She was caught anew by that tension as she spelled out how this threat had shattered her confidence in her husband and challenged her assumptions about what marriage and motherhood could provide. When the affair exposed and broke down the hypothesis upon which she had always depended, namely, the unconscious assumption that making the fixed choice of a mate would assure her identity, her loss of faith reverberated against the lapse of confidence she'd suffered during labor. Her sense of herself as a free agent jarred, her reliance on marriage as a framework for experience and a guarantee of protection collapsed.

Left with "nothing whatever to count on," Megan was stricken with a painful loneliness—a real paradox considering that she was hardly alone in any concrete sense, given the continuing presence of her husband to say nothing of the incessant demands of her infant son. But she was alone in a more profound sense in the loss of protection her assumptions had provided. Her dependence on those assumptions had afforded her a certain security—the sort a person does not even know she has until it suddenly crumbles. An existential isolation overtook her when the crisis with Mark occurred.

Megan seemed to be at a loss even as she recalled that aloneness when we talked some six years later: "I felt alone, completely alone. It just didn't matter that I was married, I was still alone. I realized that my husband could not make me happy. In fact, he could make me very unhappy. I asked myself, 'Who can I trust now? I have to trust myself. I have to be responsible for my being happy. I have to do it.' And that's when I said to myself, 'OK, what do I want to do?' "

In demolishing her unconscious assumptions, the crisis forced Megan to grapple with the discrepancy between the way life was supposed to be and the way it was turning out to be, and it led her, finally, to forge an identity of her own. A curious counterpoint between you and I ensued as she recalled this dialectical process: "During that crisis, I began to assess myself and my place in the world. I began to see that you had to be an independent person, that it wasn't viable to think that I could be part of a couple and that would give you a way to be in the world. I really began to see that I had to define myself. In marriage I had a life, but I did not have a *self*. Getting my self was something I postponed."

Creating her own life was something she had not expected to have to do at all. Its necessity showed her what she had lacked: identity itself. In a statement Helen could have learned much from, Megan described how the crisis in her marriage forced her to carve out a sense of self—within the matrix of adult relationships: "This crisis showed me that I didn't have an identity. I did not resolve the identity crisis in the prescribed adolescent years. It was the catalyst of Jonah's birth and Mark's affair that forced me not to postpone it any longer. That's when I really faced it. That's how I found out that you have to create your own life within the context of marriage."

Megan uncovered an important contradiction when she considered how motherhood too had affected her identity development. As she examined its impact on her sense of self, she realized that although motherhood requires a self, it demands *selflessness*—literally, the absence of a self. It was only when she considered this conundrum that Megan realized she had looked to motherhood for a life purpose. Instead she found that "having a kid could not be a purpose. A sense of purpose is synonymous with providing a sense of self. Being a parent requires maturity. It's an experience that has to do with the self, but it's not enough to have to do with the self. It requires a self."

She described just how caring for a baby drew her away from a sense of self while appearing to supply one: "Having a child could keep me busy and deflect me from thinking about this issue, but it was not going to provide me with a sense of self. It could not sort out questions like what to do, how to have purpose in the world, how to find direction and goals—in short, how to be in the world. Being an adult means taking a look at yourself to shape your life, to make the difficult choices consciously. Having a child does not accomplish that."

Megan felt keenly disappointed when she discovered that having a baby was not going to give her a life purpose. Nor would feminine roles and the domestic realm suffice. There was a real difference between depending on those roles for an identity—as she had until then—and acquiring the authority of self-determination.

Acknowledging the magnitude of the disappointment and accounting for the difficulty that followed from it seemed in itself, however, to help her gather strength by dislodging a certain passivity that had framed her expectations until then. Being forced out of a passive stance itself launched the pivotal process of self-definition: "The identity I acquired came from feeling that I had to take responsibility for creating my own life. It wasn't just going to come, it wasn't just going to grow. It had to be built. I knew that I had to make choices and take responsibility for my own happiness and for the direction of my life. And I had to set some goals, I had to make a purpose for my life that was just for me and just from me, one that wasn't fulfilling somebody else's needs. To do that, I started from nothing."

Ironically, it was the collision of choice and choicelessness that forced Megan to create options within a relational context: "Before, I'd had the option to run away, to rationalize, to justify rather than change. But in this situation I had nowhere to go. I couldn't support myself, I had a six-month-old baby I couldn't leave. You get to rock bottom. So then you are left with these limited choices, and if I wanted to do anything, I had to choose something, to work for something. There weren't any other options."

But the disappointment over what motherhood failed to supply was not without a saving grace. Consciously coming to terms with her situation and developing her abilities to care for her child tested Megan's inner resources—and provided a sorely needed bridge to an identity of her own. That bridge was built from a new sense of choice, one that emanated from self-knowledge and self-examination: "I began to know myself a little bit better by taking care of Jonah," she said. "I felt, 'I can do this, I am good at this. My choice is to do this, to take care of this child. It is hard, but I can manage.' I did cope, and I felt like I was good at this. It was a fuller way of looking at myself, the first real experience of 'I am a person with certain characteristics that are viable because of this experience.' "

Being able to see herself from an outer vantage point and to label herself as "a person with certain characteristics"—the essence of self-reflection—were key to Megan's development. It was this ability to articulate who and what she essentially was that would later unlock Megan's forgotten girl, the child who harbored a natural ability to choose. In the meantime, Megan realized "that I wanted to shape a life"—to develop her competence beyond the domestic sphere.

"Being home and being married wasn't sufficient. You have to go out in the world and accomplish something. I wanted to secure my sense of competence, to be good at something, acquire a measurable skill, something that I could say, 'I have learned this, I am good at this, I can do this, I know this.' I had to use my potential and mold it."

But wanting to shape a life was not enough. Megan also had to come to terms with her own inertia. She sounded determined as she recounted an inner battle with what she saw as adolescent fecklessness: "I had to make choices and had to work for those choices, even when I didn't want to. I had to follow through and set a goal and reach it. I had to sit down and decide, 'What am I good at? What do I like to do? And what career choice would fit these criteria?' And that's when I decided to go back to school—and to stick with it."

Curiously, the paid work she had done "out in the real world" before she got married counted for little in the active self-ownership and competence Megan sought. Megan had to determine her own course and actively forge a solution of her own choosing to acquire real competence: "I had worked since the age of eighteen," she mused, "but this was different. I was going to acting school, and the voice teacher told me I had a good voice, the potential to be really good. And that carried me along. I studied music then for several years. I wrote songs, did street singing. I got club jobs, here and there. It all sort of happened to me, floated to me. It was easy to do those things. But I never made a decision to do it myself. I never said, 'I want to be an opera singer and I'm going to work at it.' None of it was generated from a sense of purpose."

Apparently even extraordinary abilities failed to count to Megan if they were not driven by purpose, choice, and intention. Situations that drew on her talents did not help her construct an identity because of this lack. If they came about by luck, they felt inauthentic: "The singing didn't make me feel competent because it wasn't something I chose. It was something that I happened to have potential for. Through a fluke of chance, somebody encouraged me. But it didn't feel legitimate. Because I didn't generate it for myself, it was doomed."

She pointed to the link between competence and choice, and exposed passivity as the enemy of self-ownership when she clarified, "Not choosing it myself meant there was no fuel to keep it going. I was in the passive mode. It lacked a self-determining aspect. I don't think I had enough sense of self to make a choice of my own. It takes a sense of self to choose to do something."

"How do you feel you got a sense of self?" I asked, and I learned how crucial the self-examination born of crisis can be.

"It's all in that one year after Jonah was born. The disappointment, the hurt, the feeling that I was alone. Having to take a look at myself, having to say that I was partially responsible for what had happened, having to confront my own culpability." She nodded toward the door as though someone was just outside as she added, "My husband was not an ogre. I had to examine the consequences of my own actions, to look at them and say, 'OK, what are the characteristics that led you to this? And what do *you* want to be?'"

It was a mystery how Megan had navigated such a devastating crisis and come out of it with any sense of self at all. She pondered on how all this had led not to an utter loss of self but rather to the acquisition of an identity. As she reflected on the nature of identity, she grew pensive about its evolution: "I feel that there has always been a thread, a sense of solidity about myself. But before all this, there was just that thread of a self without an identity, enough to cope with crisis but not enough to define that self, to shape it. At least I had not been conscious of the self before."

She seemed to be considering something more as she contemplated the process further. "The self wasn't conscious until it was jolted to awareness, or *I* was, that I had certain characteristics that I had to take over actively by myself. I had to take a look at the myths I had wrapped myself in. A great part of it was looking at myself and not liking what I saw, and recognizing that I'd have to change this emerging conscious self. That was primary."

Having survived this crisis early in her marriage, Megan decided a few years later to separate from Mark. Her decision was not made without ambivalence. Part of her reluctance to leave the marriage stemmed from "parting from a man who knew that me, before I grew up." Ties to childhood tugged at her when she found herself hesitant to put the marriage behind her. As she described this sore spot, Megan turned up a memory that gave me a glimpse of the root process at work in female identity formation.

In a discussion that oscillated between present and past, she began to uncover the girl as mother to the woman. "A good mother learns early that she must always be letting go," she had written on the test I had sent her before the study began. She amplified that statement as we spoke together. "And you let go of who you were in the past, of childhood and growing up, of your childhood house. Letting go is painful," she added with regret. "You need to go over it again and again."

I first caught sight of the girl as the touchstone for a woman's identity when Megan made this loop back to her childhood—her initial allusion to the girl she'd been and to that girl's meaning to her. Her womanly strength would be somehow linked to the act of retrieving that girl—even as she let her go. Her glance fell and her voice was nostalgic as she went on. "Maturity is to see the child you were and own that caring about your self." Making a figure eight with one hand she added, "As it gets clearer, it moves further away."

As she recalled her girlhood experiences, the elusive girl within sallied forth: "At nine, I can remember walking on a fence, all around a park, thinking I really liked being nine years old and I wouldn't mind being nine forever. I was finding out about the world, not doing anything particularly momentous, just thinking those thoughts to myself as I walked along the fence. I remember having a real sense of joy, of confidence about negotiating the world on my own. The image I have is of a child with a long string to hold on to, one she can move freely around. I felt secure and self-contained. I had a sense that 'I can get by in the world, even if it means I am alone. There's a way for me to negotiate it. I can do it.' " This self-possessed girl, a child in step with the world, playful, spirited, autonomous yet connected was the girl that Megan recaptured and sharpened to build her sense of self as an adult woman who could take the rudder of her life into her own hands.

The childhood root for the adult Megan had become took form as she recollected the girl: "When I was nine, we moved from New York to the suburbs. I had been going to a small private school that was connected to a church where I was studying to be confirmed, but we moved before that happened. I really wanted to be confirmed and I pushed for it. So the nuns at the church sent me the homework. I would complete each lesson and send it back to them, and I managed to get confirmed in that church, which was very important to me." The girl proved determined. "Even at nine I was able to say, 'This I want, this is important to me, it's something outside of myself and I'm willing to work for it.' "

The choice to be confirmed despite the timing of her family's move was the first to give Megan a sense of herself as "a person in the world, separate from others. I was willing to work for something that had meaning only to me. It was as if I were saying, 'I am this person who wants to do this, that's who I am.' It was part of an identity. I could see a little bit of myself, I could have some image of who I was."

Describing this realization led her to recall a later self-reflective dialogue when Megan had borrowed on the girl's initiative for an adolescent declaration of self: "I'm thinking of how I graduated from high school a year early at my own impetus. It was like I was saying, 'I am a person who wants to move on. I don't want to stay here.' To do that, I had to convince my parents, and the principal of the school. I had to go outside myself, which wasn't something that came easily to me. I had to go knocking on people's doors saying, 'I want this.' "

Both these choices involved considerable initiative—to say nothing of an ability to stand apart from herself and reflect on who she was. When I asked Megan what had precipitated the two like, though opposite, events, the same childlike, self-determining language marked her response, as the adolescent's declaration of independence echoed the nine-year-old's initiative: "These changes were catalysts for making a statement about who I was at that moment. In high school, it was a way of defining myself: 'I am a person who wants to do this. I am going to leave high school a year early,' I'd said to myself. That says something about me because the reasons for doing it were *my* reasons. I saw myself differently, doing that instead of just drifting along. My willingness to exercise choice gave me a way to see myself."

A child who could confirm herself *before* she turned to relationships to prescribe her role, this girl was the referent for Megan's essential identity. The child provided the initiative—and the language—for Megan the adolescent to make a choice of her own. Her sense that "I can get by in the world, even if it means I am alone" at age nine provided the germ for "This is what I want, this is important to me," at sixteen. The high-school student's "I am a person who wants to move on," and the mother's "I can do this, I am good at this" were foreshadowed by the nine-year-old's "There's a way for me to negotiate it. I can do it."

Megan elucidated the importance of retrieving that self-possessed girl as she spoke both to the continuity of this childhood identity and to its transformation by saying, "The image of that child, doing her confirmation lessons by herself, walking around the park with that long string to hold on to, seems implicated in the person I've become as a mature individual. I have a lot of tender feelings for that child that was me and is still me to some extent. The child carries the essence of you as a person, it includes your roots, who you came from. It's part of your past before you were, and what made you that child." Although certainly changed by intervening experiences, Megan concluded her life study by saying of herself at age thirty-one, "In some crucial way, I am that nine-year-old encapsulated in a grown-up."

Only after her marriage was put at risk did Megan unearth the competent, autonomous choice maker she had been at age nine. Only when she articulated a self within the context of her responsible, feminine roles did she find that depending on marriage for direction and self-definition had eclipsed her own choices. It had taken a major crisis to expose the danger in the widely shared womanly assumption that "somebody will take care of it"—of her—in the "continuous unfolding of life." Believing that caring relationships would ensure protection, provide a basis for identity, and secure a lifelong place in the world had deflected her identity development. The devastation of that false hypothesis had constituted a full-fledged existential and epistemological crisis.

The outcome was fortunate: Megan had been able to construct

an identity out of the rubble of broken assumptions. No less caring and no less related, still committed to marriage and motherhood, she began to balance care for herself with caring for others and to make herself the subject of her own experience when she retrieved the ability to make choices of her own. A critical shift for women, this development came from first examining and then shifting out of her passive stance.

But what had become of the self-possessed nine-year-old in the interim? How had Megan gotten disconnected from the girl in the first place?

Megan pointed to "patterns of womanhood" as the culprit in her loss, suggesting that social prescriptions entice females to assume ready-made roles in lieu of defining themselves and directing their own choices—even females coming of age in contemporary times. "Being female makes it harder to become oneself," she said. "The culture offers escapes: patterns of womanhood. Women are still seen as part of marriage, which is given a sugar coating. No one tells you that you need to create yourself as an individual within that context.

"Even though I was intelligent, accomplished, and creative, I didn't see myself as autonomous. I felt I needed to be married, have a kid, and do all of that. It was hard to see any choices other than those that belonged to the typical pattern. I followed that trajectory until the image burst. Only when my husband had that affair did I look at the assumptions it carried."

And yet, Megan was clearly a woman with her own signature, perhaps all the more distinct because she had gone through such a struggle to inscribe her life with it. She had constructed a solid identity of her own in the face of crisis—without abandoning her relationships.

What clues could her life study provide to this constructive process? It seemed that hitting rock bottom in a state of existential aloneness had had much to do with Megan's coming to a bedrock sense of self. She'd laid the groundwork for building her own identity when disappointments leveled her adolescent expectations and ripped apart the mythical trappings of femininity she had wrapped herself in. The foundation for her newly wrought sense of self was forged by grappling with the discrepancy between the way things were supposed to be and the way things turned out to be. And the abandonment of long-held assumptions that leaves a woman feeling abandoned herself served as a cornerstone for the new identity she built. Feeling alone appeared, in fact, to have been a necessary support to reconstructing an identity that would meet and match her own specifications.

Equally important was the intermittent dialogue she'd had with herself, reworking a scaffolding of assumptions to accommodate the hard realities she stumbled upon[2]—realities that exposed the fault in forfeiting choice and depending on relationships to ensure a firm footing for her life. But the strongest buttress in acquiring a sense of self consisted in making choices of her own. The source for those choices was the nine-year-old fence walker, the girl who chose to confirm herself, independent of her family.

I left that simple apartment at the end of our final meeting with Megan's words ringing in my ears: "Being female makes it harder to become oneself. The culture offers escapes: patterns of womanhood." Indeed, ready-made patterns of womanhood had masked her autonomy, diverting her from an authentic sense of self. Did such patterns of womanhood deny other women the needed chance to make choices of their own, deflecting them from self-determination? What do Megan's comments suggest about the impact of marriage on women's identity? How might the "typical trajectory" of marriage pull others off course? And what is it that tamps down the young choice maker, covering over a female's primary identity so that the girl within lies buried, hidden even from the woman she herself could become? When Megan pointed to patterns of womanhood as the culprit, I wondered how broad cultural, social, and gender expectations had operated to shape other women's sense of identity—or to separate them from it.

I turned to the narratives of two older women, each one old enough to be Megan's mother or even her grandmother, to see how such expectations—or the rejection of those expectations—had functioned in their development. Both of them had grown up in an era when women's choices were blatantly constricted, a time when a woman either subscribed to patterns of womanhood or risked cutting herself off from the mainstream. The stories of these two women unfolded on separate tracks. One, determined to be independent despite the expectations of the times, rejected patterns of womanhood—but lost her grip for decades on "the person I really was" anyway. The other subscribed to Woman's Life Plan, harnessing her energies to the goals of her husband. For her, the plan proved nearly lethal.

6

THE DIVISION OF PURPOSE FROM SELFLESS CARE

early old enough to be Megan's grandmother, Sophie had grown up in an entirely different era. A woman of her generation was not expected to make her own choices or to forge an independent life. Rather, she was expected to marry. While Megan had had all the advantages of a middle-class child of the fifties—suburban neighborhood, well-chosen friends, and private schools—Sophie, a child of the Depression, had lived close to the edge even as a girl. Her parents were Polish immigrants; her father a tailor, her mother grateful not to work outside the home. How was Sophie to escape this marginality? She knew that if she was not fortunate enough to be chosen as a wife, she would end up as a spinster teacher or nurse, or a nun. She shuddered at those destinies. There was but one way out: Woman's Life Plan.[1] The plan was simply to marry well, to bear and rear children who thrived, and to forward her husband's career.

Sophie did not realize that the plan depended on woman's subordination—and that subordination itself would make self-possession impossible. In fact, self-possession was entirely too abstract a notion for her times. Sophie was concerned solely with survival, and she knew that survival hinged on marriage. She had only one choice: to embrace the plan and make it her own.

Beyond survival itself, marriage held a certain allure, for it provided a focus and a role. It gave a woman a place in the world, fending off the bleak anomie that afflicted an unmarried woman. Sophie certainly did not expect to lose anything by it. She "did very well," as they say, after a fleeting liaison in her early twenties, by marrying a promising young doctor. When she took this step, she became "frau doctor": she helped her husband build his practice by answering phones, making appointments, keeping books, and managing the office. Soon enough, she delighted him with three healthy children— all boys. She hardly noticed her authenticity slipping away while she tended to their needs.

Little did Sophie suspect that she would ultimately lose her reckoning when the husband she'd buoyed up and the sons she'd launched charted courses of their own. Only when her children grew up did she find she'd lost her own moorings by enshrouding herself in the mythical trappings of femininity and jettisoning her girlhood hopes to the currents of Woman's Life Plan. Her desperate attempt to shed the trappings of womanhood when she realized she'd become no more than ballast nearly cost her her life.

But when I met Sophie at age sixty-eight, she was the picture of stability. Straight-backed and elderly, she had made that crisis fade beneath her calm composure. Her children, all in their thirties, had established families of their own. Her husband suffered from Alzheimer's disease; feeble and unable to communicate, he had been placed in a nursing home. Sophie lived alone in a stately manor house.

As she served tea from a silver service on the sideboard in the dining room, I heard a grandfather clock chime four in the hall. A welcome breeze from a screened-in porch cooled us this late summer afternoon as she fastened a loose strand of hair with a comb and began through her own life story to shed light on the questions Megan had raised about patterns of womanhood. Her account illuminated all too well, in fact, just how patterns of womanhood can obliterate the girl within by virtue not of marriage itself but of something even more important: a woman's separation, via the plan, from her own sense of purpose.

I began to sense how the dichotomy between the selfless care that forms the backbone of the plan and the purposeful nature of the girl would deflect a female from her own purposes as Sophie recalled her girlhood aspirations. Her life story cast in bold relief the consequences to females of dividing the human world by sex, of polarizing such common human qualities as work and love, purpose and care, competence and femininity, selfishness and devotion, intellect and feeling. What I realized stood behind her composure turned out to be a despair that resulted from shearing away a girl's own hopes and supplanting them with marriage. The proverbial hope chest of her times suddenly looked more like a coffin as she described how she'd buried purposes of her own in the process of becoming not someone in her own right but someone else's wife.

From behind her glasses, Sophie's eyes took on a faraway look as she twisted a sapphire ring and sifted through memory to the girl she had been long ago. When she was a child, she "wanted to lead a useful life" but found she "had no models for doing so." She was determined not to be like her mother—a woman, Sophie noticed, who did not stand her own ground. Even as a little girl, she wanted something more worldly than a hidebound domestic life. She was bright and ambitious—but her aspirations conflicted with society's notions of what a female was supposed to do and to be. She learned early that professional ambitions were not suitable for a girl. Boys were meant to study, girls to marry.

"I grew up during the Depression, our economic situation was poor. But my brother was encouraged to study and I was not. As luck would have it, he was reluctant to study on," she began. "But I wasn't encouraged. No one ever said, 'Well, why don't you?' Mother didn't and my older sister didn't, no such thing. I had an uncle I was close to, but even he laughed at my ambitions to be a lawyer, because I was a girl. It wouldn't have taken much, but nobody lifted a hand. It wasn't expected."

A girl who wanted to be a lawyer while Sophie was growing up was subject to ridicule: "I was made to feel very strange in wanting to be or do something on my own," she explained. "Because I was a little girl, I was expected to get married. And when the whole world tells you something, you begin to believe it." The influence of "the whole world" and its attitudes was strong.

By the time Sophie married her young man, she had long given up ambition. She felt lucky to escape the common cramped boardinghouses that surrounded her during the Depression. Having a house of her own gave her privacy and status. But instead of the fulfillment she expected from supporting her husband in a growing practice and rearing children who thrived, she found herself isolated—the same paradox Megan had encountered, for Sophie, like Megan, was in the constant company of her children. While she took pleasure in devoting herself to them, she had the uncomfortable feeling that something terribly important was missing. She could not define exactly what it was, but she knew she was dissatisfied.

Unable to identify what was wrong, Sophie focused her concern on an absence of intellectual activity. To compensate for that lack, she organized a course of study at home, systematically reading the classics. But these efforts proved empty as she, like Megan, was cowed by an essential loneliness that compounded what was actually a loss of self—a loss that had wiped out her intellectual goals and gone beyond them to sweep away the sense of purpose she'd embodied as a girl.

In retrospect, Sophie could explain how her relationship to her husband and children had limited her development, and see how she herself had made their needs far more important than those she might have claimed as her own. She realized that putting her life in the service of their development—without developing her own purposes—had covered over her needs to a dangerous extent, impinging even on the joy of mothering itself. In playing out the domestic role, she'd put aside the question of what to do with her self: "I was very dedicated to my kids and did only for myself to sustain my desires, but I was secondary. My interests were never equal, never on a par with the interests of my family. My husband didn't share the responsibility of the children—everything was up to me. I didn't really take myself, my own development, seriously."

In the process of neglecting her development, she lost her sense of self. Any individuality she'd had as a girl was obscured by the mother role. Her devotion to the family all but eclipsed the natural autonomy of youth—and the natural authority of the self. Nurturance and empathy, when they depended on selflessness, made for a poor substitute for an identity of her own: "Not only did my development languish because my identity reflected the children's achievements and their development, but it was worse than that: I was losing my own identity. I was Mother. I was trying to make a profession out of Mother. No one had ever said, 'Well, Sophie, what do you really want to do with your life? You—the inner soul of a person?'"

Only when Sophie's sons were nearly grown up did she recognize that "motherhood was not a profession." She felt locked away from experiences of her own, and wanted to taste independence. Frustrated by professional objectives that seemingly could not materialize, she began taking college extension courses and got a part-time teaching job—opportunities that had previously been precluded by domestic demands. "I finally got a little job that was my own. I couldn't do that before because my husband was used to depending on me. But I wanted to experience for myself being in the world on my own. I wanted to take things on their own, by myself, with my own judgment. I was out there to find myself again. I was on my own two feet. I wasn't depending on anybody. And I could stand on my own merits, so to speak, not on those I had gained by association. I made my own decisions."

But the job Sophie got was a temporary one, and when it ended she all too easily lapsed into the selfless role she'd occupied for a quarter of a century—a role she was drawn to simply by virtue of its familiarity. The feminine model she had conformed to for so long was both empty and ever-present, a vacuum that drew her back inside: "It was difficult to oppose my husband and his wishes that I stay at home, to break out of the mold I had been encouraged to sit in happily."

What happened then exposes the dangers of abstracting a woman's psychology from her biological status: "Finally, when it came to menopause, I fell into a depression. Everyone blamed my feelings on menopause and they kept saying, 'You'll get over it.' "

The passivity of Sophie's syntax, the stasis of her metaphors, suggests she'd lost her own volition: "Molded" into a frame of mind in which she could not act, she could not avoid "falling" into a depression. But a part of Sophie knew that menopause could not explain what was happening to her. This was a depression that struck at the depths. "I thought it was the end of my life. I didn't believe it was a passing thing. I thought this depression was final, that this was it." As if to impress me with how serious it was, she added, "It was severe."

In taking over Sophie's life, Woman's Life Plan had obliterated Sophie herself. Caught on a hook of selfless devotion, she'd been left to dangle above the real world that vitalized her husband and sons, suspended apart from her own vitality. So accustomed to fostering the needs of others while she neglected her own, she could not imagine an existence without the structure of motherhood, yet she could not abide that structure. Unable to tolerate the plan, yet unable to live without it, what could she do but cross off the whole dilemma?

Sophie became so separated from her own purposes by succumbing to the domestic press that she no longer felt she knew herself: she made a serious attempt at suicide. "I had to burst out of the vise I was in," she explained. "I felt as though I were absolutely somebody else, a terrible feeling. I took the risk of a suicide attempt because I wanted to be extricated, saved from the life I was living, to burst out of that stagnation."

Had it not been for an early morning call to her doctor husband at home, one that awakened him, but strangely, he thought, did not disturb her, Sophie certainly would have died from the sleeping pills she'd taken at bedtime. When he found her sleep unnatural and was unable to rouse her, he realized that she was nearly dead. He summoned an ambulance; she was resuscitated and rushed to the hospital. Much to his distress, she was admitted to a psychiatric unit and treated with psychotherapy.

Sophie's nearly fatal suicide attempt at age forty-nine could easily evoke a psychiatric diagnosis of menopausal depression—even in this day and age. Fortunately, the resident assigned to her case avoided falling into that ready trap. He resisted the usual pressures to label her condition "involutional melancholia," a diagnosis often affixed to women, denoting a depression that arises from passing the peak of life and heading into the inevitable decline.[2] He avoided too the handy explanation of "the empty nest," which would have been natural considering that she was "losing" her children to adulthood. Had he appropriated such stock explanations to direct the course of her therapy, Sophie surely would have languished.

But this young psychiatrist recognized in Sophie a lost soul, perhaps the "inner soul of a person" she had named when describing her experience as a girl—the inner soul that had been neglected for the decades that had passed since her girlhood. Instead of simply treating an illness, he treated Sophie by meeting her on her own uncertain ground.[3] He approached her not as Mother, not as frau doctor, not as aging matron, but as Sophie, just Sophie—a person he did not yet know and wanted to come to understand.

As the therapy unfolded, Sophie rediscovered and reclaimed her girlhood purposes, uncovering the primary self that had been submerged by feminine roles. Through the therapeutic relationship, she not only retrieved the ambitions she had lost as child but also recovered the feelings and vitality of the long-buried girl who'd held them. Rediscovering the girl and her ambitions was an experience so powerful that Sophie compared it to being reborn: "I was reborn from my old youthful ambitions of what I wanted to do with my life, those

I had as a youngster. It wasn't just the education I wanted, I also wanted independence. What I wanted was to develop my intellectual interests, those I'd had since elementary school."

At this point, Sophie began to construct a life that stemmed from a sense of self that was clearly her own. Instead of molding her identity to the shell of roles that had encased her, she turned her attention to her inner resources. She enrolled in the university's extension program. "The fact that I could develop my own inner resources delighted me. And pursuing what I wanted to do gave me an identity that no one could take away from me. Those other identities could be removed: if you are a mother and your children go to Australia, you've had it. What are you?"

She saw education as something no one could take away from her: "But if you develop yourself in your mind, what you know and what you can do, no one can take that away from you. I wanted to have an open-ended pursuit that I could develop to wherever it would lead me." Pursuing a graduate degree at the time we talked, she pointed to the bachelor's diploma over the sideboard.

By reclaiming her youthful ambitions and permitting them to take first place in her life, Sophie recaptured her primary identity and made it her own. In recovering the neglected purposes of the girl within, she restored the sense of meaning and integrity that girl embodied. She conquered loneliness by connecting firmly with herself—retrieving the girl who'd been neglected in favor of female stereotypes. The girl now defined Sophie's way in the world, directing her life from a clear sense of self.

In the pleasant dark of the late afternoon, I had been unaware of the many pieces of sculpture that were placed around the house until Sophie walked to a corner of the dining room and turned on a lamp. I saw that in this corner stood a porcelain piece on a dark wooden stand. The figure of a woman, it had fallen over and broken just before Sophie was admitted to the hospital. She explained that she had worked to restore it during the outpatient phase of her treatment. She had promised herself during her recovery that if she could repair the figure, she could repair herself. She showed me with pride that every fragment had been saved; she had restored it completely. Her ability to glue together her original identity when it had been fractured by the force of domesticity and to brace it with her original goals paralleled her restoration of the sculpture.

Sophie's life pattern was one in which the caring role of traditional womanhood deflected her from her own purposes. Her early hope of worldly competence yielded to the domestic pull; her purposes were incompatible with the selfless devotion of domesticity. Like most women born before the Second World War, she had had to attend to the two domains of love and work quite separately in an alternating sequence. Sophie tended to domesticity first, putting her own purposes at risk. She retrieved her girlhood purposes and developed her own competence only at middle age.

Willa, Sophie's contemporary, reversed the traditional female pattern, devoting herself first to a career. Although she avoided the trap of domesticity, she too realized at middle age that her growth was stunted and that she was losing the struggle to become herself. For her too the domains of love and work were held separate—not only in her experience as a woman but also in her imagination as a girl. She remembered at age seventy-two that as a child she'd pictured herself both as writer and as wife and mother. The disparate parts of the dual image floated free from each other, the one forming the "flip side" of the other. Willa's life study indicates that a girl has two root images of the self, each essential to forming her adult identity.

Willa's dual image reflects the dichotomy in our culture. Her life study, like that of Sophie, demonstrates the destructive consequences of turning against either root image to pursue the other one exclusively. Her story shows how tending to either aspect of the dichotomy alone fails a woman in her project of "becoming the person you really are." Her narrative demonstrates the direct connection between early images and later experiences, and shows how important it is to heed both sides of the duality. Willa provides important clues about what permits their integration.

Aware of the all-consuming nature of a career, Willa assumed as a young woman that pursuing her own goals would depend upon repudiating her attachments. Becoming a writer seemed to rest on putting the image of husband and children behind her. Unlike Sophie, whose worldly purposes were suspended by domestic life, Willa set aside her image of herself as wife and mother. A professional first, she married later in life, "escaping from one image into the other." Only when she found that she was unable to have children did she begin to reconcile the two images. She became mature by her own standards when she combined them, putting her purposes as a writer into a framework of relational care.

"When I was a girl, I always thought that an ideal situation would be to be married and to have two children," she said, sitting in the window seat of her upstairs study. "But where the children would come from, I had no idea. And the husband—where would I meet the husband? That was just kind of a dreamworld. Of course I always knew I would become a writer. I wanted to put words on paper, to tell stories. But there was no connection between this image and the one as wife and mother. The one was a kind of flip image of the other."

Willa had grown up in the South. She was the older child and only daughter of parents who had made their own way. Her mother, "a woman ahead of her time," left home against her father's wishes at the turn of the century. Bound for St. Louis, she was determined to learn photography. Her father, a New Yorker, came south to start a business and met her mother when he had his portrait made. Although Willa decided early to have a career of her own and grew to accomplish a great deal, her description of her life was a chronicle not of achievements but rather of family relationships. It was natural for her "to divide my life into chapters, as if I were doing a book. And I thought I would do it in hats, four hats."

The first chapter was titled "The Hat with Pink Roses." It began with her parents' romance and carried the disappointing message that things are not as they seem—something she first learned through her mother's experiences as a young woman.

"When my mother was engaged," she began, "she had the traditional Victorian engagement—a year hemming linen dish towels, staying home and preparing herself for marriage. When she married my father, his job took him on business to Ohio, and when she told about it, it always seemed romantic. They hired a horse and buggy and they would drive, just those two, from town to town and stay in little hotels. She loved it so much. And she felt the way Victorian brides do—very protected."

With a rueful smile she then explained, "But she felt that way more than my father made her feel that way. Walking after dinner one evening, they passed a milliner's shop and there in the window was a lovely hat with pink roses. My mother stood in front of the window and admired it. My father said: 'Why don't you buy it tomorrow when the shop opens?' She was so pleased that he wanted her to have it. But then something terrible happened. He said to her in all her radiance, 'I'm sure you have enough money to pay for it!' And the minute he said that, she was crushed.

"The next morning she did go in, and she discovered that he had paid for the hat. Why did he tease her? Was it that he wanted her not to feel too certain of him?

"Well, that hat really was a preview of the rest of her marriage—expecting so much from her standpoint, and having it not turn out the way she thought it would be and all that. The first ten years of my life were a reflection of that happening over and over and over—in her marriage and therefore in my childhood and my brother's childhood: things not being the way they seemed."

As her mother had had the rug snatched out from under her when she'd been teased over buying the hat, so Willa had had a childhood that was a series of dashed expectations. For her, too, disappointment collected around her father: "For me that meant wanting my father to be home and expecting him to be. I adored him. He said he would come home at a certain time, but he didn't come. And he'd leave to follow anyone who caught his fancy. He'd be gone an hour, a week, a month sometimes. There were excuses and reasons why, but they were never the real reasons. And when he was home he would be drinking, and my mother would always say, 'Your father is taking his medicine,' and my brother and I knew it wasn't medicine. Early on I learned from my father's behavior that men cannot be trusted."

One of Willa's earliest memories was of a precipitous move that confused her. What she saw then led her to conclude that emotions belong under cover, as though hidden by a fashionable hat: "When I was four years old, my grandfather bought land in Texas on the Rio Grande, and he asked my mother to drop everything and come down and help him. My brother was just six weeks old, and without a question my mother, my brother, and I left home and went down to southern Texas and lived with my grandparents.

"I wondered why we left my father behind. And why there was no discussion at all. You can see why it would be plain that there was something amiss. My mother must have told her autocratic father what was wrong, but we never heard quarreling or discussion, we never saw my mother cry. It was a sudden disruption in the family, and even I could sense that my grandfather did not consider my father worthy of respect. But," she hastened to add, "it was all smooth and covered up, all under cover."

To keep things smooth meant that Willa had to ignore the obvious, and conceal her disappointment. It came as no surprise that the first book she published, years later, was titled *Susan Be Smooth*, "advice to young women on manners, style . . . on how to present your best self to the public."

"The Black Hat" was the title of the next chapter of Willa's life.

It was ushered in by her father's death when she was ten and lasted until she left home at age twenty-six. Dominated by a sense of loss, the image reflects the mourning she endured—not only for her father but also for a lost sense of the family as it had been. Her mother moved the family into an aunt's household. It was hard to make ends meet, and the tensions ran high with so many people crowded together. "My brother and I simply had to conform," Willa remembered. "There was no way I could be myself."

Although her brother, too, had to bend to straitened circumstances, he was not so limited as she in feeling or behavior. Feminine compliance confined her identity. "When my brother would erupt with frustration, my mother would hand him a little riding whip. 'Beat the devil,' she'd say. 'Whip Satan out of the house.' Oh, how my little brother loved thrashing this fictitious character!" Willa, however, did not have the privilege of externalizing anger, displaying it, or discharging it—because she was a girl. The duality between feminine compliance and what she really felt—a duality that took her far away from the person she really was—was something her brother was not subject to. " 'That's enough—he's gone,' my mother would say when she saw that my brother's anger was relieved. As witness to it, I felt really very responsible. I *had* to be good, good, good. The riding whip was never handed to me!"

Only when Willa left home for college did she begin to bring into view an image of herself as a person who did not have to comply and to stay under cover. Part of this shift had to do with a latent identification with her father. As a sixteen-year-old who had left home for New York, he had kept a diary of his experiences. She had read his journal after he died. Much of what he'd written revolved around his inner thoughts. He hoped, for instance, that his older brother and his wife would ask him to live with them in the big city—but they never did. Eventually another brother sent him down south to establish a branch of a business the family had started. Willa's identification with her father's adventurous spirit brought forth an entirely new side of her personality when her own social milieu changed.

"When I went to college it was the first time I was away from home, away from Mother, and I discovered that I could be very entertaining. People laughed at what I said, and I thought, Well, I must be like my father. He had lots of attractive qualities, and I thought I must be like that." Out from under at last, she could begin to search out and express who and what she really was—apart from feminine compliance—and revive her girlhood image of herself as a writer. She abandoned the other image she'd carried—the one as wife and mother. But she, like Sophie, was pressured into marriage, despite her nascent independence from it. She married a man she did not know well, only to discover that his intentions were malignant: a homosexual at a time when homosexuality was not tolerated, he wanted a wife as a cover. Willa had unwittingly encountered, once again, the early lesson that things are not as they seem and must be kept under cover.

In a chapter titled "The Hat with the Straight Brim," she described how she escaped from marriage and returned to her girlhood objective of becoming a writer. She was convinced that her success as an author would depend on putting her mother and her home behind her. She determined to "do it or die."

"Not until after I married the first time and was immediately divorced did I begin to do something about this other image. And that's when I left home, made a really mature effort to grow up and do what I wanted to do—and put this other image behind me." Willa took a bus to New York, her father's city, hoping to make her way in the publishing world. But she found herself out of her depth, and came home within weeks. After gathering the courage and the means for another journey she headed north again, this time to Boston, which struck her as far more congenial. She knew that a writing career was not ready-made, and for seven years she "did her time," first writing advertising copy, always telling people, "I'm going to be a writer!"—until she was stopped short by a friend's remark: "Then why the hell don't you begin?" This shocking question was just what Willa needed. In ten evenings after work she dashed off the ten chapters of her first book, *Susan Be Smooth*. It was an immediate success: department stores featured Susan fashions, the book was serialized in newspapers across the country. Willa was in demand as a speaker and a writer. Other books followed. Then came stories and magazine articles.

To pursue her career as a professional writer took concentrated effort: "The Hat with the Straight Brim was a single-minded phase full of drive." In her determination to achieve what she set out to do in her career, Willa was not so different from women coming of age today, women now in their twenties and thirties who feel that they, too, must adopt an exclusive sense of purpose in order to survive in our contemporary culture—one that puts the spotlight on work and pushes love into the shadows. Women who have grown up amid the devaluation of attachment and care, women who now distrust relationships and seek to avoid the denigration that comes with a devotion to them, are as hell-bent on careers as Willa was. These women experience the same duality that shows up in Willa's images.

Rosabeth, for instance, the Renaissance eight-year-old in Chapter 1, defined herself at age thirty strictly as a career woman. She claimed to be free from male-female stereotypes and asserted that her work came first. But when I asked her how she would describe the milestones of her life, she, like Willa, pointed to changes in social ties, framing her response with relationships. Like Willa and Sophie, she kept achievements and relationships separate—even in her mind's eye. In a comment that reflects the wedge the culture drives between relationship and achievement, she outlined her experience this way: "The milestones are graduating from college, getting married, having kids, parents dying. I'm not going to put career in there. I don't think it's a milestone."

During the course of our interviews, Rosabeth canceled wedding plans because of an exceptional career opportunity. At first, I was shocked by her decision. I could not understand why she had not tried somehow to manage both the marriage and the professional leap. But as I understood more about the division in this culture between attachment and autonomy, I concluded that Rosabeth was right: she had correctly ascertained that the culture does not permit a woman the chance to tend to a new marriage while undertaking the commitment that a career demands. I realized as I analyzed the "new" context women are contending with that it was I who had rung it up wrong. In sensing the forced choice, Rosabeth was ahead of me: she probably saved both opportunities by postponing marriage until she made her professional mark. She might have lost both possibilities by taking them both on at once.

Willa helps us understand what is wrong with forfeiting attachments and dedicating oneself solely to a career, making clear why it is not enough simply to reject Woman's Life Plan and pursue a career in a single-minded manner. Her determination to accomplish the work she wanted to do was both necessary and admirable, and it did protect her from the devastation Sophie suffered. But its exclusive nature arrested her emotional growth. The girl she'd been in the first place, one who'd carried both work and love in her images of herself, was displaced by negating her relational needs just as Sophie's sense of self was eclipsed by denying her needs for achievement. By pursuing a career on one track and putting relationships on another, each was kept from becoming her own person.

Willa continued to compartmentalize career and relationships throughout her thirties. She explained how the hat with the straight brim separated her from her feelings, how an exclusive focus on her professional endeavors held her emotional development at bay. As long as she kept career on one track and relationships on another, she remained immature: "As far as the way I handled getting a job, keeping a job, getting a better job, and finally breaking off from the routine of nine-to-five jobs altogether and getting to the point where I could be a free-lance writer, that certainly was not immature," Willa asserted. "But in relationships with other people, especially with men, I showed great immaturity. I was easily swayed by the feelings of others, unable to make my own decisions. I was just not my own person.

"I had set out to become a writer, and I did become a writer," she explained. "I succeeded at my career. But emotionally, I was not learning. While one side of me was very clearheaded and going in the right direction, the other side of me was just doing anything to please. So I 'arrived,' so to speak, at my destination, but with all of those conflicts unsolved. It's a wonder I didn't have a mental breakdown, because I was still a person going haywire."

Willa's emotional growth stood still until she integrated the duality that had divided her. Although she had had friends, some of them men, while she worked at her career, her work took precedence over relationships. She had her share of romances while she put the writing first. But there had been no temptation to make them anything more than secondary, perhaps because she had not been taken seriously as a person. "Nor, to be honest, did I take any man seriously, as a person." The disjuncture of love and work continued until she made an emotional commitment that wove the world of care into her world of purpose.

Willa claimed that "real maturity came with marriage." "My emotional growth began when I was nearly forty and decided to marry John," she said. "John and I began by being friends. That was the difference. We talked about things I cared about and he cared about. We had a firm, good friendship before there was any thought of love or marriage. Now at last I was in a relationship as an equal. That was the beginning of my emotional health.

"Men really are desirable creatures, but I'd so early learned not to trust them. With John, for the first time, I saw that I could have a relationship with a man and it didn't have to be sexual. It could be on an equal basis. I'm a woman, he's a man. We both have brains, we both have interests. But I don't have to be a sex object, I can be just myself. John was the one person, the one man, who was a solid friend, not an aggressor."

With this relationship, Willa began to realize that her life as a career woman held a certain sterility. Despite the realization that work itself was not enough for her, however, she had mixed feelings about giving up the taut life of the straight-brimmed hat for marriage: "It was such an absolutely single-minded, engrossing, enjoyable time. The things I did, the things I wrote about, and my success in getting them published were all very pleasurable. My mother always told me that if you're going to be a writer you have to give up everything else—and she's right. But that isn't enough. At least it wasn't enough for me."

Still, she did not see herself integrating the dual images of herself that she'd carried since girlhood. When she married John, she expected to trade writing for wifehood and motherhood, maintaining her tie to the literary world through her journalist husband. But she did not conceive—and the assumptions that had been held in the domestic side of her girlhood image began to fade. As the image of wife and mother failed to replace that of writer, Willa was shocked to find that in abandoning the hat with the straight brim she had made herself vulnerable to all sorts of disappointments and doubts. And she missed the focus on work and the comfort that it offered: "In the beginning I did a lot of crying, a lot of thinking that maybe I shouldn't have married. I missed the good, old, secure, single-minded feeling that all I wanted to be was a writer. I hadn't grown up, that is what I was really crying about."

In a fourth and final chapter, which she titled "The Hat Made by Hand," Willa began to piece together purpose and care. With this hat, she "came back to the two things I had always wanted: a home, which I made with marriage; and a career, which I had in the writing." Creating the hat made by hand involved basting together parts of both of her early images and stitching them with bits and pieces of the other three hats to the fabric of her marriage. Refashioning the hat meant taking out the mother piece, making a hat that did not include children. She gradually found a way to combine her writing and her relationship, and integrate the separate images of herself. Balancing them was key.

"John encouraged me to keep on writing. I kept my hours, my discipline. But I made a choice not to give all of myself to my work. When the time came for John to retire, so did I. I still do special projects now and then, but the time had come for me to stop going my own way. It just seemed better to shape my day together with him."

She redefined relationship as an achievement: "I would describe myself as a person with a very successful and happy marriage. That is an achievement. I think I'd put that at the top of the list, though I hasten to say that I'm glad I can look back on that marriage and know that I had more than that—the writing."

In a comment reminiscent of the "joint independence" and "joint decisions" Katherine described, Willa spoke to her future goals: "What I want to accomplish is much more than simply success in my work. I want success in myself. I want to be able, with John, to make the right choices."

As we concluded our discussion, Willa added to the metaphor for her life: "My basic philosophy has always been, in spite of my muddy emotional times: I really want to make of my life a fine art. Fine art is work and discipline and giving. Fine art is something that people can look at and say, 'That's something, I see a lot in that, I can use that in myself. I can think about that and be a more useful, fulfilled person because of what I am looking at.' A woman's life should be that to her and to other people."

She expanded on her description, showing how fine art is a purposeful endeavor of relationship that goes beyond a single-minded pursuit of a career. Work is part of it, but fine art makes its statement through relationships with others: "To really be an artist, I once read, you must give yourself to something bigger and better than you are. For me that has been life itself: marriage, my work, my friends, the choices I've had to make, accepting the fact that I have no children and not feeling sorry for myself. The thread of my life has been to make my life amount to something that is worthwhile. It's much more than being *happy*. It's rather a sense of deep satisfaction that you're getting where you want to go without trampling on people, by helping other people and helping yourself too. It is having a life that adds up to something." A true artist, she had shaped and balanced the elements of her life into a single piece.

Willa's narrative illustrates the tremendous press of the barriers between the domestic and the professional realms in our culture. Although a girlhood sense of purpose inhabits both these spheres, they are kept on separate bands of experience in women's lives and lived out sequentially. Her metaphor of the hats conveys the profound difference between a life that covers relational needs with professional competence and one that integrates love and work: the hat made by hand was far more complex—and much more her own—than the hat with the straight brim. She consolidated her identity by hand-stitching the elements of purpose and care together into a beautiful, unique pattern. In the tapestry of Willa's adult life, work first became the figure. Later, love stood in the foreground. In weaving together the different elements of her life, Willa by no means lost the figure of herself. Rather, she found a way to give herself to others without giving herself away.

7

THE POWER
OF FEMININE IDEALS

hat of women who went against the cultural grain, breaking with tradition by refuting feminine conventions? Some early sized up the lesser status assigned to women and turned against traditional roles, making the choice to define themselves in opposition to them long before they came of age. They realized that women's roles were subordinate and found women's subservience distasteful. They determined even as girls not to fit themselves to the usual female pattern. At age eight or nine they crystallized a sense of self based on freedom, independence—values that conflict with stereotypes of females as nurturers. Often they were drawn away from the domestic realm and into the outer world by their fathers, and enjoyed a special relationship with them. Determined as they may have been, however, to depart from the traditional female path, these women too became enmired in sex-role conventions that overtook them and separated them from an individual sense of self at least during adolescence, when the power of feminine ideals, rampant in the culture, overwhelmed individual self-definition. They threaded their way back while women to an original girlhood identity through a complex weave of self-reflection and life experience.

Jillian, a fifty-year-old language teacher, provides a good example. She had an easy way about her as she pushed her spectacles down her nose to speak with a good deal of ironic humor about her perspective as a lesbian in a heterosexual world. Surrounded by the tasteful decor of a light and airy condominium that was somewhat Japanese in feeling, we talked. She'd been born in New Zealand, "where there were no lesbians at all." She'd come to the United States at age thirty after living for a time in Australia and Europe, and had worked as an overseas telephone operator to put herself through school. Although she had occasional contracts to teach English to adults through university extension programs, she was supported primarily by a trust fund she had inherited from her mother that was combined with monies from her eighty-year-old father's sheep ranch. She'd recently returned from a year in China, where she'd been on the faculty of an international English-language teaching program.

In accounting for how she had come to be a woman who defined herself against the usual female pattern, she said, "I think I rejected a lot of it at an early age. I can remember hideous Christmases at home. Christmases were nightmares to me. I dreaded them. One of the things I hated, especially, was the preparation, all the chores that I'd be stuck with because I was a girl. Living in the country, that would involve going out in the fields and picking peas and beans for hours and hours. My stepmother would say, 'Go pick peas for fourteen people.' It's backbreaking! All these men sitting around and the agony of preparation I had to go through for those goddamn dinners.

"I resented deeply one particular Christmas when I was about twelve. I'd spent days picking peas and beans and hours getting things ready, laying all the tables. And then the dinner was eaten and all the men sat around burping, drinking brandy. I had cousins my age, boy cousins who were allowed to go outside and play after dinner, but I had to scrape off all the food from the plates, dry all the dishes. And then we had to start cleaning the place up. The men were sleeping all over the same room that we were tending to, lying all over the sofas, snoring away. And I can remember the absolute feeling of outrage I had then. Even as a girl, I felt 'damned if I'm going to do this!' Part of me did, anyway. Another part thought that it was inevitable that I would end up being somebody's slave. I think that was when I first became a feminist.

"Now, too, when I go home, the men will sit around, expecting to be waited on hand and foot, and will make obnoxious remarks about women. They would deny, of course, that they are sexist, but New Zealand, like Australia, is a man's country. Women were the caretakers, totally, in our society—and still are. My father doesn't know where a single thing goes in his own kitchen. I saw very young this really privileged position of men. It made me angry at a very early age—and tell you what, mate," she added with a laugh, "it still does!"

Reflecting back on even earlier memories, Jillian grew subdued: "When I was three and my mother died, there I was with an older sister and a father who couldn't provide a home for us. He couldn't ever have gone off and gotten a house by himself, like a woman would have. He couldn't take care of us, he couldn't even put our shoes on in the morning. He couldn't take care of himself! Some woman or other always had to look after us, first a maid, then an older sister of his, then my stepmother. He couldn't manage without a woman to do the tending. I saw women as holding everything together, which they did. I always saw women that way."

After her mother died, Jillian remembered her childhood as unhappy—"except for that little window of time when my father, my sister, and I went to live with my aunt when I was between the ages of five and eight. Those were happy, laughing, fun, joyful years with a lot of giggling memories. My uncle was there, and two cousins too. My father had his own apartment, built onto the house. He was separate, but he was there. Every Sunday morning, I used to call him on the telephone from the main house. He'd invite me to come down; I would always go down and jump into bed with him on Sunday mornings. That was our time. That ended at eight because he married. After that, we could never do that again."

Eight was a pivotal age for Jillian; the existence she'd had for three years surrounded by warmth and love turned sour. When her father remarried, she was dislodged from her special position with him, left out in the cold. To add insult to injury, she suffered her stepmother's antagonism. "Eight was a real bad year because that was the year my father remarried. And I left my aunt, who was—it was like the loss of a second mother, really. And then I had this kind of young and pretty stepmother. My auntie Pearl was a lot older and

I wanted a mother who was young. I thought she was young and pretty and I was so excited about having a young and pretty mother.

"But she just hated me, really, resented my presence. She didn't want me there. And they did a lot of drinking. They'd be drunk by six o'clock and send me up to bed. I used to jump from the doorway to the bed because I was afraid of monsters! She would lock me in the bathroom for hours on end, taunt me about my natural functions. My father was so hungry for whatever she gave him that he didn't notice. And my sister, my only other link, had gone off to boarding school. She was first sent away at eight, but much nearer to home. When my father married, she was sent to school a long way away. I lost everything that year."

Cut away from the family, Jillian made of her forced independence a tool to sharpen her sense of self. With this tool, she turned a noxious situation into a formative one by carving a niche of her own. A repeated, solitary experience provided bedrock features of her childhood identity that came to anchor her self-definition: "At eight I learned to fish all by myself. I used to get up very early in the morning and go off with my little rod. My stepmother could have cared less if I'd been swept off a rock. She was pregnant, and it was her pleasure that I get up and disappear every morning to hang out on the beach all day. I'd go down to the beach at dawn in my bare feet, my little pea-stick legs sticking out of my shorts, holding my sandals and rod in one hand, and clamber out over the rocks. I'd go right out onto the biggest rock in the middle of the lagoon and fish for herring."

Her father endorsed her early morning forays: "Every summer my father made me a new rod to fit my size. He bought my catch at a penny a fish, for bait, for bigger fish. I provided him with bait for snapper."

Like many a female heroine of the heterosexual persuasion, Jillian grew up as a father's daughter. The fishing was something special between her and her father, something exclusive that reflected her favored position with him: "I knew I was my father's favorite child. I went with him once to a Maori *whare*. The Maoris love pork, and he used to swap pork bones from the backbone of a pig for the elusive whitebait or other fish they'd caught. They'd call him up and say, 'Hey, I've got a pint of whitebait, want to trade for some pork bones?' I spent a lot of time with him. I was a substitute son to him. There's some pain around that, too, because the only way I could really have made him happy would have been to have been a boy, and he made no secret about his longing for a son. I resent that deeply now. It's just hateful, it's really wrong to do that to a child. Yes"—she sighed ruefully—"I was his son. I had guts, grit, all the things he wanted in a son.

"But the fishing brought me something of my own," she considered. "I kept my bait in a little tin that I would fasten onto my belt. The bait I got by putting a wet sack out on the ground at night. Every morning I would crouch down and lift this mat, and the wet of the mat would have drawn the worms up. So I'd pick off some juicy worms and put them in the tin with some dirt, stick it on my belt, and I'd go creeping off in the dawn in my little shorts and bare feet, with my rod and a knife I kept in my belt. I used the knife to cut my bait, to cut the fish, to cut the line if I needed to. The beach was always deserted, except for an occasional white man or two. But the men wouldn't be fishing with a rod, like me. They had guns that would shoot a line out for bigger fish, or they'd be in boats.

"And the Maoris would be there, fishing. One morning I remember this Maori fisherman came over to me. He'd been watching me go out over the rocks and plunk my line in every day, and he finally came over to show me how to catch these tiny fish. He scattered a little bit of bread on the sea and the fish started jumping up. And he showed me how to cast my line and keep it moving all the time, how to hold the rod so I could feel the end of it tease my palm. He taught me how to get *paua*—shellfish like abalone—off the rock, by slipping the knife in at a certain angle. He also showed me how to kill the fish quickly, by sticking my fingers through the gills. And I'll never forget, after I learned all this from him, one of the Maori fishermen once said to me, 'You're the best *pakeha* fisherman I know'— *pakeha* means white. I knew that it was a great compliment.

"I fished at dawn from the time I was eight until I went away to boarding school, when I was eleven. Those were intensely happy times."

Although she'd lost her mother, lost her aunt, lost her special relationship with her father, and suffered the antagonism of her stepmother, Jillian managed somehow to salvage a core value through this experience. "I was given a freedom to explore and to have these experiences that were not at all usual. There were no other little girls down on the beach by themselves at six in the morning, in the dark and the dawn, carrying their sandals, walking across the sand with a little rod in their hand. I can't believe now that I was allowed at eight to go down to the beach to climb out over those rocks, totally unobserved. The tides were in or out—you could have been drowned. In fact, my stepmother would have been delighted had I been swept out to sea. There's no way I could let my eight-year-old do that! I couldn't do that! It's amazing to me that I had that experience but I'm actually extremely grateful for it. It was a privilege. I was lucky: It gave me a certain amount of freedom."

A mother's absence, a father's preoccupied presence, and a stepmother's malevolent intent all intertwined to force Jillian back on her own resources—as they have for other women who have come of late to the world's attention. She likened her situation to the circumstances of other European girls transplanted to foreign soils, girls whose maverick youth was left to chance. Like her, they were abandoned to the wild, given over to the natives, permitted experiences they never would have known had their own mothers tended and supervised them. Taken out of civilized habitats, they learned about the natural world and found their own competence through experiences their unwitting fathers allowed.

"Look at Kenya's British women, independent women who've done unusual things: Beryl Markham, Karen Blixen. These were girls who were given experiences and given access to experiences that were very unusual for girls—through their fathers—usually through a kind of benign neglect, or through being special in an alien culture. They were given certain privileges that normally would not be afforded to females, but were afforded to foreigners because foreigners were given a different status.

"My circumstances were a lot like theirs: I was a little European child eight years old being taught to fish by these Maori fishermen. They taught me skills that white kids aren't taught. I knew that. There was not another European on the beach. There was not another female on the beach. I was smart enough to know that this was unusual, that what I was experiencing was not being experienced by other people. It was an extraordinary childhood, really. It was a weird mixture of pain and privilege to be able to do these things," she reflected. "I was conscious of that, aware of my special status. And I've thought about this a lot recently. . . . It laid a real foundation for me."

But at age eleven, Jillian, like her older sister, was sent away to boarding school. Unlike her sister, however, she was no scholar. Her stepmother had undermined her confidence; she'd been the brunt of many a cruel joke and made often to feel like the family dummy. Going to school was being forced into exile. "I hated boarding school. It was unbelievably strict, it was like a prison. It *was* a prison. A

dreadful, bloodless prison. Eleven years old in this cold environment—with a lot of old maids from England who were really vicious
to us young girls."

It was at the school that Jillian first realized she was a lesbian—
although she hardly knew what to make of what she felt in that
repressive culture: "I remember clearly the day I knew I was a lesbian.
I was about fourteen, I was in that British boarding school. We were
allowed out every three weeks to see a movie. We were allowed to
see the movie *Carmen Jones* only because it was based on an opera
and the authorities had absolutely no idea it was this hot movie with
Dorothy Dandridge and Harry Belafonte. I was with all my little
girlfriends, and we were so starved for stimulation that one thing we
did was go over the movie together. And we were going over this
movie *Carmen Jones* and I realized that every girl in my group was
fantasizing about kissing Henry Belafonte and I was fantasizing about
kissing Dorothy Dandridge! That was the moment that I knew. It
was like a penny dropping. *Boing!* Just like a penny dropping! I had
a lot of anxiety over that realization. I went up to the library, looked
up the word *lesbian*. I had no idea how to cope with it. I didn't know
one other single lesbian.

"I think you really have to be in a country like New Zealand and
know that you're a lesbian at fourteen to know what hell really is. I
can't imagine anybody living in a more hostile environment than I
did to discover that I was a lesbian. It was completely unacceptable.
There was no one even to discuss it with. There was no freedom of
life-style.

"When I was in China last year, there were no lesbians. There
are no left-handed people in China either. The woman who served
as our liaison was surprised at all the left-handed people in our contingent. She said, 'You know we don't have any left-handed people
in China.' 'They don't give you the option of being left-handed in
China,' I told her. She couldn't get it. It's the same with lesbians.'"

Jillian succumbed to social pressures as a teenager, however,
losing her identity to a heterosexual frenzy. She even got engaged to
marry one of the eligible men she dated just as she turned twenty.
"I always had boyfriends, boys were always attracted to me. I had a
lot of sexual experiences with any number of boys on holiday. I just
figured that the more I did it, the more I'd like it. I was trying to
get myself out of lesbianism. It wasn't as though I disliked hetero-
sexuality, or didn't respond. My sexual experiences with boys were
very exciting. But I always *knew* it wasn't what I wanted. It was

something I could have, and it was fun, but it wasn't what I wanted." Submitting to the norm and yielding to the imperatives of heterosexual behavior separated Jillian from who and what she was: "Not only was it not what I wanted," she proclaimed, "*it wasn't even me.*"

Having taken this wide detour, she did not lay claim to her sexual preference until she was twenty-eight. "I went to Australia about then, and sold books door to door. One of our team leaders lived in Sydney and rented out rooms. She told us she rented out a room to this woman who was a lesbian. I became obsessed with it, and had to meet this woman. And so I did, and we went to bed. This was years ago, when there were only dykes and femmes, and that woman was an absolute, complete dyke—totally mannish. As bad as it was, though, it still felt natural to me. It still felt more comfortable to me than all those experiences I'd had with men."

Identifying herself as a lesbian was a slow and painful process for Jillian, however: "Women held far more emotional interest for me when I was very young, and my sexual feelings for women were strong—since age fourteen. But I denied it for so long. That one encounter with the bull-dyke was a real test case for me. That was my first conscious, adult experience as a lesbian. An absolute, deliberate seeking out of that. And as sordid as it was, it still felt cleaner than anything I had done in the past. It confirmed what was natural to me, what was comfortable." Most important, it returned her to her sense of self: "Even though this encounter was so awful, *it still felt more like myself.*"

Jillian discovered her sexual preference in a repressive culture in restrictive times. There was no women's movement to support her, no political context for her identification against the norm. Her self-definition was hard won in a way that is nearly unimaginable to women coming of age in contemporary society. She told of an incident that brought back the pain of her isolated self-realization: "I was with a friend's brother at a restaurant a couple of years ago. He happened to be gay. We were seated next to these two young dykes who assumed we were a heterosexual couple. They proceeded to make sport of us, to make disparaging remarks. I wanted to kill them. I thought, If those little twerps had gone through—how *dare* they!"

At age thirty, Jillian fell in love with a woman with whom she moved to the United States. Having failed her exams at the British boarding school, she lacked even a high-school diploma. But this woman was accomplished academically, and she inspired Jillian to start college. "She was very instrumental in providing me the confidence I needed to get through. She always told me I was bright. I knew that she was bright, and I thought, Well look, she's bright and she thinks I'm bright, so I can't be as dumb as I've thought all these years. She also provided an atmosphere. If we had a day off and I had a paper due, she'd go and do the laundry just to leave me the house to myself." Much to her own surprise, Jillian graduated from college summa cum laude.

Jillian's degree provided a stepping-stone to a new occupation: "I got my degree and ended up as a manager at the phone company, where I'd worked nights as an operator to get through school. I enjoyed a lot of financial gains, my salary seemed like a fortune. And I bought this little place. But I hated that work, and was miserable there. Then the company needed someone to teach an English course and I popped out of the computer because I had a B.A. in English and teaching experience. So I did that, and I knew right away I was doing something I liked to do and was good at. Out of that, I became interested in these people and their language backgrounds. Some of them spoke languages that had no tense, some had no plurals! That was fascinating to me. That's when, after years with the company, I left and started teaching English as a second language."

But it was difficult to develop her interest into a career, Jillian found. She had a string of part-time jobs teaching foreigners in high school. She grew restless and discontented. A close friend died; she lacked a soul mate. All she could think to do was get away, to leave the United States entirely. She sought a geographic cure for her ennui. "I wasn't doing well here. I had been under an enormous strain to survive, financially. I had a terrible time trying to find a job. I'd eventually found one, but we got something like twelve dollars an hour. I had a trust fund but I had to put myself through school, so I had accumulated debts. I'd had a series of rotten relationships. I was tired of that cycle. I wasn't involved with anyone at the time, I was sour on American culture, my life-style in particular. I was ready for a change. When the opportunity dropped into my lap to go to China, it seemed as though fate had presented me with an opportunity that I should take. I wanted to devote myself to work, and I wanted to see if I could endure something that was that difficult. It was like testing my own ability to survive. I decided to do it in a flash."

China was an odd place for feminist Jillian to escape to: "You can't find a more repressive place than China, for a woman to be," she commented. "I simply can't imagine the fate of being female and

Chinese. The bones of your feet, crushed so that your feet always remain the size of a four-year-old's. That's just one aspect. It's stopped now, but I saw women with bound feet. They're now in their seventies, but that's uncomfortably close. And there are other oppressions, a million oppressions for Chinese women really. I mean, a woman is always addressed as a child until she's married in China. So I would have absolutely no status there at all, were I Chinese."

Jillian, though, enjoyed the special status of a foreigner in Asia, just as she had enjoyed being a lone European among the native Maori. Combined with being a foreigner, her status as a teacher nullified the onus of her gender as far as the Chinese were concerned, giving her a bridge to privilege and independence unique among females in that society: "The fact that I was a foreign woman, outspoken, looked up to in a way teachers never are here, meant that I was actually treated more like a man than a woman there. I wasn't part of anything. I was just a very successful teacher. I was given total respect and all kinds of privileges. At banquets, they would offer me cigarettes and drinks and things they would never dream of giving to their own women. I was separate from the women's world and its unbelievable limitations."

The limitations of the primitive culture forced the restoration of a part of Jillian that had been lost since girlhood. "In China, so many things were stripped away that you really felt like you got down to some essential place. I found I got enormous pleasure in certain basic, minimal actions: bathing, keeping clean. Connecting with a different people. Managing on the survival level, just these basic, essential things. Somehow coping on an elemental level cleared away the clutter, got me—I felt very real."

As she described this process of "getting very real," Jillian discovered that her solitary journey to China paralleled her sojourns to the beach at age eight. The elements were much the same: in both instances, she left familiar surroundings for unknown territory with rudimentary tools at her disposal. In both, she would find herself an alien European among natives. In both, she would receive special privileges, be treated more like a male than a female. In both, she would be thrown back on her own resources. Perhaps most important, in both, she would recover a core value: freedom.

"Going to China was a desperate thing for me. But I knew that it would push me to a whole other view of things, that it would force me out of the box that I had trapped myself in—and it did, in a way I didn't anticipate. It made me appreciate what I had: freedom. The freedom to be female. The freedom to choose a life-style. It was right under my goddamn nose. I lived here in this country where I was free. I had to spend a year in Beijing and lose that freedom to know what it was, to realize that I was a woman, and that as a woman I really was free. It gave me back the freedom I had had at eight."

She ruminated on the feelings the journey to China had evoked: "The year in China really changed me, I don't know exactly how. It began with desperation. I felt like I couldn't cope anymore. I went back to New Zealand on the way to Asia: I was at such a low point I wanted my father to take care of me, and my stepmother." She confided, "At a very low point when I was in New Zealand on my way to China I went up to the cemetery and I sat on my mother's grave. And I read the tombstone, and it said, Age twenty-nine years. And here I was, forty-eight. And I realized that she was a child. I'm the mother, she's the baby now. I realized that I had to be my own mother. It became very apparent to me that I couldn't go back home. Nobody can. This fantasy that you can go back home to a romanticized dead mother or to the arms of a loving father wasn't real. My father is a lovely man, but he's very weak. And he can't—he was the twelfth child in his family, raised by bossy older sisters. And so he married a bossy old bitch who bosses the britches right off him. To him that's love. He's not a strong man. He's a very loving man, but he can't protect me. He couldn't when I was a child, and he's not going to be able to now. That experience was the beginning of actually growing up."

The desperation of the forty-eight-year-old on her way to China mirrored that of the eight-year-old on her way to the beach, the girl whose experience held both the potential for self-realization and the danger of despair—at once the zenith and the nadir of the essential self. Beyond her special status in both situations, she traced the return in China of who and what she had been in the first place to the foundations of her experience fishing on the rocks. The simple things were what began, again, to make sense to her. She found herself bound to the basic elements. As she turned it over in her mind, she realized that the world of the rocks, the world of fishing, and the world of China were closely related to one another.

The year in China returned Jillian to a bedrock sense of self, one that had been carved out at age eight: "When things get bad for me I revert to that—I want to go out onto the biggest rock in the lagoon and see if I'm going to be swept away and see if I can catch another fish. I remember those years fishing because those experiences were valuable, they taught me lifelong lessons. They were deep experiences. But those were depressed times. And that's where I was before I went to China."

She explained what fishing at age eight had taught her: "I think that fishing teaches you a kind of patience. There's a sort of a waiting that you have to do when you're fishing, a kind of attentive waiting that has taught me something. Something central that I use in teaching. It also taught me how to be with other people. I had a little inroad to the culture that other people didn't ever mix with. It gave me a special sort of knowledge. Somehow, I knew something that other people didn't."

The inroad into a different culture, derived from being a European girl with a rod in her hand among the Maoris at the age of eight, was something she'd used again and again—when she'd moved into a variety of cultures in Europe, America, and Asia. The early experience had given her a guileless rapport she'd used in China, and something she relied on repeatedly in teaching languages to people of diverse nationalities.

"What it is exactly, I don't know. It gave me a certain confidence in being able to mix with people, different people. A withholding of judgment. When I was in China, I was able to mix with them in a relaxed way. That started right back then, with that extraordinary experience at eight." Considering the self-reliance she'd borrowed upon, at midlife, from her girlhood experience, she added, "Somehow I tapped into my own strength then. And so much later, at forty-eight, I tapped into it again. It has to do with certain circumstances that enabled me to survive. And I did it really *well*. It was easy for me. It felt good to get in touch with that part of myself again."

Having retrieved the elements of her experiences at age eight in her experiences at age forty-eight, Jillian felt at peace with herself and happy at age fifty. Just home from a photo safari in Kenya, she said this of herself and her present situation: "I have a great life now, and I appreciate it, I really do. I feel for the first time in my life, at fifty years old, content. I loved going to Africa, I'm excited about going to the Great Barrier Reef, about meeting my sweetheart in Hawaii next month. I just taught a great seminar with the woman I work with. I feel like I pushed and shoved and struggled all those years. And during that time I used to tell myself that I would reach this point, but sometimes I'd feel overwhelmed and miserable. And now I've reached a point of joy. Of enjoying my life, a real fullness. I never thought I'd get to this point where I am now, where I feel happy."

Commenting that she felt more herself at fifty than she had since the age of eight, Jillian returned to the theme of freedom: "I grew up begging for my stepmother's love, and she was not about to give me love. I was so sensitive to other people's opinions, and now—it's not that I don't care, but I am free. It's very liberating, but it's taken me fifty years to reach this point. I think about going home next month, all those people and their opinion of me, and I feel like I am strong enough now to not give a shit. I'm not going to be suitably dressed, I'm not going to be sufficiently feminine, I'm just going to be me. They'll like it or lump it. I feel a certain equality with them. That's a wonderful feeling."

The rock of the lagoon reemerged in her description of herself at fifty: "And I don't feel there are any mysteries in myself or the world. Things are what they are and I am what I am. Even the world seems—after spending time in Asia and Africa, touching those continents—even the world seems less mysterious to me, conceivable somehow. I have a sense of the globe, and of me. I don't feel like there's any huge rock within me to overturn, that something hideous might suddenly crawl out from underneath. And I feel *known*."

Asked for an image of herself, she returned to themes of freedom and patience when she likened herself to a bird and a turtle: "A bird because all of my important dreams contain birds. Birds in constant flight. Freedom. And a turtle because it's been a long, slow journey for me. There's something about the slow but patient movement of the turtle."

Jillian rejected female stereotypes. Jo felt rejected by them. She viewed female roles as pleasures she could not obtain because she saw herself as ugly. She was born with Marfan's syndrome, a congenital disease that affected her appearance, making it impossible for her to match or even to approach feminine ideals. The condition she'd inherited resulted in severely limited vision, excessive boniness, and extreme height. Although she escaped a heart defect also associated with it, she was over six feet tall and very thin; her shoulders and hips protruded, giving her an awkward, bony look. She had straight white hair cut short around her face. Her glasses were Coke bottle thick. Although she could see well enough to get around, she was legally blind.

Jo felt undesirable as a female while she was growing up. Thinking she'd been forever barred from feminine privileges, she turned against the natural femininity she embodied as a girl. Although she eventually married and had a baby, she continued to feel that the essence of womanhood eluded her. It was through an oblique, platonic relationship with a male employer that she finally reclaimed the neglected girl within and recaptured the femininity that girl kept in reserve.

Working as a part-time typist for an academic man, Jo, age fifty-eight, proudly titled her life "Steps toward Becoming a Woman." She gave me the details of her painful story in an offhand manner, almost as though delivering a simple package. The first of these pertained to the conditions of her family life. Her mother, who had the same affliction, was a near invalid while Jo was growing up. Her father was a housepainter. She was born during the Depression, like Sophie and Willa. Her family, too, lived in desperate poverty. One of her earliest memories was of her father putting bootblack on her socks when the toes of her shoes wore out: "We were very poor. One time when we went out I had black shoes and white stockings. My father blackened the toes of my stockings so they would not show up through the worn-out shoes. And then he made caps for those shoes."

Despite this context, Jo felt that she had a "normal childhood" and thought of herself as perfectly feminine until she went to school—the point at which she became a social outcast: "When I went to public school, the kids made fun of me, they called me names. Until then I had no idea what I looked like. I didn't know I wasn't attractive, always ugly, always too big and nearsighted. The only thing I had was this differentness. I was alone. Nobody associated with me. I wanted a normal life but I was not getting any feedback from a normal life. There were just so many things that said to me, 'Look, you're ugly, you're not on a level with other people. You're just different.' "

Jo had been unaware till then that she'd been afflicted with a disease. But once she was rejected and humiliated in first grade, she concluded that everything a female could obtain in life hinged on physical attractiveness: "When I was young, I felt that the most important thing in the world was to be attractive. A woman should be attractive so a man will marry her, and if she isn't, she's going to be an old maid, her life is bleak, there's nothing else in life for her. Even if you were stupid, I was sure that being attractive would take care of it. And since I wasn't physically attractive I thought there was nothing in the world for me."

Unable to match ideals of femininity, she pushed away her wishes to be womanly. Since her femininity was of no use to her, she tried to negate it. "As a little child, I always wanted to be a woman. But I was so big and awkward that being a woman was not—it just wasn't—

I was afraid that *nobody would ever want to marry me.* Nobody would want me for a wife. I just figured I was going to be an old maid."

Other experiences made her sure she could not possibly achieve a womanly life: "Somewhere along the line when I was ten or eleven, an elderly woman who was a friend of mine took me along with her when she went to an optometrist and he took a look at my eyes. Then he looked at me and said, 'The worst sin that you ever can commit in this life is to have a child.' That really nailed it down. I already felt that nobody in their right mind would ever want to marry me. By then I knew the condition might be inherited. But to be told that this was the worst sin—

"You know how little things affect your life. Once I visited my cousin and we were trying on bathing suits, and she said, trying to be nice to me, 'You mustn't mind that you don't look good in a bathing suit. You've got as much right to go out on a beach as anybody else.' Gradually these things bore in on me. I really felt that I was not going to get married and have children, which was the perfect life to have. So then I figured, Well, maybe I should be a lesbian."

Once she came to feel that a normal female life was unattainable, Jo began to reconstruct an identity based on alienation from physical perfection. The trouble was that this new identity was not her own: "So then I started wearing pants and shirts and ties, and trying to be masculine, which of course was not me."

She struggled with being female in a culture that defines the feminine in such a narrow way that she could not possibly approach it: "Through it all, I was very definitely feminine. But I didn't want to be because I felt that it was going to be of no use to me. My mother used to say, 'It's too bad that you weren't a boy,' because of my size. If I had been a boy it would have been all right to be the size I was. So I felt I should be masculine."

Failing to meet ideals of femininity, Jo rebelled against all kinds of norms while she attended a school for the blind between ages seven and fourteen. Her rebellion during what she calls "a scrambled, unhappy time" led the school to kick her out. "After I was finally expelled from school, I went to a psychiatrist for a while, until both of us got sick of that arrangement. She was the type that made you lie down on the couch and she would sit behind you. Then, bang, she decided this was it—it was getting nowhere."

For the next four years, Jo was kept at home. "I spent most of my time in the attic alone," she said. "It was a lull. I used to go to church once in a while and the old ladies there were nice to me. It was like a dull sleep." Her life was limited not only by her physical handicaps but also by her conviction that she had no future. "I wore glasses and was flat chested. So I knew I might as well hang it up."

The feminine conventions that provide females a place in the culture could not pave the way for her: "During that time my cousin came to visit, after her mother died. There was this fellow that we both were absolutely crazy about, a friend of my brother's. He was married, but he used to come to the house with my brother. My cousin started having an affair with him. It blew my mind because I would have wanted to have an affair with him myself, you know. But there again I was the one who was flat chested, I was ugly; my cousin had a nice shape, and she was aggressive. She could do everything. Nobody was interested in me.

"So many things happened to shake my confidence. Once during that period, when I was about sixteen, my mother was away. I wanted to clean the house for her, but I had never done housework. Of course, we didn't have a vacuum cleaner, so I did what I'd seen my mother do—take newspapers and wet them and put them on the rug. That collects the dust and then you sweep them up. Well, of course, being as nearsighted as I was, I didn't do a good job. But when my aunt drove my mother home she said how nice it looked, and I felt kind of good. Then my father came home and had a fit because he saw all the dirt on the baseboards. He flew into a rage. It seemed no matter what I did, nothing was right."

After that "long, bleak period," things looked up when Jo started to work at age eighteen, stitching pillowcases at a workshop for the blind. She held the job for seven years. "It was dull, but it was something I could handle. I had more sight than some of the others, maybe seven or eight percent vision. My mother pointed out that from the time I was eighteen on, I earned a week's pay every single week up until the time she died.

"And I began to get acquainted with people and go to clubs. That's when I met a fellow I could have married. I wanted to get married because I was tired of working. Sewing for seven years can get pretty dull, you know. But he had multiple sclerosis, so common sense was against it. And then I had another opportunity, an Italian fellow. He had limited vision too. He would have made a very good husband. But you can't marry someone just because they would make a good husband."

When Jo later fell in with a neighbor who was similarly marginal, she was half glad to find that she was pregnant. But she was also terrified that the baby would be a girl. "I didn't think I could stand looking at anyone like myself," she said. "When the doctor said to me, 'Open your eyes, you have a beautiful baby boy' it was the most wonderful thing, because I knew that he would not go through what I went through."

She and her husband stayed with her mother in the household Jo had grown up in. Having a baby only overwhelmed her, however, and marriage put her "beyond my depth." "When we got married, neither of us was an adult, and I was very dependent on my mother. I would go into rages because my husband would go and spend his money, and then we wouldn't have any. I wasn't used to that. I was used to not having much, but what I had, I had. He'd take the money and say he was going to pay the bills, but he would gamble. And I would lose my temper and scream and howl. And my mother would calm me. She'd say, 'Why don't you go out and go to the movies?' I just left the baby with her. She lived here. This was her home."

Jo began to take responsibility for herself and for her son only when her mother and her husband died—within six months of each other—when she was in her middle thirties and her son was just a toddler. "I'd always been frightened when I was away from my mother. I remember when she went into the hospital when I was three or four. My brother and I had to stay with an aunt. And all I remember is my brother having to sit and read 'Little Red Riding Hood' to me, over and over again."

At first Jo remembered little of her father: "My relationship with my father was not too good. I was always afraid of him. I never touched him. I do remember one time, before I started school, when he had to put some iodine on my finger. I remember him painting iodine circles so I'd have little red rings on my fingers.

"Once my mother had an eye operation. She lost her eye. I remember when my father and I went to see her. He went in and told her, 'Now, don't you worry. I'll read to you. I'll put ropes around the house for you.' And it was the only time I ever saw my father cry. That's when I realized how completely dependent he was on my mother. He only lived a few years after that.

"When my mother died, and six months after her my husband, I was completely alone. It is a little scary, if you're used to having someone, to know that you are completely responsible for yourself. She used to close the windows at night; she used to tell me, 'Five minutes to get the bus.' Only after she was gone did I realize that if it rained during the night and I did not get up to close the windows, no one would close them. By closing those windows whenever it rained, by catching the bus on time without my mother's reminders, by doing the grocery shopping before we ran out of milk, I began to see, gradually, that I could manage without her."

The double loss impelled Jo to find a job that really could amount to something. She was hired to do some typing for an academic who needed research tapes transcribed. Her blindness had led her to develop her ear, and she had been trained as a typist at the school for the blind. Still dazed from her losses, she was not sure the job would suit her, but right away she found the professor eminently approachable. In fact, she mistook his identity at first: "The first time I met Bill, after I was hired by personnel and had started the transcribing, I went down the street to the secretarial office to copy something I had typed. The door was locked, and Bill came down the hall to let me in. I thought he was the janitor." She chuckled. "I had no idea who the man was. I said to myself, 'My God, nobody gets to work around here on time. It's ten o'clock already, and nobody's here but me and the janitor.' I didn't find out who he was until much later. Eventually he asked me if I wanted to work in the building where he had his office. He really valued the work I did for him. He never failed to say, 'Jo, you're fantastic. You've got those tapes all done!' "

After she started working for Bill, she "began to see the world in a different way. That was a time of waking up in the morning and wanting to get up. And colors—colors. When I was younger, I thought it reflected a shallow nature to like bright colors, cheap jewelry, or cheap perfume. And now, I like bright colors, I like to buy perfume that costs three dollars a bottle instead of ten dollars. And oh, did you ever know how beautiful a ten-cent store is if you haven't been in one for a long time? The colors and the brightness. And the people there are wonderful."

Over time, the job and the relationship Jo had with Bill came to replace the disarray she'd made of her identity when she'd concluded she could never be what a woman ought to be. In fact, the relationship was critical to restoring a sense of self she'd been estranged from long before. So transcendent was the experience that Jo, like Sophie, felt reborn. She, too, used religious terms to describe its impact: "This phase of my life began with the advent of Bill. It means something to me that he chose me to work for him. He accepted me with all my faults. He didn't seem to mind that I was ugly. He didn't seem to mind that I was nearsighted. He renamed me, by the way. My name is actually Joanne. When I went to work for him, he was so vague on names he called me 'Jo.' And I liked the way he said it, so I just changed it. Now everybody calls me Jo except people who have known me for years. I feel I was actually reborn. I was renamed and reborn. It has been a reincarnation."

Bill's appreciation of Jo countered years of social rejection. His acceptance of her was the first challenge to the "not me" identity she'd built around being unattractive and therefore unacceptable: "Bill accepting me was the big thing. He just accepted me. He didn't seem to mind my handicap. He didn't seem to mind the fact that I read everything with my nose like this, tipped up in the air against the paper. He didn't mind the fact that I had to clip my papers to an old newel post and move it close to see them. He didn't mind the fact that I was ugly, long legged, flat chested, and the rest of it. One reason I feel very accepted in the world is because he accepts me."

Although Bill's acceptance of Jo was key to reversing the rejection she had suffered from the time she went to grade school, her ability to care for him was even more important in reclaiming her identity. Much attention has been given to being cared for and loved, but Jo's account points to a new vector in development. She made a critical distinction when she identified the key ingredient as actively caring for another person:[1] "It's not what *he's* done that has made this the happiest and most important part of my life. It's that I cared for him right from the start. I mean, I created that caring. He doesn't, of course, care about me, except in a certain sense of the word."

Jo's ability to feel affection for Bill hinged on her certainty that the relationship would not become sexualized. Having a relationship in which she would not be exploited as a sex object was crucial to finding and expressing her feelings. The benign safety of the relationship was the essence of its expansive nature: "He provided me with someone who I could become all absorbed with and yet not become physically involved with. I could wait on him and mother him; he loves to be mothered, you can mother him absolutely to death. I could be as close to him as I wanted to. I could discuss things with him, not terribly intimate, but family things—without any fear of sexual involvement. So I could go as far as I wanted to.

"Before I started working there, I didn't know that men and women could have relationships without it being sexual. Low-income people who work in factories don't have colleague relationships. Blue-collar workers have relatives and they have friends, but they don't have colleagues. So this was something new. He was the first one I ever had this completely free relationship with, a happy, free relationship. He is a wonderful person!"

Being privy to Bill's faults and failures also played a part in Jo's swell of feeling: "He's someone that I always had the inside track on. He was mine, he was my boss. Even now I feel he belongs to me— and to his wife, of course. I have to manage him, he's often in a cloud. He does the darnedest things. Like he was supposed to meet his wife when her mother died so they could go together to the funeral. I was taking care of their son for the day. And he got all confused and ended up in the wrong place. His wife waited for him as long as she could and then she said, 'Well, I've got to go without him, I just can't help it.' And then by some miracle the route she chose took her past a corner where he was standing waiting by mistake. So he got to the funeral. You can see why I feel like a mother to him, the old wife in a harem," she clucked.

More serious and most important, the relationship and the caring Jo expressed within it restored a critical component of her identity, returning to her the femininity that had long eluded her: "These years of working for him have turned me into a woman. I feel feminine now in a way I haven't felt since I was eight or nine. I like being a woman. But it's taken a long time. I do like being a woman. I really do."

This realization stirred an early reverie that conveyed the essence of the natural femininity she'd embodied before she realized she was strange in the eyes of others: "When I was young, I didn't realize that I had all these problems. I loved clothes. I can remember my mother making me dresses, and I remember I wanted a white dress with two pink bows up here"—she pointed with both hands to the bodice of the dress she was remembering and then to its skirt—"and I wanted two pink bows down here. I wanted those bows very much. I didn't realize that I looked any different from anyone else."

She elaborated the memory, associating her newfound femininity with her feelings for her father, remembering the affection that was blunted between them when she was a little girl: "And I remember feeling very happy going out with my father when I was little and he took me places. I really loved my father. I wanted to hold his hand. I wanted to put my arms around him. But in those days father's weren't affectionate, and he came from a German background."

Other recollections of her father came to her as she spoke. "One time when I was living at that school for the blind, I went into the hospital for an operation. He used to come for me every weekend, and he'd take me back to school on Sunday night. He said before I went to the hospital that when I came out, he'd bring me home. Well they didn't tell him when I came out, and they took me back to school. He came that night, he got a friend to drive him. He had to carry me home because I'd had a foot operation. And I remember when he carried me, I was afraid to let myself feel him physically.

"Later when I was a teenager and went out on a weekend night, he would wait by the window till he saw me coming home from the bus. Then he would go to bed before I got into the house. My mother told me later that he never went to bed until he made sure I got home safely. But I never knew these things. I didn't know until much later that he had been a good father. If only I could have held him, if I could only have put my arms around him. I wanted so much to love him."

This melancholy memory startled Jo into realizing that the feeling, feminine self that she'd reclaimed through caring for Bill was the same self she'd had as a child, a girl obscured in the meantime: "I was always the person I am now, but I didn't realize who I was. I was in there all the time!"

She pointed out that she was no different physically from how she'd always been. It was her sense of self that had been changed by her retrieving a core component of her identity: "I'm no different than I was before. I'm just as big, just as ugly. I've still got the hips, the long legs, the ugly neck, the flat chest. Truth is what we see: I'm not any more attractive now than I was then. I'm the same person— worse because I'm older and dumpier and gray haired and wrinkled. But because I think differently, I see differently. I just feel *me* in a way I never felt. I feel physical. I put clothes on and I can feel them physically. I am aware of the physical. And I am aware of *men*."

As if to reassure me that she really meant it, she went on, "I pay attention to the way I look. I put feminine clothes on now, clothes I feel will look attractive. And I pay attention to fixing up my house. I am proud of what I do to decorate it. I made these curtains for the kitchen. I didn't want to take away any light, but I wanted some kind of a soft frame for the windows. So I used this white material, and gathered it at the top." She turned back to me as she explained: "A window without a curtain is like an eye without a lash."

8

NATURAL PATHS
TO THE GIRL WITHIN

wo women in my study drove their emotions underground and hid a whole spectrum of feelings that constituted their
identities because of damaging relationships with their mothers. They
struggled to protect themselves by locking up and burying the girl
within. Carol and Ruth echoed Jo when they told their stories: both
of them restored as women a whole, original identity that had been
kept in hiding throughout girlhood. Like Jo, they struck a path back
to the original girl through care and connection. The relationships
that released the girl for Ruth and Carol, however, were as intense
and personal as Jo's with her boss had been limited and abstract. For
one it was marriage, for the other motherhood that provided the active
expression of care essential to rediscovering and reclaiming the girl
within. Their experiences point to the developmental impact of active
caring in adult life, particularly where the damage to the nascent self
has been severe.

Carol, a forty-three-year-old photographer, was long divorced from her first spouse and had recently remarried. She and her new husband were building a split-level house an hour outside of New York. Lean and lanky, she slung her camera over her shoulder and loped along to her studio, beyond a pond in the back. Under the skylights at the north end of the gallery, she bent over some prints of children just developed in the darkroom—portraits in which the children were caught in action rather than fixed in standard poses. Carol was especially interested in these action shots because of her own restrictive childhood. "Pushed underground while a small girl," she was the only child of wealthy parents and grew up on an expansive estate. She had always had a nanny—until she'd been sent away to boarding school at the age of twelve. She'd written of her New England family before the study started, "My father was very passive, sweet and jolly. Mother was explosive, frustrated and frightening. I was an only child, quite timid, brought up by a nanny."

Carol explained how she'd become separated from her girlhood self: "I lost who I really was by growing up with a mother who just demanded of me what I couldn't be. I could never satisfy her, I just wasn't like her. So I went through that whole time trying to please her. But I just never felt that she loved me. She wanted me to be something that I couldn't be. So I struggled with that. Of course, you want your mother to appreciate you, and I just never measured up. I didn't do anything right. That was bad."

Not only did Carol feel unlovable as a child, she was also made to feel inadequate in her capacity to love. Failing to meet her mother's standards in both respects was what made her stash her feeling self away. "I never felt I was making it with my mother," she reflected. "There was no affection. She would chastise me because I wasn't able to get out the kind of emotions that she thought were appropriate for what she gave to me on Christmases and birthdays. So I went underground. I mean, I had my own self underground."

Carol made a valiant, typically female effort at adaptation. As a child, she molded herself to give what her mother needed: attention. "I thought the only way to get over hating my mother was to try to understand her, to figure out where she was coming from. When I was eleven or twelve, I decided that the best way to get along with her was to learn what made her tick. If I understood her, I could handle her abuse. So I went about getting to know her. I would talk to her. I would ask her things. That helped."

In place of the girl she really was, Carol substituted "a kid who somehow got to be a very understanding person at a very early age."

Understanding itself became the organizing force for her relationships and the axis of her identity. That modus operandi further supplanted the natural self she had pushed underground until she finally came to feel that she had only "a self based in selflessness." The authentic, feeling self became remote as what began as a survival tactic with her mother developed into an all-encompassing style that saturated her personality and perfused the essence of who and what she was: "I didn't have any identity aside from understanding everybody. My role was to please and to help. That tied me up from being myself, in retrospect. I was terrified of upsetting anybody, so I never had any feelings. I never was sad, I never had a tantrum, I never was angry. It interfered with allowing feelings, with being myself."

She replaced her own identity so completely with understanding that the self she had pushed underground began to elude even Carol herself. The false, compliant self that she acquired covered her authentic identity with an overlay that suited her mother's specifications. Anger, frustration, competition, and needs to love as well as to be loved were hidden under the "veneer of a wonderful person."

As a teenager, Carol knew only that she was not herself: "I wanted acceptance, for people to like me. The way to get it was to be as nice as could be. Underneath I wanted to be a great person. I had a lot of talent in various directions. I didn't have Olympic goals, but I wanted to be an excellent person. I was a good rider, a good swimmer, a good skier. I was a good photographer, a good musician, a good writer. I had a lot of competitiveness, but then this passive, outside part of me took over." She lost herself in female selflessness and understanding: "I tried and tried all the time to understand everybody, so I lost myself. I got my sense of self from doing for others. I didn't know who I was. I was just an understanding person."

Although she went away to boarding school and then to design school, Carol still felt oppressed by the relationship with her mother and subordinate to her. Like many another young woman in her position, she decided to escape the household by getting married. She adopted a daughterly stance toward a man she met at a nearby college. Seeking in him perhaps the decisiveness her own father did not possess, she married him, expecting him to direct her life and resolve her problems. But she soon found to her horror that she had married not the strong father she might have sought but instead a man much like her mother.

"Inside I felt confused. I was a kid and I was all mixed up, and he was so straight and strong, so opinionated and so firm. I looked to him to say, 'This is what you need to do.' I thought that he was going to straighten me out. And I thought he would get me away from my mother. But what I was doing was going from one mother to another. He was exactly the same as she was."

When she found she had simply transferred her dependence from one figure to another, and when that transfer failed to free her from an inner dependence, Carol became even more removed from herself. In a desperate effort to reclaim and articulate an identity apart from her immersion in the dependent roles of daughter and wife, she decided to have a baby. "Marriage separated me from my parents. It was an escape for me. I didn't have to live with Mommy and Daddy anymore, I didn't have to depend on them. But then I became dependent upon my husband. And when we got married, I lost myself totally. I lost my name, I lost my identity. I was just my husband's understanding wife. And so I had a baby to separate me from my husband. When I had it, I finally had something that was just mine, something that I was really good at. What I was trying to do was get myself back."

Despite her efforts, the situation worsened. In fact, it was compounded after Carol had a baby—when her husband and her mother joined forces to defeat her sense of self. Her mother remained a vivid presence, continuing to dictate Carol's mental standard and also to intrude on her life as wife and mother.

"After I was married, I had my husband and my mother fighting. They competed for who would handle me and how. My mother was worst during my early years of marriage, when my children were babies. She told me everything that I was doing wrong. She made it clear that I wasn't good at anything. At the very beginning she said to me, 'You can't possibly breast-feed this child. You don't have any nipples.' Later it was, 'You can't raise a child in this apartment, there's no air in here.' When she could not change my mind herself, she would call my husband up and say, 'You can't bring up a baby in that kind of environment.' He would never defend me, but they disagreed about everything. I was a perfectly docile person, stuck in the middle between them."

Carol felt as subordinate to her husband as she had felt to her mother; he took the upper hand in their family life together. She continued to live with the voice of her mother speaking constantly in her head, a voice now amplified by that of her husband, disparaging everything she thought, felt, or did as it grew louder and clearer: "The problem was that I didn't get away from my mother. She was

my mental standard until I was in my thirties, when I finally got up
the guts to have an argument with her. I always would think, no
matter what I did, 'I bet Mother won't like this, or approve of that,'
you know, when I bought clothes or changed something in the house.
But it went much deeper than that."

Carol linked losing herself—and refinding herself—to confront-
ing her mother, which helped her thread her way back to the girl
she'd buried. The incident was a pivotal one: in the wake of splitting
up with her husband following a decade of marriage, she took her
children to her parents' summer house at the shore—a visit that
radically changed her relationship with her mother and finally muted
the voice in her head.

"I first thought that I must be an adult when I had a child to be
responsible for and take care of, but I didn't really feel grown-up
until I told my mother off. And I was really old when I did that. I
think that I was thirty-one or thirty-two when I told my mother off
for the first time ever. That was something. She had said something
vicious about me behind my back, and it got back to me. When I
thought about it, I just went bullshit. I had come to my parents for
help and understanding. All I wanted my mother to do was to say,
'I love you, you're all right, you're my daughter,' but I got this insult
instead. I was livid. I told her I didn't ever want to speak to her
again. I shouted at her, 'Don't call me up, I don't want to hear your
voice until I'm ready to!' And then I left. We were supposed to go
sailing, but instead I got the kids together and told them we were
going home. We packed up and drove the three hundred miles
through raging thunderstorms. As we pulled out of the drive onto
the road, I could see Mother hunting stones on the beach—which is
what she does when she's upset—in spite of the wind and the threatening sky.

"It was a great experience for me because I had never been able
to get angry at her before, overtly. I was always seething inside, but
I was always scared of her. Until then I had been tied to her opinions.
That keeps you a child. I always worried about what she thought
about every single move I made. I stopped doing that at that point.
I got her off my back. I had gotten rid of my husband, whom I
shouldn't have married in the first place, and I got rid of my mother
too, when we had that fight. That's when I really became a grown-
up." Carol reflected, looking back, on what this encounter had meant
in retrieving her identity: "It was a long process, finding me. And

that was the first step. The force she'd had over me went away right then."

Breaking out of the internalized relationship with her mother was a nodal point in her development, but it did not suffice to retrieve the self Carol had pushed underground as a child. The understanding, selfless style she'd initiated with her mother and elaborated with her friends and husband continued to form the basis of her new relationships. The confrontation could not release her from the dynamic that lay at the crux of that style and directed its evolving path. The understanding style had become entrenched; it was difficult to dislodge. After the argument at the shore, it not only persisted but also combined with the morés of the hippie era to produce a series of self-abnegating affairs. Each time Carol became involved with another man, she first felt free and then found herself duplicating it again—a pattern that encroached upon and all but blotted out the possibility of reclaiming and asserting her own identity. She titled the ten years after her divorce "Carol Trying to Find Herself and Not Being Able to Do It."

"After my husband finally moved out I felt I was reborn. It was a time when I went to bed with anyone I wanted to. During those times, people were ecstatic over the chance to do that, you know, free love and all that. I really got into it—the freedom of it. I sort of dropped out of society, which seemed to be falling apart anyway. I would meet someone walking down the street and take him home to bed with me. He might stay just the night, or he might stay six months. I was absorbed in this new way of being, a nondefined, nonprescribed way. I seemed to attract all kinds of rootless men, some good ones, some not so good. One of them really loved children. He pushed himself in and infiltrated my life for a year. But the real me was not what he wanted. When we broke up, I lost my social life. Then my former husband got remarried, and he and his wife made a play for the kids. The oldest two were almost teenagers, and the new couple had everything to bribe them with. So those two left and I spent a year without them, a time of great unhappiness and emptiness."

She placed her hopes in another man: "Then I met Brian, who was a lot younger. He accepted me exactly as I was, without the usual I-wish-that-you-were-something-else. He moved in at my request and stayed for five years. We bought a house up in the mountains. We went there for the summer. We worked on that house together, all

summer long. We were equals, he was a partner—until he got lost
to the bottle. The last two or three years with him I realized he was
a desperate alcoholic. I went to AA and to Al Anon. I tried everything."

In accounting for how she stayed with Brian after he became an
alcoholic, Carol explained the underlying dynamics of what would
otherwise have appeared to be a masochistic relationship:[1] "I got swept
up in saving another person, society's role for a woman and one that
I knew well. I'd had that practice with my mother. I'd had four
children, so I was always doing for them, worrying about them, car-
pooling them, going to their schools and talking about them, feeding
them, clothing them, the whole bit. Taking on Brian was more of the
same, though he was a joy when he was all right. I can remember at
a women's group people saying to me, 'What are you, some kind of
masochist? Do you like this sort of thing?' But I kept hoping he would
be all right, that he would conquer his drinking problem."

In what was perhaps a peculiarly female orientation, she focused
not on Brian's problem behavior but on his deeper potential: "Brian
had great potential as a person, and I was interested in that. We had
so much in common, our likes and dislikes. And he did accept me.
I needed to be accepted. That made it hard to let go of my hope and
belief that he would change. Every time he'd have a few sober days,
I'd think, It's going to be all right now. He'd say, 'I'm going to cut
back, I'll get a job, and it will all be wonderful.' When that happens,
you say to yourself, 'Oh, gosh. Do I dare believe?' "

It was disciplined self-reflection that finally extricated her from
the damaging relationship: "I went through that over and over to the
point where I finally started writing this diary. I wrote in it for a
whole year. That's when I finally saw that I'd been sucked in to this
pattern. And then I gave up hope that he was ever going to get better.
It had been obvious to everyone else, but then, the others had not
seen his potential, the good things about him that are really there.
When his drunken abominations began to bother my youngest son,
I kicked Brian out. That was the end of my help-everyone-on-earth
phase."

Enduring Brian's problems also had the curious consequence of
bolstering Carol's attitude of superiority—a feeling she both needed
and despised. Although this attitude may seem surprisingly at odds
with underlying feelings of worthlessness, it is harbored by many who
are cut off from the spontaneity of the natural self and tied to the
nurturing, caring stance of the false self. "If someone comes to you

for help and you're nurturing someone, then you are innately superior to them. I always felt superior, even when I was a little child when I was being browbeaten by my mother. I was shy and meek, but I still felt superior. I never showed it, but inside I always thought that I was much smarter, much better. Understanding my mother made me sure of that. I felt that way with my husband, too. I went right on feeling that men were stupid."

The understanding yet superior attitude that Carol took toward her mother was simply transferred down the line in her relationships with men. Only when it interfered with her relationship with Brian did Carol link her superiority to hostility and begin to find it alien: "When that feeling cropped up with Brian, I wanted more than anything else to get rid of this superiority. I began to dislike my superior feelings, hostile feelings that bordered on hatred and disdain. I detested my superiority, I hated it in myself. It was a burden. It kept me from being vulnerable, from being myself. So I decided I was never going to have another man. That's when I decided to be celibate."

Carol decided on a period of celibacy to free herself from entanglements—and from her smug superiority. During the next two years, while she was on her own, she began to feel that she could exist apart from a dependent, selfless, superior dynamic. She also began to rediscover some of her own competence: "I really for the first time felt that I was free. I didn't have anybody telling me what to do and I could figure out myself what had to be done and do it. I'd been terrified of being alone. When my husband left when I divorced him, I didn't know anything. He had always taken care of all the money and given me an allowance. I didn't know how much it cost to live in this house. I didn't know anything.

"When I decided to make it without a man, I realized I had already learned how to take care of myself. I'd had jobs, I'd learned to budget money. I found that I could keep this house and make it work all by myself, without moving any man in. In fact, I had been doing that all along, but there had always been people masking it. I suddenly felt, 'You can take care of yourself, you really are there.' I realized I had become self-sufficient. It was wonderful. During that period of rampant celibacy, I started getting really good feelings for the first time—feelings of myself, just myself."

Toward the end of those two years, when she began to find what she called her "selfness," Carol met a man who seemed to appreciate that selfness rather than seeking the selfless understanding others had depended on. Sensing in him an "equal partner" who could strengthen rather than threaten the person she was becoming, she decided she would marry him: "My decision to get married again was totally based on the fact that I would not give up one particle of the selfness I had gained by being alone. I was going to keep my self-esteem. Finding my own selfness was really hard. My selfness is 'This is the way I am.' He seemed to accept that instead of resenting it."

Part of what she valued in the new relationship was its departure from the compliant past: "One of the things I liked about him was that we started having fights right away. He will fight and I've been able to fight back. He would yell at me and I would yell at him. We have really thrashed it out, we've had some real struggles, some real fights. Having never fought before, it was really wonderful."

She did not return to a natural self without a sense of loss, however. This time it was not a part of her original identity but rather a component of the false self that was given up: her superiority. "It really was hard in the beginning to give up my superior role, to give up being the boss. I don't have that superiority, which I hated, any-more. We are equal partners, we can quarrel equally. And when you can quarrel equally, nobody is the boss of anybody else."

Carol reflected on the impact of the marriage on her own de-velopment: "I think what matters most is feeling loved. Somebody cares about me and will tell me and show me. That has never hap-pened before."

But feeling loved, as important as it was to Carol, only formed the context for the critical development that finally freed her primary identity and all the feeling it contained. She made an important dis-tinction when she shifted the emphasis from feeling loved to loving itself: "No, let's see, feeling loved isn't quite it. Lov*ing*. Actually loving somebody is even more important than that. I can't tell you what a wonderful feeling it is to be just crazy about somebody, totally involved and loving. It's just a great feeling, *daring* to love some-body."

Daring to love provided the final impetus Carol needed to break out of the prison in which she'd locked herself as a child. The power of loving—rather than of simply being loved—served to remove the impasse that had arrested her development. She connected daring to love, the impulse that had been frustrated in her relationship with her mother, to uncovering her original, authentic identity. She gained enormous emotional freedom—freedom from female perfection, freedom from superiority, freedom from selfless giving—through daring to love her husband.

"I've been able to become not only more loving, looser, warmer, but also more fallible, more forgiving. It's allowed me to free up, let myself go, to let myself be vulnerable instead of trying to be perfect. I've dropped my superiority completely, come down from where I had placed myself up high as the perfect person. I've dropped my guard. I feel good about myself. I've been able to be more emotional, to give myself in a different way, sexually, to let somebody give me pleasure instead of always thinking I was giving the pleasure. And I feel my creative juices flowing. After years of neglecting my photography, I'm being more selfish about time in the darkroom without feeling guilty about it. I was always a person who had to be strong. Before, I was always whatever I was for someone else, never just for me. I never as a child was able to be immature, if that's what self-ishness is. I guess I'm going back a few steps to immaturity to get mature."

Long separated from the hidden self, Carol explained the importance of being able to be vulnerable in reclaiming herself, making an important connection between vulnerability and the restoration of an original identity: "I've allowed myself, finally, to be unsure, to be *vulnerable*. I can give in to normal feelings that I've never allowed myself before, I can make a mistake every now and then, I can feel bad or cry. I was just the bravest kid. I would never cry. I would try never to be sick. If I was sick, I would never let my mother know. I didn't even know me. I wouldn't let myself know me."

The equality of her new marriage turned the key to the prison in which Carol had locked herself, lifting the latch to the identity she had closed away as a girl. Finally coming out of the prison was the direct result of marrying a man with whom she was on equal footing—establishing a relationship that did not threaten her selfness but encouraged it. The power of a partnership of equal give-and-take—and equal vulnerability—restored her original sense of self and liberated her as the confrontation with her mother had been unable to do.[2] "Telling my mother off in my early thirties was kind of getting out of that prison, but the sort of general prison, let's see. I was underground, and I don't think I ever did come out before. I am going to say that it's taken this new marriage. I am going to say that I really have just come out!"

Unearthing her original identity altered all her relationships. She clarified that it was the nature of the relationships—rather than their presence or absence—that had changed: "It's not that I've stopped caring about people. My identity is basically that I love people. That is my basic thing. So it's not stopping that." The difference lay in being vulnerable and being able to demand things. "I am finally able to say, 'I hurt, I hurt bad.' I can just be bitchy. It feels OK to do that. Never as a child could I do that. I didn't even have normal feelings. I was always so scared. I was just ground down to a little smudge of nothing. I really could not allow any kind of feeling."

Relationships proved both the source of jeopardy and the source of salvation in Carol's identity. With a whole spectrum of feelings at her disposal, they became a source of self-esteem. The freeing of her self depended not on independence from relationships but on a sense of self within them. "Unless you are a total intellectual or, I suppose, an inventor, someone who lives completely for the mind, completely inside themselves, you've got to interact with other people and it ought to be good. If it isn't good, then you're not going to feel good."

It was not toward solitary self-sufficiency that she aimed, although it seemed that for Carol, as for others, solitude was an important component of unearthing a core identity. She headed toward increased selfness and a kind of mutuality in relationships in which she could be whole. New ties permitted the release of an ability to love that had long been sequestered. "I'm pleased with myself. I think I help people a lot without having to do any more than talk to them. And I enjoy that. I'm productive in my relationships with people. And my basic thing is that I love people. I come back to understanding. Women have been endowed with an ability to comprehend both themselves and others. Men seem to lack that ability. They lack understanding. Women understand. Women understand because they have to. They take care of the children. They take care of the men so the men can go out and work. Women are the ones who make things work. They are the backbone of life."

Through an intricate, relational process, Carol had unearthed her original identity: "I am just now beginning to have a real identity. I'm somebody, I'm somebody! What it means is that I can be a whole person—finally! And I am forty-three! It's ridiculous because it should have happened sooner. I feel like a real person for the first time. I know it sounds like a cliché, and I cringe to say this, but I have really learned to love myself."

Carol summarized her story by saying of her original self: "It was here, I had it right away. I don't know how I got it, but I had a self fighting for myself, inside. I was very aware of who I was right from the beginning. But then I became a prisoner.[3] The self I had when I was small was all locked up inside. All my assertive or angry feelings were buried inside it. I was in there feeling both superior and hateful. I couldn't break out of that prison. My self never came out. But it was in there the whole time. It is just such a thrill now to be able to come out. I really feel out! My authentic self was in there from the beginning and I have finally let it out!"

Although Carol's account of a nascent self imprisoned in early child-hood may seem unique, Ruth had a story strikingly similar to hers. Ruth too hid herself in a fortress as a child because of a noxious relationship with her mother. A forty-year-old college teacher, she described the overriding task of her development as "coming into my own." That process had been long and arduous, for the girlhood relationships she had with her parents had left her badly damaged. As for Carol, the pivotal event that led Ruth to unbury her identity turned on a powerful relationship in which she could freely and actively care.

According to the family folklore, Ruth was stubborn and difficult as a girl. The second child of Jewish parents who lived in the Bronx, she was a force to be reckoned with, but her parents could not contend with her: "I think I was born sturdy and struggling. But I knew early how my mother felt about me, how ambivalent she was. In many ways she had it in for me, so that while she was telling others how much she cared about me, what I was taking in was: 'This lady be-grudges me the air I breathe.' " Ruth's "problem" was the opposite of Carol's: "I was supposedly impossible, always emoting or throwing up or having a bad tantrum. And I was accident prone. I slit my mouth open at about two and waited in my father's waiting room for him to finish with his patients so he could stitch my mouth up. I fell at two and a half and cut my hand open. My father botched the repair, but I was blamed for not exercising my index finger. My theory is that that's the reason my brother has become a plastic surgeon. He was eight when I had these accidents, and he remembers blood all over."

But Ruth would not complain, for, as she said, "my mother is not a lady around whom one would wish to be vulnerable. If you let a chink show, the arrows were poised. If you complained, she went straight for the jugular. I put my vulnerability away early because it was a suicidal act to have it out in her presence."

Survival meant retreating into a fortress where Ruth struggled to keep her identity intact. She described in detail the feelings she had, and the way she defended herself against them: "The sense I had as a child, and the sense I still have around my mother, was of being swallowed up by another person, of being absorbed by her wants, her needs, her craziness, her view of the world. So I went into hiding with her. I thought, I'm retreating inside of a small fortress. I had the sense of being overrun, again and again. Of being made to cry and then being ridiculed for crying. It was like being a country surrounded by hostile states. Very early I erected a wall around me, an electric fence that would defend my borders. I created space by taking my feelings and going inside, underground."

In self-defense, Ruth modified her active temperament, a keystone in identity, to accommodate to her perception of her mother's resentful feelings about the trouble that she supposedly caused: "I was viewed as a doll, something still and passive that could be dressed up with pretty clothes," she said. "And like a doll, I was neither seen nor heard."

The sense of danger that pervaded her relationship with her mother contaminated her view of the world and her place within it: "I became mistrustful of feeling things, expressing things, of other people's expression too. I grew up with a sense of privacy and shame."

In danger if she let her mother invade her fortress, Ruth was also endangered when she was apart from her: "I was somehow led to believe that the world was a ghastly place, and that separate from my mother I would die, I'd be destroyed. Standing by myself was an incredibly courageous act. I was certainly in double jeopardy."

Ruth credited being able to manage to her relationship with her brother, especially after her father went away during World War II: "My father volunteered for the army despite a 4F deferment, and went off to invade Normandy in Patton's army when I was two and my brother was eight. That left me in the untempered hands of my mother. The reason I survived it is because of my brother. I got a tremendous amount of nurturing from him, though he did not get so terribly much himself. He was really my father when I was a little kid. There wasn't much sibling rivalry between us because we couldn't afford it. We were at the end of the world with only each other. He took quite good care of me all the way through. Even when I went off to college by myself on the train from New York because my father, as always, could not take time off, my brother met me at the station. He used to call me almost every night and take me out to dinner every week. It was important. He did all the things that daddies are supposed to do."

What relationship she had with her father contributed to Ruth's insecurity. When he came back from the war, he wasn't willing to pave her way in the world because she was a girl: "I can remember going to concerts with him and my brother when I was ten or eleven, and he would meet a friend in the lobby. He would introduce my brother, but he wouldn't introduce me. So I acquired a sense of 'not being.' "

Being female put her in a lesser position from the start: "When my parents had people come to visit, the women all sat in one room and the men all sat in the other, and it was clear that the men were talking about important things. My family was very sex-role divided. My father came from an impoverished, immigrant family and worked his way through college and medical school. My mother came from an immigrant family too, but they were quite well off. But she wasn't permitted to go to college because you shouldn't educate women. She taught me that educated women didn't have any common sense."

The conflict between femininity and accomplishment was central: "The mixed messages I got all the way along were wild. I was supposed to be very smart, but I wasn't supposed to do anything with my brains or my ambition. I was always told that no matter how talented you were, women didn't go into medicine—and this in a family in which medicine was the only thing in the world worth doing. It wasn't until I was thirty that I stopped wincing when I met or heard of a woman doctor. I was far brighter than my brother, but he's the surgeon. I've gotten three degrees and followed a circuitous route to the career I have today. If it hadn't been for my parents' prohibitions, I'm sure I would have been a psychiatrist.

"I'm also sure that all my education has made it hell for my mother to have me as a daughter. When I headed for my academic degrees, my mother discounted my ambitions by saying, 'When I was your age, I wanted to set the world on fire too,' as though I would get over it. I still want to set the world on fire. Not on fire, rather I want to set it in bloom."

The incompatibility between being a woman and being ambitious almost kept her from academic success: "Being female made it hard to succeed at my accomplishments. I came within months of finishing another doctorate ten years ago, but I kept hitting a brick wall. That brick wall was clearly 'Thou shalt not take thyself so seriously and be so committed and really be a professional, a lady Ph.D.' And getting educated made it hard for me to come to terms with my femininity. My mother claimed that as her turf. I thought of myself as odd, as aberrant, as abnormal for having the education, the work."

She labored with that damaged self-concept through two college degrees, several teaching jobs, and the birth of her two children. Still, it seemed to Ruth that femininity was impossible to integrate with intellectual purpose. The split between thought and feeling was emphasized by the patriarchal institutions of higher learning she attended—until she came across a graduate program that consciously integrated intellect and experience: "It wasn't until I got this last degree that I found out how smart I could be, how I could use the womanly aspects of smartness in learning. Before, when I had gone to college, you were expected to be cool, analytical, deductive— neatly. This last program has been the opposite: it was experiential, relational, and qualitative. Divergent thinking was OK, it was OK to have some feelings. Out of twenty-eight years of formal education, those were the only four when I really learned things—where I changed because of what I learned."

Ruth attributed her survival to four things: "One of the things that saved my life was my brains. Being able to think made it possible for me to protect myself from my parents." The first time she remembered putting her brains to use on her own behalf was at the age of nine or ten: "I can remember then saying to myself, 'I'm never going to tell my parents anything that matters to me again.' I was clearly self-reflective then.

"Another part of my salvation was figuring a smart way out of a crazy family—and that was to marry. By the time I was sixteen, I had chosen whom I was going to marry: I decided the first week we went out that I was going to marry Michael. He was bright, and I had felt so strange through my growing up because of being smart, that I wanted someone who was at least my match. I wanted someone close to me in age, somebody kind and sweet and nurturant. He had a reputation for being brilliant. And we had fun together! We could talk and talk and talk. When people start out together very young, they don't always grow at the same pace. So it's been a leapfrog process where we've caught up with each other time and again. It's been a sustaining, confirming, and growing relationship, for the most part.

"The third part has been psychotherapy. Going into therapy was a wild, outrageous thing for me to do. My father didn't believe in reflectiveness, and he thought psychiatrists were crocks. But if I had not gone into therapy when I was twenty-eight, I am sure I would not be alive today. It was uncrippling, an unbinding of my feet. Through it, I gained courage and came to see myself as understandable."

But by far the most powerful element in restoring her true nature was the experience of becoming a mother: "The piece right through the middle is the children. They showed me the way."

The revolution in her self-concept started with pregnancy. Ruth's experience of gestation began to counter a misperception her mother had passed along to her about her femininity—or its lack: "I always assumed that I wouldn't be able to get pregnant, and with each of the kids, I got pregnant right away. And that was the first inkling that my mother's myths didn't fit reality. Especially the myth that being smart would keep me from nursing a baby. When I did that, I found that I could be smart and . . . womanly." That came as a surprise, for while Ruth was growing up, femininity had stood in opposition to intellect and her mother had stressed how smart Ruth was. To Ruth that meant she couldn't be womanly. "I think the most important part of the first pregnancy and birth was the sense of 'Oh, I really must be an honest-to-goodness all-right woman after all.' I always thought I was too smart to be a woman, that I wanted too much, that I didn't know my place, that there was something wrong with me—that I wasn't quite right."

Recalling the experience, she added, "And I loved being pregnant. I absolutely loved it. And that was a great shock. I was one of those people who looked beautiful pregnant and I felt better than ever. I felt terrific physically. I played tennis till right before my daughter was born. I felt so much in my body, and was enjoying my body for the first time."

As powerful as this experience had been, it was one Ruth nearly denied herself. She had been convinced by her childhood messages that she could not possibly be a good mother: "I was the one who was a lousy daughter, and I was afraid that would mean I would also be a lousy mother. It was like being in a sandwich, an awful sandwich. And I was terrified of having kids because I feared that my kids would feel about me the way I felt about my mother."

But the conventions of the times overrode her personal fears: "It was inconceivable then not to have kids. You grew up, you got married, you had kids. I was particularly terrified of having a daughter, because my brother had been the favored child in the family. And after all that panic about having a daughter, my first one was a girl, and I was in love with this incredible baby. I hadn't realized that being her mother could be an act of self-restoration. In fact, if someone had given me the choice I would have chosen not to. When I hear people anguishing about whether or not to have kids, I can't figure it out. They tote it up like buying a car. How can they know what it will be like in advance?"

Pleasures she did not anticipate and aspects of feeling particular to Ruth's neglected inner girl were revived by mothering itself: "When the children were small babies, I could nurse them and hold them. I don't know what that means to most people because I've never been most people, but I think I will always have a touch hunger. So for me there was a kind of healing in that holding and closeness, and finding out I was not a destructive human being. In taking care of them, I took care of me. A piece of me was restored by being a mother, the piece that is someone who wants to take care of."

Restoring that part of herself, Ruth transcended the walls of the fortress she had built as a small child. The fortress that walled off her own feelings was essential to her survival then; caring deeply for her children was pivotal to reviving her authentic self. "In terms of becoming me, there isn't anything in the world more important than what I've had with them. There were things I was willing to do because I loved them before I was able to love me. What they've done is made it possible for me to restore my core, which was really deeply wounded."

She illuminated the developmental potential that becoming a mother holds in the process of reclaiming an original, unwounded identity when she described how becoming a mother brought her into contact with the self she'd hidden in the fortress: "I think of an incredible line in one of [D.W.] Winnicott's books where he says, what the baby sees when he looks into his mother's face is himself. I suspect that what I saw when I looked into my kids' faces was me. That brought me into contact with a part of myself I had put away out of great necessity: my vulnerability."

Allowing herself to feel vulnerable in her relationship with her children—as Carol had in her relationship with her husband—restored Ruth's sense of self. The intensity of her attachment to them and the vulnerability it exposed led her to unearth her core identity. The extraordinary effect her feeling for her children had on her sense of self testifies to the developmental impact attachment has not just on children but also on adults.

Once she restored her identity, Ruth conquered her mother's view of her by becoming a person entirely different from what her mother had expected her to be: "It's been a long swim through cold, deep water to get back to me. I always had the sense that I would die around forty and my mother would dance on my grave. I have triumphed over that. About ninety-five percent of what I do is different from what my mother would have predicted for me. I am a different kind of mother, I'm a professional, a different kind of person. I wasn't supposed to be strong, I was supposed to be fragile. But now I can run six or seven miles. I've overcome her sense that women aren't supposed to be interested in sex. I feel sexually strong and whole and right. I enjoy dressing as a way of decorating my body.

"Living well is the best revenge! And part of my living well is seeing little kids now, seeing a child with a sense of her*self*. It reminds me of how stubborn I was. I am so delighted to have been stubborn. That's what I owe my survival to. I am a survivor. I take a lot of pleasure in that. And I never would have unearthed my sense of myself as a survivor without my kids."

Carol concluded her life study with a reiteration of the central effect that mothering had on the process of restoring her authentic core: "I've thought about it lots and lots of times since we've talked about it first, how incredibly important it is to look into your kids' faces and see pleasure, see love really. It's strange. So much of the stuff on child rearing talks about the nuisance of it and the pain of it, and so little of it talks about what kids give you. Of all the things we've talked about that remains most central."

9

RECKONING
THE RELATIONSHIP BETWEEN
DAUGHTER AND MOTHER:
TRANSFORMING
A CRITICAL TIE

Not all women become mothers, but all women begin as daughters. Each and every one of us is "of woman born."[1] No book about women's psychology would be complete without at least a sideways glance at the relationship between daughters and mothers. Although I did not ask specifically about this bond, women I interviewed spoke spontaneously of its importance. Coming to terms with their mothers had such a profound impact on their adult identity that many of them singled out that pivot decades later when we met. A key aspect of arriving at a fully adult sense of self seems to have much to do with resettling this relationship—long after women have taken on adult commitments such as marriage, motherhood, and careers. A radical shift that almost never occurred before a daughter had left home and established a life of her own, this renegotiation took a variety of forms among the women I interviewed. A wrenching confrontation for some, it proved a subtle psychological process for others. The striking finding that shot through these accounts was that no matter how self-sufficient a daughter had become, reckoning this woman-to-woman relationship was a nodal point in her psychological development.

The importance these women placed on the mother-daughter tie may seem incongruous given their ages, accomplishments, and psychological maturity. To linger with one's mother past the years of childhood is at odds with social expectations. Traditionally, American women have been expected to maintain only a superficial connection to their mothers as one component of a broader life plan in which a wife typically tends primarily to husband and children. Against this template, women's attachments to their mothers hardly figure in. Only in certain ethnic groups is a persistent close involvement with one's mother considered "normal" or deemed worthy of scrutiny.[2] Others who struggle with the attachment past adolescence are considered suspect if not stunted—failures at the task of separation. We assume that women coming of age today will make it their business to separate from their mothers and cleave unto their husbands—or their careers. Unused to thinking of adult daughters as showing evidence of continued attachment to their mothers, we expect adults to keep their mothers at a vast psychological distance.[3] Growing up American means banishing one's parents.

The accounts by women in my study of a continuing attachment might even seem to bolster the official, standard notion that separation is indeed a developmental end point women fail to reach. "Aha," the follower of Freud may remark, "you see, women *are* by nature immature, still wrangling with their mothers when they're supposedly adult." But these women indicate that something far more complicated than simple separation is at work. Certainly daughters in the study wished to terminate their dependence on their parents. But what they sought was to balance that lopsided dependence, to get out from under by righting a subordinate stance. Instead of breaking away to stand on their own, they reworked their ties to their mothers so that those ties reflected who and what they had become as women. The rapprochement that they described hinged on refashioning the relationship so that it became reciprocal. They did not want to break the mother-daughter bond; they wanted to transform it. Given the cultural ethos that urges separation on adults, the burden fell on each individual daughter to rework the attachment without forfeiting it. In a culture hell-bent on separation, this activity took on an almost subversive character.

Why should this relationship, formative in the early years, hold so much power during adulthood? Part of its power lies in the many strands of female identity a mother will always embody, for mothers and daughters share a long and intimate past. It is against our mothers' skin that we first encounter the smells, tastes, and physical sensations of life itself. It is at our mothers' breasts and in our mothers' laps that we first find comfort, warmth, and nourishment. It is in our mothers' faces that we first see joy and delight. In these faces too we first see mirrors of our own faces and feelings. We learn in our mothers' arms about being human, and about being female. But it is also at our mothers' hands that we first meet disappointment, frustration, and sorrow. We carry these feelings—all of these feelings—with us from the earliest moments, and we associate them with our mothers throughout life.

Many of us arrive at adulthood with mixed feelings about our mothers—and confusion about ourselves as women. Some of us lead adult lives quite different from the lives our mothers have led. Many of us have daughters who will lead lives quite different from our own. Often we are not sure what we want to keep from our feminine heritage and what we want to reject; what we want to pass on to our daughters, what is best left by the wayside. Even those of us whose lives resemble our mothers' cannot replicate theirs, for we live in different times. Today's times, in fact, pressure women to break out of the confines that have hobbled mothers and kept them from re-alizing worldly goals. The culture broadcasts the message loud and clear: women are expected to get beyond the household and take up a role in the workplace. At the same time, however, women are whispered about if they do not keep things humming along at home.

An intimate tie between adult daughters and their mothers may seem particularly dangerous now because it appears to risk hard-won feminist gains. Feminine roles that prescribe traditional female be-havior—wife, mother, daughter—seem to threaten women's move toward independence. The present cultural press toward autonomy turns women away from relationships of nurturance and commitment. The mother-daughter relationship is especially perplexing for the con-temporary woman who pursues achievement. In striving to be a full-fledged member of the real world, she rejects the roles that bound her mother to the domestic realm. She sees in her mother's history traps she is convinced she must avoid. Determined not to sink in the quicksand beneath her mother's feet, the woman of today resists the pull of this relationship as she strikes out on her own.

Motherhood itself has become the target of popular and scientific treatises alike as mothers have suffered widespread blame for all sorts of psychological ills.[4] A number of feminist scholars—among them Nancy Chodorow and Dorothy Dinnerstein—have become so concerned about perpetuating traditional female roles that they submit that mothers should cease playing the dominant role in rearing their children. They direct the new woman away from her tie to the previous generation because they perceive it as bondage to an archaic view of womanhood that will only lead to what one calls "a crippling identification" with her mother's ways.[5] These views push a woman toward breaking—rather than transforming—the mother-daughter bond. They dictate isolation from those who might beckon us back toward dependence, making our mothers onerous figures.

But proponents of these notions overlook the elementary fact that mothering itself takes place in a far-reaching context that diminishes the worth of females—mothers *and* daughters—to say nothing of devaluing the dynamic of attachment itself. Women who choose today to focus on the traditional feminine domain of hearth and home, as so many generations of mothers before them have done, risk being viewed as "doing nothing"—and they are prone to thinking of themselves that way. Yet they do not escape the extraordinary demands made of today's woman. Whether she works exclusively at home or also has work in the marketplace, she is expected to play her feminine role to the hilt. The pressure is on for her to be superwoman and/or supermom. A magazine advertisement addressed to working mothers places a tall order for such a woman: "Mother. Breadwinner. Playmate. Nurse. Dispenser of TLC. Disciplinarian. Pal. Chauffeur. Wizard of the kitchen. Problem-solver. Budget keeper. Source of comfort. Worker of minor miracles. Diplomat. Super-achiever. Juggler of time. (Is there ever enough for yourself?) Overly busy, often unappreciated lady. In a word, *you!*"[6]

Another ad, equally imperative, compels the reader with a rosy baby's face. Underneath the picture is the caption: "LEAVE THIS FACE?" And then, beneath that, the text: "It won't be easy. But if you're going back to work, lots of things won't be easy, like finding someone you trust to care for your baby. And making time for all the parts of your new life—job, child, husband, home." The magazine then promises to "help you choose the day care that's right for you. Help you deal with separation fears (yours and the baby's). We'll be your child care expert. . . . We'll tell you what to do about colic . . . how to get the baby to sleep . . . why your baby cries. And we'll help you get over that rough adjustment period. Help you get back to work, back in shape, and *still* get dinner on the table."[7]

Whether by taking on careers, defining themselves as home-makers, or braiding together some combination of the two, whether by striving for excellence within the domestic realm or taking ambition beyond the walls of the household, women today are responding to an underlying imperative reflected in the image of that rosy baby and the verbiage that describes the ideal mother who inspires that baby's smiling face. This demand is specific to females: *the demand for perfection*. Females are intent—because of the culture's expecta-tions—on the perfect weight, the perfect shape, the perfect curl, the perfect makeup, the perfect dinner, the perfect mood, the perfect marriage, the perfect orgasm, perfect childbirth, perfect children.*

This ideal is closely aligned with yet another ideal particular to females: the ideal of nurturance.[8] The need to be nurtured is one that all mammals share. Women have been held accountable for nur-turance, naturally, throughout human history. In fact, women have been quite invisible in human history except when they have been in nurturant or reproductive roles. Females fill the need for nurtur-ance, however, not just for their offspring but also for a host of sup-posedly independent adults. Husbands, colleagues, bosses, and even fathers all depend on females of all ages to tend to their needs for physical and emotional succor. This assumption of female obligation, situated in bodily need and response, finds its extreme in the wide-spread sexual abuse of little girls by fathers, uncles, and stepfathers and the physical abuse of women by their husbands. But even mem-bers of the female sex who are not exploited become responsible routinely for the nurturance of children, fathers, husbands, and bosses in their roles as mothers, daughters, wives, and secretaries. Females still grow up with the expectation that they will put aside their own needs in favor of tending to the personal comfort of those who sur-round them *simply because they are female*.

The demand for perfection is yoked to that for nurturance in the ideal of perfect nurturance that drives us all. Many women grow up, become mothers, nurture others, and grow old without ever realizing that this dual ideal is an impossible one to meet, for the culture

---

*Perfection as a female standard is not limited to adult women, rather it afflicts females from a tender age. A recent TV show that "listened in" on the conversation of teenage girls found them talking nearly exclusively about perfection: the perfect figure, the perfect tan, the perfect bathing suit, the perfect boyfriend, the perfect this, and the perfect that.

devalues the very nurturance it seeks. Thus women are simultaneously given the responsibility for nurturance and blamed when such
nurturance falls short of perfection. Women accept the impossible
responsibility and swallow the inevitable blame as readily as mother's
milk.

One reason mothers are so susceptible to blame is that the un-
supported act of mothering lies hidden. Our society divides work
from love, placing the activities of work in the public arena while it
secludes love in a private domain. In cultural ideology if not in fact,
the world of work belongs to men, that of love belongs to women.
While the domain of work involves public recognition and material
compensation, the domain of love is hidden from view and devalued.
Child rearing is part of that shadowy realm. Although relationships
themselves hold a power to transform the individual that is sorely
lacking in the realm of work, worldly work is what the culture rewards.
The culture's exaltation of "male" qualities—independence, rationality, competition, success, and worldly power—is paralleled by the
debasement of women's work and the devaluation of the entire realm
of relationships, nurturance, emotional effectiveness, and the work
of the household. Simply because they carry out the demeaning tasks
associated with caring for the young, women are discounted as weak
and subordinate.[9] Discredited through their identification with emotional aspects of living and assigned to the private sphere, females
are rendered powerless.

Thus social arrangements and cultural values conspire to create
a paradox in which the mother-child relationship is intensified at the
same time that it is rendered impotent.[10] A mother exerts a powerful
influence on the development of her child as an individual while she
is relegated to a powerless position in society. She cannot help but
pass along the culture's devaluation of the feminine to her daughter.
Powerlessness, because of its associations with females, gets handed
down from mother to daughter like an unwanted family heirloom.[11]
Daughters cannot help but resent their disabling inheritance.

Mothers do not set out to victimize their daughters. Daughters
themselves, they are keepers of the powerlessness *their* mothers acquired and passed along. Each daughter in this study, like all women
in our culture, is responding not only to the idiosyncratic relationship
between herself and her mother but also to the cultural context they
are embedded in. That context diminishes the worth of all females—
and devalues the activity of attachment. When a daughter looks at
her mother through this cultural lens, she sees a reflection of de-

pendence and weakness regardless of her mother's individual strengths. In order to escape that powerlessness, a daughter must negate the reflection. Her immediate impulse often is to destroy it by breaking the mirror. But to break the mirror, or even to turn the glass against the wall can only perpetuate this shared predicament.

A more sophisticated and complex response would take into account women's wish to sustain relationships as well as to empower themselves. By acknowledging the patriarchal traditions that frame and give form to female powerlessness, daughters and mothers can give the lie to the weakness and dependence the culture attributes to women. By sympathizing with the desperate position of a woman of whom both husband and culture demand perfection, a daughter whose mother demands perfection of her can temper her anger toward her mother. By recognizing the cultural pressures that set the borders of her life, a mother can temper her demands on her daughter. Mothers and daughters together can resolve the common predicament of mother blame by building on womanly strengths—a sense of connection with others, an investment in sustaining relationships, mutual empathy, a commitment to cooperation and mutual care—important qualities, often trivialized and demeaned by the culture.

This reflective stance can give women a power to change that far exceeds the power derived from changing a single relationship no matter how central that relationship may be. By putting mothers in their places, we try to put the powerlessness of being female in its place—but that is a step in the wrong direction. By putting ourselves in our mother's places, we address powerlessness at its root. Coming to terms with the mother-daughter relationship involves freeing the feminine qualities the culture denigrates and by reclaiming and revaluing feminine qualities women share. It is critical to come to terms with the mother-daughter relationship and what it represents, to find a way to reckon the relationship rather than to jettison it at the threshold of adulthood.

But little girls are hardly capable of such critical reflection. They know only that their mothers embody something that they need to distance themselves from—even though their mothers are like-beings whom they may also want to emulate. Girls are quick to grasp the devaluation of the feminine when, according to the women I studied, they try to decipher what the future holds for them as women. Rosabeth's account provides an example of the deleterious effects of the cultural dichotomy on the new woman who is "liberated" from the restrictions of old gender roles. Although her mother was a woman of accomplishment, Rosabeth avoided identifying with her. Having swallowed the culture's exaltation of "male" qualities, she reached the conclusion that masculinity is superior to femininity during a preadolescent assessment of her parents that still held when she was thirty: "My mother has been a model for what I don't want to be," she stated. "Now it's true that she's not a very feminine person, but that's not why I don't like her. In fact, some of the ways in which she is headstrong and willful and intellectually aggressive I very much like and appreciate, and I have adapted some of those things to round out some ways in which my father is—not quite proud enough of himself. So she rounds out some of my views of what I want to be like."

In this statement, Rosabeth aligned masculine qualities with the positive, which she sought to acquire, and feminine qualities with the negative, which she sought to avoid. Sensing the greater social power of the male, she appreciated in her mother only the masculine qualities that would have added to her father's force. She fell victim to the culture's disparagement of femininity when she explained how she had constructed her own self-concept in opposition to femininity, which she viewed as an impossible limitation: "I have a full sense of what masculinity is, and only a sense of what femininity is not. I have a very stereotypical view of femininity, and have little use for women who are helpless and make silly conversation and appear to be not doing anything with themselves."

The negative stereotype of femininity is so strong that it overwhelmed Rosabeth's personal experience of the accomplished mother she grew up with, the day-in, day-out contact she had with a woman who hardly fell victim to silly conversation, or "not doing anything."

"A lot of it has to do with thinking of femininity as negative," Rosabeth continued. "I think of women as less self-actualized in general; I'm afraid I'm beyond them. I really resisted women's movements and female movements and things like that because I didn't understand what I had in common with any of those people." So extreme was Rosabeth's aversion to the stereotypical feminine that she referred to women as "them," and as "those people."

Despite her mother's achievements, she allied herself with her father: "I've made a real attempt to be more rational, to be able to explain things, to know what I'm doing rather than just doing things or feeling things. I want to be rational and to experiment. I got that goal from my father, through comparing my parents."

Femininity does not draw women forward in part because it

excludes so many human qualities. Stereotypes of women that depict females as less rational, more emotional, and "less actualized" than men contaminate women's identification with their mothers and with womanliness itself. The incompatibility the culture forces between male and female, work and love, rational and emotional led Rosabeth to disparage all she saw as feminine—complicating her identity development rather than clarifying it. In fact, she demonstrates how claiming one's own womanliness, once a matter of simple identification between daughter and mother, has become a thorny process. In avoiding that identification, she was sharing in the renewed cultural devaluation of the feminine. In rejecting her mother to avoid the pitfalls of femininity, she not only discredited her mother but also disparaged traditional feminine qualities in herself.

This wholesale rejection of the feminine—and of the mother who embodies it—left many another woman lost at sea when it came to founding a bedrock sense of self. Liz's story is a good example. A British expatriate, she was a forty-nine-year-old secretary when we met. Her husband was a businessman. Her three sons were mostly grown. As a girl, she had deduced that her mother's pattern was one she must not follow: "When we were small, my mother was always overworked, always complaining. She associated all of the traditional female stuff—the housework, the cooking, the endless round with children—with misery. She was never joyful about any of it. I knew you didn't have to be like that, but I couldn't see how else to do it. I had to find my own way, I couldn't use my mother as a role model. I mustn't be like her—miserable, fractious, undeveloped, caught in a cave of womanly doings." Reflecting the denigration of the feminine, Liz remembered how she'd tormented herself over her natural impulse to identify with her mother: "All I knew was that I could not be like my mother. I was obsessed with that. How could I not be like her?"

Her personal issues with her mother were intertwined with girlhood observations about the lesser status of women in general: "I remember, too, being very angry at eight or nine when the teacher in my classroom was talking about cheap labor, which of course was female. I remember turning around and looking at these pimply little boys and thinking to myself, Why are they going to earn twice as much as me?"

Liz began to go beyond these dual limitations when she tapped the inner realm: "In my reveries as a girl, I would wait for things to get right. I somehow sensed that other people had something else, an inner life." But it was through relationships themselves, first as a girl and later as a woman, that she found that there was more to life than female misery and exploitation: "When I was not yet ten," she remembered, "there was a neighbor with a very small kitchen that she obviously lived in. And I spent a lot of time with her. She had a parrot—a huge parrot. This woman was happy. I became aware that there was another way to be. Not until I left school at fourteen and worked as a maid did I firm up that notion. The woman I worked for was always thrusting books on me, and I remember reading lots of Hardy. I could see then that one could create an inner life to fall back on."

Another adolescent relationship began to alter the sense of female inferiority that Liz had acquired as a girl. "After I failed my exams for grammar school at ten, I was a cowed, pathetic child," she recalled. "That did not change until I reached about eighteen, when I met my older son's father. He and I had a passionate affair and I had a baby. Having a baby in the fifties without being married was a pretty dicey business. But Andrew himself turned out to be very bright. He was a handful, but he was a great joy. I started to think, If he's that bright, I can't be all that thick. That's when I started to work things through. In spite of living with my mother, I felt success with Andrew. He was a great beacon for me."

What she called "emergence of the real person" began when Liz was twenty-four. An inner psychological departure shifted her out of the disabling relationship with her mother then. She lived at home with her mother, who was unutterably depressed. Over time, Liz got bogged down by her mother's mood and even grew convinced that her daughterly failure lay at the heart of her mother's depression. "My situation was really quite ghastly," she said. "Andrew and I lived with my mother, and she was a real guilt slinger, miserable and depressed as always. I knew my mother was immobilizing me, but I couldn't bear being alone."

Musing on these difficulties as she walked Andrew home from the nursery on a perfectly ordinary fall afternoon, Liz was struck with a moment of clarity that liberated her. Picking over all the things a daughter might do to relieve a mother's sadness, she suddenly realized that nothing could dislodge her mother's misery: "Suddenly I got this charge. I really came round to realizing that my mother's problems were not my responsibility, and that her wanting me to take them over was something that I couldn't do—and it was very sad." The insight that she could do nothing to dispel her mother's despair changed everything. An epiphany she pointed to a quarter of a century later, this inner moment of reflection had remained a central feature of her development.

The experience was remarkable for its internal nature: "There was nothing external going on, nothing I can really pinpoint. It was purely psychic. But it freed me up somehow. I started to read more creatively; I would insist on having a decent Sunday newspaper instead of the rubbish my mother wanted to read. I felt a surge. Whatever was dormant within me started to reemerge, an awakening and flowering. It was a breaking away."

Liz awoke to a potential for being different from her mother during this moment. Her flowering inspired a lasting romance. But that awakening was not to last. She became a married woman—like her mother: "That awakening and flowering was so strong that I suddenly felt that I could make a marriage work without being like my mother. But when I got married a year later, I was sucked back into a cave of womanly doings. It all swamped over me."

The female convention of marriage, unlike the unconventional act of having a baby out of wedlock, thrust Liz backward, in her words, "slinging me back into the destiny I'd feared." She quickly lost the distinction between her life and her mother's and began to grieve for the loss of what she thought she'd had, a certain independence from her mother's ways. Stepping into marriage, she found, put her in danger "of my mother swallowing me up again."

Powerless to resist the pull of her mother's depression, Liz then felt that depression become her own: "I had time to be doing all sorts of things, but I wept it away," she said. "Sometimes I was weeping because I was furious at my husband because he wasn't doing what I wanted him to do. Sometimes I was weeping in a rage against my mother. It was almost as though I'd got weeping to do, and had to do it."

Searching for a model of womanhood that was not saturated with melancholy, Liz befriended a woman who was different from her mother in mood and a dozen other respects. Paradoxically, she set about learning how to get out of "the cave of womanly doings" through that friendship—and she finally came into her own.

"But then I met Lydia," she related. "She was the perfect role model for me. She showed me how to be happy with a traditional female role. She was just smashing. She could run a house and be happy about it. If she dropped the mashed potatoes all over the kitchen floor and half the dinner was missing, she'd sweep them up and get the bread out. It was just a great big giggle. Nothing was a trauma for her. I'd had flashes of knowing how to be happy, but I couldn't sustain it. Lydia knew how to sustain it."

This friendship provided Liz the leverage she needed to complete the process she'd begun when she'd realized she was not responsible for her mother's distress. Lydia "got me away from the mental impression of my mother. I hadn't crossed my mother off before I got to be friends with her. Without that friendship, destiny could have led me to repeat my mother's life."

Ironically enough, Liz's relationship with Lydia was both a refutation of the "womanly qualities" she saw in her mother and a reinforcement of femininity. The attachment steadied her, providing a rudder during the next female experience that might have washed her back into the cave: having another baby. "By the time my next baby was born, and I had known Lydia for a year, I knew exactly how I was going to handle him. There was no danger of being swept down by my mother's images. He was very demanding, a baby who cried, but I didn't let it get to me. I did my growing up through him."

The feminine aspects of affiliation, nurturance, and emotional activity, contained in the act of mothering and in the friendship with Lydia, were what helped Liz to come to terms with her relationship to her mother, and reclaim her sense of self. With these experiences she conquered the negative female legacy she'd inherited: "I've made myself over, countered destiny," she proclaimed. "I've got hold of my own fate, realized that nobody could do it for me. There were two distinct routes I could have taken. And I did not take the path into the deep, dark cave. The path I took was up a hill, covered in brambles, snares of all sorts ready to reach out and trap me. My life's been a gradual shoring up along that path. I didn't allow myself to be caught."

Liz shifted her relationship with her mother through a two-step process: first the inner psychological departure, then the friendship. "My mother's not been laid entirely to rest," she confided. "Sometimes I feel as though she is sitting on my shoulder filtering what I say. But she's receded into the background. The pattern that had gone from her to me has vanished."

Other women in my study trod a well-worn path littered with angry confrontations to transform their relationships with their mothers. Some had to hammer home the point that they were no longer children in order to step fully into adulthood. Those who felt oppressed by the mother-daughter relationship found that they had to "get out from under" to come into their own, as Carol had related. "Don't call me up," she'd shouted to her mother. "I don't want to hear your voice until I'm ready to!" The confrontation helped restore her to herself. It also led her to feel genuinely grown-up. "I first thought that I must be an adult when I had a child to be responsible for and take care of," she explained. "But I didn't really feel grown-up until I told my mother off." Wendy, too, reclaimed a bedrock sense of self only when she confronted her mother's petty demands of her after her husband was killed: "I had to confront my mother and say to her, 'You've got to stop this! Look how old I am! I'm not thirteen any longer!'" She herself was surprised at what it took to assert her natural authority: "That was harder to do and took me longer to do than to make a proper marriage, or to have a child. That confrontation effected some final growing up."

But some daughters, especially those who had close, nurturing relationships with their mothers, grew up when they faced their mothers' deaths. Their experience and that of those who told their mothers off points to the positive part separation can play in the process of maturing. A psychologist stated without hesitation that she became grown up when her mother died, although she would have defended herself as an adult many years before. Upon learning in her late twenties that her mother was terminally ill, she reorganized their already close relationship, in part by expressing more honestly how certain differences of opinion between them bothered her.

The shift in their relationship began when the twosome did their weekly grocery shopping together shortly after the mother was diagnosed with incurable cancer. At the produce counter, her mother reached for a fresh pineapple, but then drew back and refused to buy it "because it was too expensive." Of course she was right. It was winter in New England, and the pineapple had been flown in from Hawaii. But the daughter, aware that time was short and opportunity for indulgence limited, pushed her mother's objection aside, insisting that what life is all about is buying fresh pineapple. Their raging battle at the supermarket, a first disagreement, was a simple challenge that opened up deeper areas in which the daughter had remained silent. In the months that followed she and her mother shared important differences they'd held back for the sake of harmony, and deepened their relationship. Reaching a new level of individual and shared honesty before her mother's death freed this daughter to become powerful in her own right.

Jo's situation was entirely different, yet it was her mother's death

that empowered her too, a score of years before we met. A variety
of physical handicaps kept her dependent on her mother until she
was in her early thirties. She lived with her mother even after marrying and having a baby. Her mother's death finally forced her to
take responsibility for herself. As she'd put it, "Only after she was
gone did I realize that if it rained during the night and I did not get
up to close the windows, no one would close them. By closing those
windows whenever it rained—by catching the bus on time without
my mother's reminder, by doing the grocery shopping before we ran
out of milk, I began to see, gradually, that I could manage."

Other women took hold of their own lives in an entirely different
manner, still related to relationship: by borrowing on the distinctly
womanly theme of care. Helen was one of them. Although she'd
succumbed to the ravages of divorce, there was one bright spot on
her horizon: her seventeen-year-old daughter was an honor student
about to start her freshman year at an Ivy League college. But Helen
had nearly passed up motherhood. She, like Ruth, had thought she'd
be unable to succeed at it. What changed her mind was a shift in her
inner dependence on her mother—a shift that resolved her vision of
herself as a dependable, caring person.

Helen had defined adulthood as "when you stopped being a kid,
I guess—when you got thrown out of the nest." Like other women,
however, she made a distinction between that event and the point
at which she really felt grown-up. A person who had "lacked self-
confidence to a nearly pathological degree," she began to gather some
confidence in her ability to manage adult life while in her twenties,
during which she attended college, married, and learned to deal with
a complex network of people. But she did not really feel grown-up
until a friend of hers needed immediate, responsible care—when
Helen was thirty years old. "I had a funny experience around that
time. I had been married for nearly ten years then, and suddenly
there was a real shift in my perspective. A close friend of mine was
pregnant, and she and her husband came to spend the weekend with
us. She excused herself from the dinner table and she was gone for
a long time. We finally went to find out what was happening and we
found her on the bed, bleeding. She lived in another state, and was
miles away from her doctor.

"The first thing that came into my head was, I should call my
mother and she'll tell me what to do. The next thing I thought was,
You don't call your mother at this age—you deal with an emergency
yourself, which we did. It was only then that I began to see myself

as a person who could be depended upon instead of doing the depending."

This unspoken dialogue led Helen to redefine herself in such a critical way that all of her relationships changed. Coping with this dramatic situation and crystallizing a vision of herself as a person who could provide care instead of a person who needed the care of others led her to put into a different perspective all to whom she was attached. She began to feel that she was on a par with people whom she had previously held in awe—a transition that made her feel authentically adult: "Having thought that I was absolutely worthless up until that point, I began to garner some sense of worth," she reflected. "Having felt inferior to my husband and all the brilliant associates he had who were our friends, I discovered that there were a lot of things I could do that they couldn't. So I became confident on some level. Then I realized I could stand up for myself and I was aware of it. I was *aware* then of being an adult."

Reconceptualizing herself as capable of caring was a turn so critical for Helen that it gave her the confidence to overcome her mother's stand on parenthood and meet the greatest challenge of all—producing a child of her own. "My mother was very anti having children, and I was scared of them," she explained. "I was convinced for the longest time that I just wouldn't be able to handle it, and I made a conscious choice not to have any.

"After that, though, I visited some friends who had three daughters. The youngest one was three years old, and I just had the best damn time with that little girl. She was so bright, and she had this sort of baby wisdom—a whole new way of looking at things. I thought, This kid is really kind of fun. She really got to me. So then I thought, Well, gee, if I could produce something like this, maybe I could handle it after all. Maybe I wasn't anathema to every child. The result was that I had my first, last, and only child when I was thirty-three. I must say I found a lot of solace in it, a lot of resources, a lot of courage I didn't know I had."

Helen was not the only one in my study who began to see herself as "a person who could be depended upon" by virtue of an experience that had to do with womanly care. Other daughters reshaped their relationships with their mothers by beginning to take care of them in concrete ways, reversing the traditional constellation of roles. One woman grew up early by looking after her bedridden mother while she was in junior high school. Having to care for her mother pitched her into adulthood early. Her ability to care well for her mother changed her self-concept so that when her mother recovered, they enjoyed relating as equals. Feeling grown-up hinged on incidents—circumstantial and psychological—that led these women to discover that they were as caring and dependable as were their mothers. When they called upon themselves to provide responsible care for others, they began at last to see themselves as people in their own right.

Perhaps most compelling in this regard is the story of Willa, the seventy-two-year-old writer whose integration of the dual images of girlhood was described in Chapter 6. She began to define herself as an adult when she left home at age twenty-six, but she did not come into her own as a person until she changed her relationship with her mother—after she married at age forty. Her earlier success as a writer somehow fell short of endowing her with the sense of being her own person, and for many years after she established herself professionally, she felt immature. She measured maturity not in conventional patriarchal terms, such as autonomy and economic self-sufficiency, but rather in terms of acquiring an ability to make decisions in the context of her ties to others. Until she met this rational-relational criterion, she felt that, while adult by common measures, she was immature. But this ability eluded her despite her apparent occupational independence.

"As far as the way I handled getting a job, keeping a job, getting a better job, and finally breaking off from the routine of nine-to-five jobs altogether and getting to the point where I could be a free-lance writer, that certainly was not immature," Willa said. "But in relationships with other people . . . I showed great immaturity. I was easily swayed by the feelings of others, unable to make my own decisions. I was just not my own person."

Marrying at middle age and then reshaping her relationship with her mother—two relational events—were the changes that led Willa to feel grown-up. She claimed that "real maturity came with marriage" and said that the crucial turning point in her growing up occurred three years after she was married, when she and her husband moved to a suburban house and invited her mother to come and live with them.

This was not the first time Willa and her mother had lived together since Willa had left home. After proving that she could support herself when she first moved north, Willa had sent for her mother, who then lived with her through the next dozen years. But it was when she integrated her mother into her own household as a married woman that she made of her life what she called "The Hat Made by

Hand." Transforming the nature of their relationship gave Willa an ability to hold her own and to make her own decisions. In that, she met her own standard for growing up: "Growing up meant putting my mother in the right perspective. Not loving her any less but seeing myself as a grown person, entitled to a life of my own. Being able to care for her, seeing that she was fine and well taken care of, I found for the first time in my life that I could make a decision unswayed by other people's feelings."

Paradoxically, Willa had had what many would call a life of her own before she married, giving up a good deal of autonomy when she wed. But transforming her relationship with her mother by "putting her in the right perspective" is what led her to *feel* that she had a life of her own. Having been "swayed to pleasing people" all her life, unable, as she said, to "run my own show," caring for her mother in the context of her marriage led her to see herself as entitled to her own life. That caring stance also enabled her to make her own decisions.

For Willa, as for other women in the study, leaving home signified becoming an adult in one sense. But feeling grown-up hinged on changing the nature of her relationship with her mother—not by distancing her but by living in the closest proximity to her. Winning her autonomy depended on caring for the very person upon whose care she had depended. A transformation perhaps impossible without the framework of marriage, this change centered not on separation but on a shift in the balance of mutual care.

Each of these daughters attests to the importance of having a substantial emotional impact on her mother. For some, the impact was made through anger. For others, it was made through care. In either case, altering the relationship through emotional activity was a maturational bench mark. Their accounts suggest that the usual stress placed on the effects of a mother on a child has a counterpart in a child's opportunity to affect a mother. Good enough mothering,[12] necessary to a child's development, may have a direct correlate in good enough daughtering.[13] Alongside a body of literature which suggests that a daughter's relationship with her father determines her orientation to achievement, these women suggest that a rapprochement with her mother gives rise to a daughter's increased sense of agency and effectence. By learning that she could modify the frustrating aspects of her relationship with her mother so that that relationship no longer thwarted growth, many a woman vitalized her sense of competence, forging the link between work and love.[14]

Instead of separating from their mothers, these daughters were separating from an outworn image of themselves as little girls. They were shifting the balance of dependence and care to secure more mutual and symmetrical relationships with their mothers. They were reaching not for simple independence but for interdependence—a kind of rapprochement that marks relationships of equal give-and-take.[15] Once they had reworked this tie, women began to seek, recognize, and create such relationships—based on mature, mutual dependence[16]—with mates, friends, and colleagues.

Their accounts call into question the normalcy and utility of a psychological standard that rests on separation, suggesting that a model that requires adults to separate from their parents is itself an odd one. In fact, separation would seem to be a crude "solution" to a "problem" the culture itself has fabricated. Although separation played a part in most of their accounts, to characterize these women's experiences simply as separation would be to place the emphasis on the wrong syllable. By changing the tie without eliminating it, by increasing the intricacy of the tie instead of reducing it, by wrestling with feminine values without refuting the attachment or discounting the mother herself, women were able to refashion the relationship so that it fit who they'd become as people. To suggest that separation is the central process at work would be to distort the essence of that process and to misconstrue its aims.

The experiences of all these women challenge the notion that the mere fact of a strong tie between an adult daughter and her mother indicates dependence or pathology; they suggest, instead, that this bond, *when it is malleable*, supports a woman's growth. Their accounts suggest that we could benefit from determining how the mother-daughter tie functions in the lives of both individuals, what meaning it holds for each. The manner in which this tie is renegotiated represents a more sophisticated index of maturity than the simple presence or absence of attachment. In fact, the absence of a continuing relationship would seem to indicate a problem, particularly between daughters and mothers, because this is the relationship through which a girl first forms her image of who and what she is. Only through maintaining this tie *and* modifying it as she matures can a woman at once buttress the continuity of her identity and integrate its transformations.

What women want to do in relation to their mothers is perhaps best summed up by the many dictionary meanings of the word *reckoning*. They want to render the account, settle the debts that left them owing. They want to loosen the grip of old entitlements, to calculate the value of the relationship. They want to balance the ledger by figuring themselves into the equation as adults so that they carry equal weight. They want to count on the tie, to rely on it, not as dependent children but as full participants in a mutual, reciprocal attachment. They want to rectify it, put it to rights, bringing its edges together so that the fit is flush. They want to make the relationship hardy, strong, substantial. They want to take a reckoning by it, to set their compass and find their position from that relationship.

Becoming a woman in one's own right depends not on severing the connection to one's mother but on changing its nature. The intricate process these women described turns not on separation but on transforming a critical tie.

10

THE SEARCH FOR MY OWN GIRL WITHIN

nd what of my own girl within? Finding my way back to her was not an easy process. I did not unearth her by reckoning my relationship with my mother. An adopted child, I was a father's daughter. I took to my attorney father from the time I was a baby, and I remained identified with him until he died, as this book was going to press. Becoming a woman in my own right meant coming to terms with the patriarchy as it was embodied in my father and in his roots, for his family was an old and prominent one. When my grandfather died, for example, his photo was printed on the front page of the paper, with the headline "Mr. Syracuse dies." There was much to uphold, a history that went back to the Declaration of Independence, to the *Mayflower* itself. John Hancock lurked in the background; autonomy and self-sufficiency, hardly abstract standards here, were manifest in each member of this patriarchal clan.

Aware as a child that there was a lot to live up to in such a family, I came early to rely on my intellect,[1] ultimately becoming overeducated in place of becoming myself. My father was intent on educating me from the start. When I was just two years old, he gave me a lesson in the alphabet each day when he came home from the office by putting me next to him on the couch and spelling out the headlines of the evening paper. I dutifully satisifed him with straight-A report cards year after year. My grade-school teachers commented that I was a sensible child on a fine, even keel. But underneath this sturdy exterior I was as defenseless as Ruth had been. And my struggle to come into my own as a woman and a writer was painful. Like Megan, I hit rock bottom before I circled back to the girl who embodied my root identity.

My history as a woman, too, fell at the cusp of the prefeminist and feminist eras, leaving me teetering on the brink between old ways and newer, more conscious, ones. I married in 1965, just before contraception, the Vietnam War, and the summer of love broke forever the lockstep between love, marriage, sex, and parenthood that had structured our society. Nineteen years old and quite unused to thinking of myself as a person in my own right, I was glad to harness my energies to my husband's agenda and adopt his goals as my own. As a young bride, I heartily supported his ambitions in the art world—until I was brought up short by a comment from the wife of one of the heavyweights in his field. At a museum gala, she told me, sotto voce, that the most important thing a wife could do is stand invisibly behind her husband to bolster his career. All of a sudden, I knew that to do so was a form of self-abnegation unacceptable to me.

Fortunately, my husband encouraged me in my own pursuits in spite of this cultural ethos. I took writing courses at the local university, all the while seeing this as a mere avocation that would yield at the proper time to the real business of life: having a family. This I delayed until I was sure of our marriage. Ironically enough, the marriage collapsed almost as soon as our son, Tad, was born. Only months before, we had rented out our city flat and moved to the Catskills, so that my husband could accomplish some specialized work in his field. Displaced geographically, I was as physically and psychologically vulnerable as Megan had been with a newborn baby.

That first winter alone, I could barely cope. With the nearest neighbor a country mile away, I rather welcomed the skunks in the woodpile, the owls in the carriage house, the shrew who occasionally peered up at me from the bathroom register. I even tolerated the red squirrels that arced across the eaves and once enjoyed a feast of homemade cranberry bread, the evidence scattered about on the round oak table we kept in that Delft kitchen. But I was at a loss to contend with the nameless creature that came to inhabit the earth cellar of my diminutive country home. One late February morning, when I could ignore its presence no longer, I called a repairman, using as an excuse a faulty water heater—simply because I was afraid to tackle something large and alive myself. The village being small, the workman knew of my circumstances. From the bottom of the cellar stairs he called to me that the sun was climbing high in the sky, and allowed as how things would soon look up. He shooed the woodchuck out, and I clung to his remark like a talisman, but the late winter snows buried the railing from the house to the road, and the weeds burgeoned into fields all around when spring finally broke.

Not until Memorial Day could I finally reclaim my own apartment some ninety miles away. With a baby to support and no means to do it, I relied on friends to find me a job. That summer, I drove to a museum an hour away four days a week and brought work home for the other three. A teenager came in to care for Tad, but he was too cagey for her. He buttoned his litle mouth shut whenever she tried to feed him and ignored her efforts to play. Only when close friends downstairs, twin brothers who were concert pianists, came up to hold and cajole him would he finally smile and eat. Daily, my guilt level rose.

One evening after eating dinner with this duo, I carried our plates upstairs to run them through my dishwasher, as was our habit, and retired to their couch, sleepy from the wine with dinner—to say nothing of the exhaustion of my life. Listening to the familiar whir of our dishes being washed, I glanced up to see a curtain of droplets raining down from the ceiling onto their kitchen floor, directly below mine. We rushed upstairs, and while mopping up the overflow from the broken machine, began one of our endless discussions about what I should do with my life. Singly and then together the brothers insisted that I had a remarkable brain and should pick up my college education where I'd left off to marry at the end of freshman year. How, I retorted, could I? I was not making ends meet even by working seven days a week. In that case, they proclaimed, there was absolutely nothing to stop me. If it was already a financial wash, they argued, I had little to lose by going back to school. I could not fault their logic. With only half the summer left, I got readmitted, procured a scholarship, and angled my way into married student housing.

Less than two months into the first semester, Tad developed a serious illness that defied diagnosis. All I (or anyone) knew was that he had a dangerously high fever, a swollen eye and cheek, an alarming white-cell count—and a need to be constantly watched. I could not, the doctor cautioned, leave him with anyone else. With a strict limit on how many classes a student could miss without automatically failing a course, I was advised by the dean who had worked so hard to find my scholarship that I had no alternative but to withdraw—and leave student housing. Angry and desperate, I called my teachers one by one instead. Thank goodness they permitted me to keep up with the assignments on my own, and to stay in school during what became a prolonged illness.

The thin rugs literally lifted up off the floors when the winter winds blew through those shoddy barracks, built as temporary housing during World War II. I wrapped myself up by night in a beautiful mohair throw from Scotland, a wedding gift from the aunt for whom I'd been named, and studied beside the space heater in my living room. The water in the metal shower stall stood frozen from November to March. Lacking a tub, I bathed the baby in the kitchen sink. The day he took sick at the end of October, I came home from the doctor's to find the back door blown open, snow scattered over the kitchen floor. I had put in a request for maintenance weeks before when I'd moved in: not one window or door had both opened and shut as it should. The wait for repairs, I'd been told, was two years— except for an emergency. That afternoon a carpenter arrived and worked on the place until seven. Back the next morning, he worked until dark to stop the doors and windows from flying open on their own.

When I finally graduated, two years later, I moved to Boston in the hope of making a new beginning. The only job I could get with a simple college degree barely provided subsistence, and took me away from my then two-year-old boy for long hours. Leaving Tad each morning nearly did me in. He would sob at nursery school despite the kindly efforts of a middle-aged teacher named Harriet. Even his fascination with a Spanish schoolmate failed to bridge the gap. Once over the morning tears, he and Veronica, who spoke no English whatsoever, would jump on their trikes and ride around the school yard chasing each other. But the next day, it was always back to square one. I wondered what was so great about being in "the real world" when at the end of a dreary day at work I would fetch Tad, take him home, and barely find time enough to fix supper, give him a bath, and read him a story by bedtime. Grocery shopping, laundry, and what I came to call "the administration of life" were all crammed into Saturdays. Any social life of my own cut into the scant measure Tad had of me. If anybody had talked about quality time those days, I would have cut my throat.

At the end of a year, undone by this trying existence, I gave two weeks' notice, borrowed enough money to buy a secondhand camper, vacuumed my apartment, turned the key in the lock, and took the kid and drove west—all the way to the coast. The trip was a godsend. Finally I found the natural rhythms of life: we went to sleep at dark, got up at dawn, played "chase" and told stories when the spirit moved, and drove on when we'd had enough of a place. Tad's three-year-old imagination turned thunderclouds into dragons looming up out of the flat Midwestern sky, and he was fast away making friends when we set up camp at various outposts.

But after that summer, it was back to school—a master's program I undertook in clinical social work, in the hope of escaping the apparently ubiquitous entry-level job that held no future. After graduation, I was lucky to be hired by the children's hospital where I'd been trained. Lucky and unlucky that is: as a staff social worker, I had no option but to work full time and to take emergency call on a rotating schedule. I carried a beeper nights and weekends—and had to report in person within twenty minutes of being paged. This meant setting up an intercom between Tad's room and the upstairs neighbors. I had gotten an advanced degree to escape drudgery but found that I had taken on a new form of drudgery instead. In those days a staff member could not even use sick time because of an ill child.

In desperation, I plotted another escape: school, once again, promised at least temporary freedom from some of these restrictions. In addition to finding intellectual sustenance, I figured that in a doctoral program I'd be able to call my schedule my own and stay home with Tad when he needed me. Ready for a change of scene, and more than ready to get out from under the institutionalism of the Boston area, I applied for a number of programs around the country. Harvard was the only one to accept me. Besides its obvious academic appeal, it was just down the street. I went.

An occurrence during the first semester focused my attention on the conflicts women face—especially the conflict between attachment and autonomy. The struggle of tending to small children while pursuing one's own goals, one I had experienced myself, began to look impossible when a faculty member not much over forty died suddenly of a heart attack. A single parent, Marcia Guttentag collapsed at the

airport, en route to one of the many professional lectures she gave.
I was struck with the anonymity of her death, the impersonal setting—
and could not help but attribute her early demise to the stress of
rearing children singly while trying to maintain a viable professional
life. Faced with the impossible dilemma, she had paid the ultimate
price for the forced choices she had made.

That same autumn I learned that Charlotte Perkins Gilman had
given her child away, so convinced was she of the incompatibility
between her feminist objectives and the demands of child rearing.
Margaret Sanger, too, had left her child behind to crusade for women's
rights to birth control—only to have the child fall ill and die. As I
learned about these pioneering women, I began to see ambition and
purpose as dangerous, even lethal where mothering was concerned.
I was immobilized in my work.

At the end of that first semester, I knew only that women's
conflicts, especially the conflict between mothering and worldly ambition, would be my life's work, although as yet I had no idea what
form that work might take. That this led, finally, to the life studies
in this book, occurred through a combination of fate and circumstance
when, a few weeks into the second semester, I drove to upstate New
York for my father's sixty-fifth birthday party. As I set out with my
nine-year-old son to drive the three hundred miles back to Cambridge, I didn't know that a blizzard would threaten our safety. Half-
way home, when squalls and flurries became pouches of heavy damp
snow, I asked the turnpike toll taker what lay ahead. She shouted
over the wind that the real storm was coming fast behind us, and
added that it was expected to close the roads. With just a few dollars
in my wallet, I could not possibly manage a hotel. I felt I had no
alternative but to keep on. I drove like fury, but the storm overtook
us. We stopped once for gas and a weather update. It was hopeless:
the service station was blanketed with trucks, engines idling to keep
their cabins warm, lowing like cattle bedded down around the pumps.

With dozens of cars off the side of the road, I was determined
to make it all the way home, but by the time we got to Cambridge,
hours later, the region was obliterated by a whiteout. Unable to
distinguish city streets from sidewalks, I hugged the river nearly all
the way back to my house. But the driveway—where was the driveway? I could only trust that it was still approximately where it had
been when we left, for the fence that ran alongside it was completely
drifted over. I revved the engine, put the car in first gear, and hurled
it into what I hoped was my familiar place. We were lucky to make

it; the snow covered all but the roofs of stranded cars, and the street we lived on was impassable for a week until a front-loader dug it out.

During the storm and its aftermath, Harvard shut down because of weather for the first time in its nearly three-hundred-fifty-year history. Banks were closed, businesses were closed, grocery stores were closed—but Cambridge being what it is, the bookstores opened. Having triumphed over the elements, I wanted badly to get out of the house as soon as the snow stopped. Car travel was banned; I put on my cross-country skis to traverse the mile or so to Harvard Square. The mood was ebullient among my fellow travelers, and the bookstore, counter to its usual policy, was accepting checks. I found two books to carry home in my backpack. One, *Working It Out*, edited by Sara Ruddick and Pamela Daniels, was a collection of essays by women writers, scientists, artists, and scholars about the meaning of work in their lives. The other was Jean Baker Miller's *Toward a New Psychology of Women*.* These two books changed my life.

It turned out that Jean Miller lived and worked in Boston, as did Pamela Daniels. A member of my school's Colloquium Board the following year, I had a chance to engage both of them for the annual Askwith symposium, which had always before consisted of the usual panel of distinguished scholars—all male, of course.

Determined to "feminize" that one-shot, climactic format and to expand its impact, we broke with tradition and invited the authors published in these two books as well as many other women scholars to give colloquia over several weeks on the theme "Competence in Women's Lives." Each speaker not only selected her own topic within that theme but also chose the time of day that fit her schedule, the size of the audience she wanted to address, the kind of room she wished to speak in (classroom, lecture hall, living room), and the level of formality that suited her. Perhaps most important, each was encouraged to speak from whatever stage of her work pleased her most: a working draft, a roundtable discussion, a finished piece were all equally welcome. The series attracted a good deal of attention from the press in the "real world"; students claimed it was the best course they'd taken at Harvard. Had I doubted that this was my calling, I could doubt it no longer.

Soon after that, the *Harvard Educational Review* published a special issue on women, including an essay by Carol Gilligan, which formed the basis for her now well-known book *In a Different Voice*.

*Publication data for all the books I mention in this chapter are in the Bibliography.

Also in that issue was a remarkable piece by Marcia Westkott, "Feminist Criticism of the Social Sciences." Westkott's article criticized the so-called objective methods of science, supplanting them with a dialectical process that would account for the inherent interdependence of subject and object.

This important theoretical expansion came along just as George Vaillant (in *Adaptation to Life)* and Daniel Levinson (in *The Seasons of a Man's Life)* legitimized biographical studies of adults in midlife. Gail Sheehy had cast their research findings on men against the life trajectories of women in *Passages.* Soon thereafter, Maggie Scarf focused attention on women's lives with *Unfinished Business.* The ingredients for my dissertation thus fell into my hands: a developmentalist at heart, I built on this collective groundwork by devising biographical research that would delve directly into women's own understanding of the underlying processes of their psychological growth over time.

Although it was not until years later that I discovered the girl within, I unwittingly relied on that girl during that last academic stint. Without the industriousness of the eight- or nine-year-old, I never could have found the single-minded drive that led people at Harvard to call me "a blur on the horizon," a sequel to the perseverance and sheer determination that had gotten me through first the bachelor's and then the master's degree. But that kind of pursuit rarely yields the bedrock sense of self my subjects found—and it did not unearth the girl for me. The doctorate over, I continued to pursue my goals in overdrive—except that I did not know exactly what those goals were. All I really knew was that I was long overdue in leaving Cambridge and its patriarchal institutions.

During the winter of my final year at Harvard, I saw an advertisement for a postdoctoral fellowship at the University of California, Berkeley, and decided it was for me. Just after graduation, I sublet my place in Cambridge, packed up six boxes and then twelve-year-old Tad, and drove to California. A new graduate eager to share the findings from my doctoral research, I offered to speak to various groups on campus. Faculty members and colloquia chairmen alike declined my offers, repeatedly pressing me to "come up with something more interesting." Women's issues, they assured me, were passé.

I suppose this response had its fortunate aspect, for my thesis emphasized the dynamic tension between attachment and autonomy, stemming from my long-standing interest in this conflict and following quite directly from the work of Jean Baker Miller and Carol Gilligan, who had supervised the research.* I wanted nothing more than to wrest my own point from my material. But that disinterest on the part of others quieted whatever voice I'd given to my work; my impulse to speak out stifled, I lost heart in my research. Determined as I might be, I could not identify the unique finding my study held. As the fellowship year wound down and I was still in debt from the doctorate, I forsook my research and made a policy to compensate for my financial condition: I would apply for any job for which I seemed qualified, and accept any job that was offered to me, provided I thought I could do it well. At the end of August, during a single seven-day period, four jobs came along: two half-time, two quarter-time. I took them all.

Chance events finally closed the gap between the determined Amazon I had become and the vulnerable girl I'd been in the first place, events that could not have brought her to me if I had continued to manage this inhumane workweek while trying single-handedly to create some semblance of home life for my son. I realized how badly I needed a break from the heroic striving that had come to dominate my life only when Tad ended up in intensive care at the age of fifteen, stricken by a massive hemorrhage from an ulcer we did not know he had. Once again I carried a beeper, but this time to those four jobs in four different locales for my own child's emergency.

It was just after his hospitalization that the unlikely gathering of society ladies mentioned in Chapter 1 led me to the deep truth that lay embedded in my data. Although that elite retreat was the real turning point, this book might still have gone unwritten were it not for a course I taught at a minuscule doctoral program, an alternative to the alternative schools. Lots of things that happened there were out of the ordinary. Once I arrived to find the school's president serving hard-boiled quail eggs with dijon mustard. The students were full-fledged professionals who had unique personalities to boot. My class of seven included an Asian minister, a black entrepreneur, a California hypnotist, and an ex-CEO.

All hunched over, the CEO bent to our needs for hospitality. A middle-aged man, he would cluck over the others, pouring coffee as the class began. Then he'd plop down into an overstuffed chair and fan himself in the late afternoon sun, regaling us in a Jiminy Cricket

---

*Courtney Cazden, George Goethals, Robert Kegan, and Harry Lasker were also immensely helpful to me during the doctoral process.

voice with stories about his wife's and grown daughter's reactions to the ideas he was taking home from "that funky class." Until he provided this weekly entertainment, I had fallen into thinking that the "new woman," unconcerned with traditional female values, would be disaffected by my material. This man's running account of the reactions of his daughter and her friends disabused me of that misperception. Later, he became my benefactor: convinced that there was something here that mattered to contemporary women, he provided me with an out-of-pocket grant.

Finally given respite from the struggle to cope by the practical support of my benefactor and my father, I dropped one and then another of my part-time jobs and made my way back to this book.* For the first time since that trip we'd taken when Tad was just three years old, the two of us returned to the natural rhythms of life. Now I was around, could join in his concerns in a way that had been impossible in the interim. At last I felt like a real mother. We even adopted a dog. Her mother was a German shepherd, but, like me, she must have been a daddy's girl, for she looked like a short deer rather than a shepherd and carried her tail like a flag. Comely and girlish, she would cross her ankles when she languished on the couch, and would rest her velvet muzzle at various points along the edge of my bed in the morning in a mute appeal for attention, like ladyfingers playing the intervals of a keyboard scale. Her markings made her a striking beauty: a black mask outlined her ears, eyes, and mouth, giving her brindle face the look of an Egyptian princess. But there was a lot more to this canine Cleopatra than those googly eyes. Sturdy and spirited, she possessed a certain moxie I admired. Sure of her feminine prowess, she would wriggle with pleasure at greeting a friend—but she was a fierce guard, too, tearing at the bamboo shade over the front door whenever a stranger approached. She knew how to wag her tail and bare her fangs at the same time.

It was during this long-awaited lull that I began to pull into view a picture of myself as a writer. In response to a dictum issued by Dorothea Brande in her book *On Becoming a Writer* (written some fifty years earlier), I wrote out my thoughts first thing in the morning, before, as she advised, uttering a word or letting my eye fall on a printed page. By keeping to this discipline, *no matter what*, I found

---

*Feminist research still often depends on patriarchal support of one kind or another. It is ironic that this book, which challenges the patriarchy, was made possible by the material support of two men.

my own voice at last. But alas, I still did not find my girl within. Instead I found abominable spelling littering those pages. This came as a shock: I had always prided myself on my spelling. In fourth grade I had even won a prize for being the best speller in my class—a book about a mouse. I had long since concluded that I'd been born with perfect spelling, and had even attributed Tad's spelling errors to faulty genetic inheritance I blamed on his father. Now I could only imagine that a neurological disorder was threatening nature's perfection. That amateur diagnosis added to the ennui that surrounded my frustration at finding my girl within out of reach, even as she danced off my fingertips while I rendered others' rediscovery of her.

The first emotional breakthrough in finding my own inner girl came when, after I'd written some of this book's chapters, I took a three-day Christmas vacation at a rustic cross-country ski resort in the Sierra Nevada Mountains. The guests gathered at the trailhead and were carried by sleigh to the lodge. After we climbed out from under a pile of deerskin lap robes, ski instructors in navy-and-red bodysuits served us an English tea with Christmas cake in front of a great stone fireplace. Feeling well taken care of, I turned to go upstairs and spotted a book lying on top of the bookcase—with the title *Emily* on its cover.* As I opened its pages, I found the story of a young girl about to become an orphan. Having earlier lost her mother, she was, like me, a father's daughter. She lived with him and a housekeeper in a little house in the country, where her friends were two cats, the tall pines, and the "Wind Woman" who rustled the trees. She used a ledger book for writing "deskripshuns" when "the Flash" showed her special designs in the trees and wallpaper, designs that lay hidden behind what most people could only see as mundane reality. Never having gone to school, she was quite at one with herself in what others would call an isolated life. She had a certain independence that arose from solitary living. I was riveted to her story.

I saw myself in this other Emily, for I had felt like a motherless one. Although not technically motherless, I had lost my birth mother and my foster mother before I was adopted. My father was my mainstay. And as a member of a patriarchal family that looked askance at adoption, I identified with the fictional Emily when a host of relatives she had never met before set to "evaluating her" upon her father's

---

*The full title of the book, by L. M. Montgomery (who wrote *Anne of Green Gables* and others) was *Emily of New Moon*. It did not occur to me until months later that this was written as a children's book.

death.* I admired her when, as they discussed her in her presence, talking all the while as though she were either physically absent or an inanimate object, she burst out indignantly, "You make me feel as if I was made up of scraps and patches!"[2] I sympathized with her when she was later taken by surprise next to her father's casket, bidding him a private farewell. Aunts and uncles unexpectedly convened to discuss what was to be done with "the child" in the very room that held father and daughter. Emily scrambled beneath the dining-room table, only to learn from what she then overheard that she had been badly misunderstood: her brave effort at self-control had been mistaken for an absence of feeling, her lack of cloying dependence had made her seem "difficult." Her intuitive reading of her relatives' negative reactions to her and her forthright responses to their hypocritical comments had been taken as bad manners, a hereditary fault that had to be "cured." Thus criticized while she was hidden in their midst, Emily was sorely and silently maligned for her valiant qualities. Only when the group turned to criticizing her father as a failure did she expose her presence—at once confirming their ill thoughts. But her anger overcame her fear of further disapproval: she confronted the grown-ups squarely with a bravado that sustained her in the face of unutterable vulnerability.

A maverick like Emily, I too had felt like scraps and patches, illegitimate in my orphaned and adopted state.† Stricken with the same stark lucidity, I as a girl readily jolted my relatives with the naked truth, baffling them with my candor. And I too was a solitary child who had spent most of my time out of school, not because I literally lived alone in the woods with my father, but because I retreated from the boredom of school and its routines. I wanted nothing more than to sit cross-legged on the floor and type letters to an aunt who was dying of throat cancer just as I was turning nine. "This is a picture of a lady with a hat," I would mercifully print beneath the abstract crayoned drawings I sent to her. Those letters are lost now, or perhaps lodged in some buried file, but I have finally unlocked my memory of them, and come to realize that they hold a piece of my truth as a girl.

But falling on the *Emily* book did not fully bring the girl I had neglected back to me. I worked away at finding her in psychotherapy,

---

*Although I wrote this chapter in the summer of 1987, before even knowing that my own father was ill, this is exactly what happened after his illness and death in the winter of 1988.
†The literal meaning of *maverick* is "a person who acts independently because of not being labeled as belonging to any one person or group."

in life, but no matter what I tried, she would not be forced out of hiding. I began to wonder, finally, if she really had existed—for me—at all. During this protracted period of disconnection from her, I became resigned to her elusive nature, to her very absence from my life. But this resignation had its costs: the writing came in fits and starts; my ragged spelling went downhill; I grew negative and irritable. I should have realized that the girl's emergence was not subject to will, that her memory would not be evoked through conscious determination.

It was in the inner realm of unconscious workings that I began to trace my way back to her and reclaim the original identity she harbored. Months into the work of writing this book, having lived for years in a small cottage with a now enormous son, I had a dream of looking for a place to live. I was being shown through a flat where every room did dual duty: the living room served also as a bedroom, the kitchen as a sewing room, even the bathroom was also used as a darkroom. I was about to leave without taking the place when the people who lived in it showed me a back room off the kitchen, one they had nearly forgotten. Lacking heat or electricity, it was lit with a pale, late winter sun and was cooler than the rest of the house. The roof was slanted, with windows that acted as skylights. Stark and spare, it held only one piece of furniture—a writing table. I took it. Only when I had this dream did I realize how important it was to have a room of my own—a room, in my case, solely for writing. It was almost a year before I managed, at age forty, to have such a room.

Not until the approach of my autumn birthday that year, a time of reflection especially for an adopted child, did the scraps and patches that I'd been made up of at age eight or nine begin to surface and to hang together. The late fall sunrise made my early morning writing practice ever more unlikely; I fell into a melancholy mood. I was rereading Agnes Smith's *An Edge of the Forest*, an allegorical story about an orphaned black lamb adopted by a young black leopardess who was also orphaned. In one particularly touching scene, the lamb recruits an owl to remove a thorn from a leopard's eyelid—and one from his heart, a result of pining in vain for the aloof leopardess. The owl decides that a hummingbird would be better equipped for the task, but he cannot catch one. The leopardess, who presides over the hillside and has never failed at anything, is pressed into service; she bounds into the forest, humiliated when she fails too. Only then does a hummingbird volunteer to remove the leopard's thorn. I had been reading this book just before first coming on the concept of the girl within nearly three years earlier, while my mother was visiting and I was in analysis. I wondered, now, whether this earlier combination of the book about orphaned creatures, a visit from my mother, and the maternal protection of analysis had functioned as a matrix for me to conceive the idea of the girl.

One morning as I sat down to record my waking thoughts, a hummingbird hovered at my window, although I sheltered no literal leopard with a thorn in his eye. The tiny green body—no bigger than a leaf and no heavier than a letter—swung from one fuchsia bush to another, poking at the blossoms as they scattered in the rain. The reflections of that gray dawn inhabited by this iridescent wonder turned up a critical memory: a collection of glass animals I'd treasured as a child, one of them a bird. Absorbed by the glass figurines, I had staunchly resisted going to school so that I could steal them out of the closet and liberate them from their tissue-paper wrappings. I would arrange and rearrange them according to animal type, family group, color, activity, or size. Only a few defied such categorization: a glass ship given to me by a cousin, and a glass ballet dancer, but I loved those two beautiful figures too and always kept them nearby.

As this memory floated across some vast moat to me, I realized that it had taken a certain disposition to spend my childhood in these activities and to win the solitude required to pursue them. I knew then how independent and willful I had been. And I became aware, finally, that my inner girl was far from the cheery girl Rosabeth described (in Chapter 1) but rather was a solitary and determined child. This recognition was long in coming: young Emily was a girl I had sealed off long ago because she did not fit the usual female stereotype. Although that contrary girl had been much in evidence, I had always fought off her intrusion. Now that I recognized her and knew of her significance, I could embrace her as the keeper of my original identity. Her memory galvanized my energies: I resumed writing this book.

The final piece in reclaiming my own girl within took the unexpected form of a gift that came to me in the oddest way the day before my fortieth birthday. An elderly aunt whom I seldom saw called to say that she'd found a letter I'd written to her as a child. A letter much like those I'd sent to her ill sister when I was eight, it was typed, of course, on stationery from my grandfather's country estate, The Cobblestone House, where his four daughters and an abundance of grandchildren gathered for the summer. Although it bore no date, it did hold clues to the girl I'd been as a child—and one clue to the age I'd been when I had written it. Lacking in preface and completely straightforward, littered with the very misspellings I had long disavowed, it was prompted by my sending her son, Perry (the cousin who had given me the glass ship), a thank-you present in return, the glass bird from my collection.

Dear Char:

Does Perry like the bird? Did it brake before it got there? If it did tell Perry I'm sorry. I really don't have much to say but here is all I can think of anyway. We found a Chimney Swift in the chimney of the cobblestone house. The mother of the bird built the nest in the top of the chimney. There was such a wind that it blew the nest down to the bottom of the chimney, babys and all. Well 1 of the birds fell out of the nest. It was caught in a crack of the chimney. Well it fell out of the chimney and we caught it. We kept it and fed it for 3 days. Then he died. We barried him in the animal cemetary with Gaby.

Guess what? Twoie, my cousin, got his apendix out. It all started the night we went to Suburban park. when we got home he had a slight stomach ach. Then he got sick 7 times. We thought it was just the 24 hour bug. the next night we thought we had better take him to the doctors office. The doc' said he didn't think there was anything wrong with him but said they better take him in to Syr. for a real check-up. then they found out he had apendicsites. He went to Memorial Hospital. They took it out Thurs day night/ and he is still in the Hospital today which is Mon. The doctor said he could come home today if nessary but we thought it would be better if he stayed there 'till WED. Well, thats all I can think of to say right now.

And then, placed very carefully in the center of the page, and typed in red capital letters on the diagonal, was the closing:

L
  O
    V
      E,
        E
          M

Here at last I had found a concrete manifestation of my girl within, one that spelled out themes of my youth that related directly to the woman I had become: the irrepressible urge to put my thoughts on paper; their origin; the patriarch's house in the country; the concern for wildlife; the absolute presumption of responsibility for the care of the wounded. Even the Wind Woman appeared as she had in the Emily book, stirring things up in the chimney. The bald presentation, the determination to attend to the aesthetic with those red letters set on the diagonal, the spare line, even the misspellings that had begun to convince me of my neuropathology, were now welcome—because they unknowingly heralded the return of my own girl within. Best of all, by checking with Twoie's mother, I learned the year of the appendicitis and found that this letter was written during the summer when I was nine. In learning the letters that spelled out newspaper headlines from my father and typing out letters to my aunts at ages eight and nine lay the roots of my identity as wordsmith and writer. The girl within was mine.

11

WOMANLY IMAGES OF SELF AND DEVELOPMENT

his book holds a bold idea: that the real fertilization of the female is held in coming back to the girl she is in the first place—rather than in the penetration of the male. A woman's ability to sustain the original self without abandoning her girlhood essence to proscriptive patterns of womanhood rests on her ability to counter fairy-tale notions in which young girls on the verge of womanhood fall unconscious only to be awakened by a prince. Preserving the original identity of girlhood and expanding it in adult life also requires guarding against the exploitation of "female" obligation, fending off a takeover by womanly selflessness that, when cut away from a commitment to the self, impedes development. Likewise, protecting the original self and sustaining its authority involves resisting female subordination to demeaning tasks that distort womanly identity.

Perhaps a tale drawn from a different culture best reveals how automatically and pervasively women have been expected to attend to lesser tasks and how painful is the derogation that attends these chores.

The Wisdom of a Child

Once when Brahmadatta was king of Banaras there lived in a village of that region an old man and his only son, whose name was Vassitthako. Each day the son would get up very early and do the work normally delegated to women, such as preparing water and toothsticks with which the father could cleanse his mouth. Then the son would do manual labor all day, and finally he would bring home food and prepare it for his father. Finally his elder father said, "Son, you have too much work to do. I will get a wife for you who can do the housework and then you will only need to do your work outside the house."

"No, please don't do that," the son objected, "for if we bring a woman into the house we will have no peace of mind at all." But the father did not listen. He contracted for a bride, who soon came to live with them.

At first all was well, as the wife did her work and the son was relieved of his double responsibility. Then the new wife grew weary of waiting hand and foot upon the old man. She began deliberately to provoke the old man's wrath and then complain to her husband about it. After she had caused him to lose his temper several times, she confronted her husband with the problem, saying, "Look how your father makes a mess of this place, and he is always yelling at me. Husband, your father is a violent old man. I cannot live in the same house as he does. He is decrepit and is going to die soon anyway, so take him out to the burial ground, dig a grave, put him in it, hit him over the head with the spade, and bury the old man."

After repeated encounters such as that, the son finally agreed to get rid of his father, but said, "Wife, it is a serious crime to kill a man. How can I do it?"

"Here is a plan," she said. "First, go to him early one morning and speak to him in a voice loud enough for the neighbors to hear, saying that you want to take him to another village the next day to collect an old debt of his. Once you are away from the town, dig the hole and bury him and then come back pretending that robbers attacked you on the road." The man agreed to this plan and all went well except that their young son overheard them plotting, and he devised his own plan for saving his beloved grandfather.

When the man put the grandfather in the cart, on the pretense of going to another village, the son got into the cart too. When they reached the burial ground and the man began to dig a hole, the boy asked. "Father, we have no bulbs or herbs for planting, no reason to dig a hole, so why are we out here digging?" The father gave the gruesome explanation to the boy, but pretended it was a mercy killing, considering the grandfather's senility.

The grandson was not so easily fooled, however, and he condemned the act as cruel and sinful. He then took a spade and began to dig another hole near where his father was digging. "What are you doing?" the startled father asked. The boy replied, "I also will bury my father when he is old, since it is the family custom, so I might as well dig the hole now!"

"What a horrible thing to say to your own father," the man complained. "You are a foul-mouthed boy."

"I am not foul-mouthed or cruel, father, but I must speak my mind now for it will be soon [sic] too late. If a person kills his innocent father or mother, his next life will surely be in hell. But if a person feeds and cares for his elderly parents, just as surely he will be reborn in a heavenly world."

Upon hearing these wise words from his son, the man had a change of heart and apologized to his son. "It was your mother who put me up to this," he explained.

"That wife of yours, who gave me birth, is no good. You should send her out of the house before she causes another evil deed," the boy warned. His father took the advice. He returned home with the grandfather, and to his wife's horror, he beat her and expelled her from the house.

The wife lived at a neighbor's for several years until the son, now nearly grown, tricked her into thinking that her husband was going to remarry. Repentant and afraid for her livelihood, the woman begged to be taken back as a wife. She kept her promises and was a faithful housewife for the rest of her life. The family followed the advice of the wise young son, giving alms and doing good deeds, and eventually they all were rewarded in heaven.

The authors of this tale claim that "the main thrust of the story is that a man must take care of his aged father, but the duties of the wife are also made clear." They follow this story with one that quotes from the *Laws of Manu* text: "a woman is never fit for independence."[1]

I would offer a different interpretation of the story. First I would title it "The Servility of Woman and the Dire Consequences of Her Denigration." It would seem to me to tell the story of a female forced to take on menial tasks to free the male from them. These tasks, common to every household, cause the father concern when they fall to his grown son but arouse no concern when they are foisted on the woman. The work must be done; the men require the woman to do it. Disregarded as a person in her own right, the wife is finally able to tolerate servility no longer. Driven to the ultimate extreme—murder—she, as a mere woman, cannot act directly but must use covert persuasion to get the husband to act on her behalf. Powerless to set the situation right on her own, she uses the means provided to women of all lands to bring about a confrontation: she precipitates an emotional crisis in those who count—the men.

The husband is cast as the moral agent of an immoral act, yet it is he who has failed to protect his wife from the patriarch's ceaseless demands. He leaves it up to the victim to devise a remedy to her own plight, passively agreeing to the plan—until he is stopped by the intervention of a second "lesser being"—the child. Perhaps because the child is male, the husband is shamed by what he says. When the son reflects his immorality back to him, the spineless husband is horrified. Unable to acknowledge his error, he blames the wife—whom he neglected in the first place, leading to this unhappy end. The son joins him in blaming her, reinforcing the projection of evil onto the female. After the wife's exile—anathema to a socially oriented being—she repents and returns to servility. Her earthly life an abomination, her reward must necessarily lie in another world.

Among a host of legends that portray the female as servile, docile, passive, or unconscious, Atalanta provides a refreshing contrast. A self-possessed girl who seizes life, a girl awakened to her own prowess, she outwits the patriarchy's coercion of the female. Daughter of a man who wants only sons, Atalanta is left by her disappointed father to perish on a wild hillside. But a she-bear nurses her until a band of hunters finds her and brings her up. Artemis, goddess of the hunt, trains her in the chase; Atalanta becomes a daring girl who loves adventure. Skilled and fearless, she shoots and kills two centaurs who try to rape her in the forest. Perhaps because she is devoted to the hunt, perhaps because she has been warned by an oracle that marriage will bring her ruin, she shuns the company of men and determines not to marry.

Atalanta joins the bravest heroes in a great hunt to kill the Calydonian boar, a menace to the forest. Alone among a band of men, she shoots the arrow that strikes the beast before any other. Although Meleager is the one to kill the boar, he awards Atalanta its hide and tusks because she has drawn first blood.

When word of her fame reaches her father, Atalanta returns to his house, where she is welcomed as a son. Hoping she will provide him grandsons, her father sets out to marry Atalanta off. Unable to oppose the patriarch but determined to remain unmarried, nubile Atalanta devises a clever scheme: she will marry only the suitor who can outrun her in a footrace. Atalanta knows her strength and competence as an athlete; she gives each man who would claim her a head start in the race. Fleet of foot, she carries a great spear and impales the man who seeks to win her as she catches up with him.

But a new arrival in the kingdom, one who admires Atalanta's boyish femininity and recognizes her inner nature, takes a new tack in this challenge. He nullifies the phallic power of her long, pointed spear with a harmless "female" symbol of nurturance: golden apples provided him by Aphrodite. Each time Atalanta catches up with him, he throws them down ahead of her. Out of natural curiosity (or perhaps because selective Atalanta has softened to this suitor as one who really knows her), she abandons her aggressive stance and stops to pick the apples up. He wins the race and so wins Atalanta. They are wed amid great revelry and joy.

Legendary Atalanta captures the spirited self-possession of the contemporary eight- and nine-year-old, the staunch, determined girl not yet bent to feminine compliance. Such a real-life girl, when she is unfettered, as yet uncurbed by patriarchal organizations, holds in her palm the touchstone for a woman's true identity. When a woman can sustain such a child and carry her into adulthood, or when she can reembrace her, the self-determined girl can lay the basis for the very relationships women in this book have identified as constructive to development—mutual relationships such as Atalanta has with her successful suitor.

Women who retrieve this girl—through the natural experiences of life, through study groups and workshops using photographs, recollections, and guided meditations, through developmental interviews or psychotherapy—do not arrive at fairy-tale conclusions in which they are rescued by a prince. Rather they retrieve an independent Artemis, a girl who can manage the forest and all of nature on her own. One woman recaptured the autonomous girl in this ancient yet contemporary girl-within myth.

A Golden Harp

Long ago when young women of good birth were encouraged only in the feminine arts as lovely creatures for men to enjoy, beings who would paint and sew and sing beautiful ballads for them, there lived a maiden called Janeece who could do all these things but didn't.

A keen markswoman with bow and arrow, Janeece lived on the edge of a forest with her mother, who was deaf and blind. Her father, who had been a servant of the king, died when she was very small, and Janeece and her mother were left to make their own way in the world.

Janeece hunted deer and wild boar and pheasant in the forest so that she and her mother could survive. Unlike other young maidens of her time, she dressed in a green wool tunic, green leggings, and brown doeskin boots. Janeece was of the forest; she moved and breathed with it. When she was stalking game, she seemed less human and more like an animal spirit. She knew what streams to drink from, what wild plants to eat, where the mineral hot springs were, and the soft, mossy fields on which to rest after a successful hunt.

One evening when Janeece was returning from a hunt, she stopped at a pond to refresh herself. She knelt over the edge to splash water on her face, and looking down she saw the reflection of a majestic snow owl perched in the tree above her. Its feathers gleamed in the new moon's light. What a lovely, noble creature, Janeece thought. She was afraid to move for fear of startling the beautiful bird and frightening it away. She looked right into its eyes reflected in the pond, and as she did the bird spread its wings, reflecting a brilliant, blinding light, and the bird spoke to her.

"Janeece, you must kill a young deer before its first

winter," said the owl. Janeece knew well that deer are born in spring, and thought that to kill a young deer before its first winter is to sacrifice a young life for nothing. It is not good eating, it has no horns to prize, it is not allowed to mate.

"But that would be a senseless kill," Janeece protested. "I cannot do it."

"You do not see the wisdom in it now," the owl said. "But it must be done. You must shoot the deer through the heart with a single arrow. And then you must remove the heart and take it to Nedra, who lives on the other side of the forest in a kingdom far away. She waits for you. Do not delay."

"I cannot undertake such a long journey," Janeece said. "Who will look after my mother?"

"Your mother is dead," the owl replied. "You will find her in her chair as you left her but her soul has passed on. Return home to bury her now and then fulfill your task."

And so Janeece did what he asked because the snow owl is a wise, magical creature whose power and intention are not to be questioned. Janeece rested a day after burying her mother. She packed a small bag of provisions for her long journey, including a snippet of green silk from her mother's burial dress. It was with a heavy heart that Janeece set out to track and kill a deer. For while she was a hunter, and a good one at that, she was a benevolent hunter. She always killed swiftly and only what was needed.

It wasn't long before Janeece came upon a doe with her fawn drinking at a stream. Quietly, skillfully, Janeece drew an arrow from her quiver and took aim at the heart of the young deer. The doe was not aware of her presence and continued to drink. At the moment when Janeece prepared to let fly her arrow, the baby deer looked straight at her; there was a moment of recognition and acceptance. Janeece removed the young deer's heart and wrapped it in the silk from her mother's dress. She buried the deer's body so the wolves would not dig it up and placed ferns over the fresh grave.

Janeece journeyed to the kingdom on the other side of the forest to find Nedra, the king's daughter. A beautiful songstress, she had not uttered a sound for many years. It proved impossible to see her. Her father and brothers would not allow it; Nedra was kept isolated from human company. The townspeople gossiped that Nedra spent her time surrounded by birds and flowers in a beautiful garden secured by a high wall. They said that she had only animals for company. Some rumored that she was possessed and endlessly danced a solitary dance in the garden. But no one who had actually seen her was alive to tell the story: anyone who violated the privacy of the garden and beheld Nedra was immediately killed.

Unable to complete her mission, Janeece felt lost, alone, and remorseful for the killing of the young deer. She doubted the authority of the owl.

That night the owl appeared to her in a dream. It did not speak to her this time. The owl hovered over her, wings outspread, glorious, powerful, divine. The next day, Janeece awoke with renewed commitment to find Nedra and deliver the deer heart.

She did not enter the palace to talk with the servants. Instead she went around back to the courtyard and gardens in search of another entrance. She heard a canary singing on the other side of a high wall. Janeece attached a long rope to one of her arrows and shot it deep into the bark of a tall tree. She climbed up the rope to the top of the tree and swung herself over the wall into the garden, landing at Nedra's feet.

Janeece looked up into the eyes of a fair, radiant woman wearing a gown the color of the sky at sunrise.

Nedra was startled and frightened at first; she mistook Janeece in her hunting dress for a man. Their eyes met in a moment of deep recognition.

But as you'll remember, Nedra was not able to speak. She took Janeece by the arm and beckoned her to sit beside her. Janeece remembered the instructions of the owl and presented the package containing the deer heart. As she handed it to Nedra, she noticed that the fabric was no longer stained with blood.

Nedra unfolded the silk and she and Janeece stared in awe at its contents—the bloody heart had disappeared and in its place was a golden hand-held harp. Nedra began to play a melody on that harp that was at once old and new, joyous and bittersweet. She closed her eyes and gradually, strange, beautiful sounds came from her mouth in a language that Janeece had never heard before. Nedra's voice grew stronger and louder. The song, although Janeece could not understand the lyrics, brought tears to her eyes.

Suddenly, the windows overlooking the garden opened and Nedra's father and brothers cried out, "She sings! Nedra once again has voice."

Nedra took Janeece by the hand and they sat together in the warmth of the sun while Nedra played the harp. Janeece let her head fall gently against Nedra's shoulder and Nedra continued to play and sing her soft, sweet song. And the birds and squirrels and other animals of the garden gathered round them.

But the story does not end here. Janeece did not leave Nedra's garden again except to hunt in the neighboring wood. The king died soon after Janeece's arrival at the palace, and Nedra's brothers were killed in an athletic contest.

Nedra and Janeece lived in the palace and guided the people in peaceful, loving harmony. Their time is remembered for the fertility of the land, shared abundance, and the sound of music, laughter, and joy. Every morning Nedra welcomed the sun in the garden with a song on the golden harp. Janeece continued to hunt, but never the wild deer. The snow owl did not appear again to Janeece in this life, but the memory of the bird's wisdom, beauty, and majesty guided her and inspired her all the rest of her days.

The writer of Janeece's tale eliminates the patriarchy and the men who might personify it in favor of a female world much like the girl-world of the eight- or nine-year-old. But real women cannot live in the girl-world of the child forever, for in real life we do grow up and make our lives with and among men. If, however, we can carry the virginal girl into the womanly realm and honor ourselves as subjects of our own experience, we can draw on the feminine strengths that this girl harbors and provides, for she is certainly the Artemis in each of us.

When a woman is no longer a virginal girl, when she speaks in her own idiom as naturally as she mouths the language of the patriarchy, when she hits on the deepest truth about who she is and tells her story of becoming whole, when she catches hold of the girl she is in the first place, she gains access to a world as fertile and abundant as Nedra's garden. Women in this study who tapped that inner realm, the domain of image and imagination where they were free from patriarchal constructions of the feminine, recaptured an organic essence. They provided images of themselves and their development that sprang spontaneously from some inner impetus rather than being aroused by the kiss of a prince. Anita, a dance therapist in her early fifties, said, for instance, "My development reminds me of a leaf floating on a pond. At the surface there is quiet: no ripples, nothing happening, just gray, gray water. And then there is a geyser. A great geyser shoots up from a spring and the little leaf on top gets lifted way up high!" For Anita, the long decades that separated childhood from her early forties were static—"latent, dormant years." The sixties' wave of feminism finally provided the habitat for her germination: "And then I read [Betty Friedan's] *The Feminine Mystique* and got swept up in the movement. When the climate started warming up, I started to grow like a seed that had been encased in ice." Shackled by a long, unhappy marriage, she was helped to "shake off a tangle of chains" by the rebirth of the movement.

Katherine captured a generative essence when she directed her attention to cultivating her children's potential: "The personality is like a garden. You've got flowers and you've got weeds," she'd said. "What I see as my job as a parent is trying to get the flowers to grow in the child's personality. . . . And you want to nourish and make beautiful the potential that you find there."

Miriam, a consultant in her middle fifties, likened her development to "a bud blooming and unfolding." She singled out an important feature of the flower: "There are some flowers, like begonias and camellias, whose petals open slowly. It's the petals that are the most important—the unfolding of the petals. Whole layers of petals unfolding like a spiral." The synchronized unfolding of the complex blossom was stimulated in Miriam's life by the human potential movement and by reckoning her relationship with her daughter.

Liz provided a flowering image that reflected her feminine triumph. Fearful during youth that she would fail to escape the misery of female roles that had enmired her mother, she finally extricated herself from a "cave of womanly doings" when the risk of being sucked into that cave was greatest: when she married and was about to have a baby. Finding in a friend an alternative model of femininity, she averted her mother's stifling ways. Adopting her friend's optimism, she avoided female forces of submission that threatened to "nip her in the bud." She said of the last fifteen years, since she'd made herself over, "It's been an awakening and a flowering, not a nipping in the bud." At a safe distance from the pull that had coerced her mother and threatened to entrap her, Liz felt at age forty-nine that she was "bursting into bloom." She added to her metaphorical self-description this exclamation: "A garden is imminent!"

Perhaps most striking among the women's images—striking for its deep statement about how a woman must reconcile and forge, moment by moment, the organic stuff of life relying on inner initiative, responsiveness, and self-determination—was Rosabeth's metaphor for her development: "A coastline represents some balancing, some forming that I've done throughout." A shifting landform created by the ever-moving sea against the "hard edges" of her nature, it began to look like the Maine coastline as she took a blank piece of paper and inked out a line with her gold fountain pen. "It's rocky. I see it with the blue water and green land meeting. The ocean is a beautiful blue and land is made of browny-green mountains and rocks—and the land falls up and down. The line is jaggedy. That represents all sorts of experiences that have been upsetting, or exhilarating, or deflating, or instances that made me proud."

The line depicted the juncture of self and life experience rather than their division. An abstraction that stood for a constantly shifting meeting of elements, almost like the fence that Megan walked along, the line represented Rosabeth's continually evolving self.[2] "What you have here is a meeting of forces. And my life has been the path between them."

As the line took shape, she pointed to a dip in the sense of self she had suffered late in childhood, a lapse in identity. "This craggily place is where it takes a little dip," she said, for even Rosabeth, the Renaissance child, traced her identity along an uneven course. As she inked the coastline in by little fragments, she commented on her immediate conflict between taking on a new career and getting married. She explained, "Right now, I would say one force, the ocean side, is a pull to be calm, relaxed, to enjoy and fit into life, moving along and creating things in a kind of normal way. The land side is my desire to make an impact with my career, to shape exactly what I do, to have a presence, even though I might be more agitated doing that. That is how the two forces are operating for me now." Pointing with the pen to a dot along the coast, she said, "And where I stand right now would be this little itty-bitty piece of coastline. And there is terra incognita up ahead."

Rosabeth's Maine coastline borrows on the purposeful autonomy of the inner girl. In that girl's ability to balance the known with the unknown, rock and ocean, competence and care, conscious and unconscious, masculine and feminine, in her willing engagement of the dynamic tension between autonomy and attachment, male and female, work and love, lies the reconciliation of the dichotomies that divide us against ourselves.

Women's images, filled with generative power, embody a tremendous generative force. It is up to the culture not to rob women of that force, not to expect women to forfeit female power to the patriarchy. By attending to these organic images and revaluing the essential feminine they convey, by reconciling and respecting the interdependence of self and surround, we can retrieve an intersubjective "I-ness" and restore generativity to the culture—a sort of generativity that has been lost to the sterility of patriarchal values.

One woman in my study likened this essential interdependence to Mao Tse-tung's metaphor of the egg and the stone. "According to this metaphor, there is an internal basis for growth, for transformation, but it requires the proper atmosphere," she explained. "An egg, even if it is fertilized, can sit in a hostile, cold environment forever and not hatch into a chicken. And likewise a stone can sit in the proper conditions forever and never hatch because it doesn't have the internal basis for becoming a chicken."

By reclaiming the girl's sense of self as subject, by countering woman's position as object, women can stay true to the generative potential of the fertile, feminine world that survives apart from the patriarchy's hierarchical devaluation of the female. Just as the line Rosabeth forged can exist only between the forces of land and sea, so the generativity of the human race depends on each sex maintaining its own generative power and integrity, and on the mutual pooling of generative halves. Only when the culture revalues the generativity of human life and when men, women, and social institutions make it their task to provide the individual with a rich soil for germination and growth can women (and men) cultivate the garden of human potential. Women's contemporary, organic images speak to the essential shift we need to become fully human beings: the shift from object to subject and the embedding of the subject in a fertile soil.

The girl of eight or nine has much to teach the woman about how to seize the subjective stance that lies at the heart of generative power. She naturally synthesizes the dualities of female and male in

her androgyny, fuses play and work in her purposeful activity, reconciles love and hate in her lack of contradiction; utilizes dependence
and independence in the tenacious pursuit of her own interests. She
embodies both sides of competence, encompassing social and relational mastery as well as concrete skills. Separate yet connected, she
is both autonomous and attached. Brimming with initiative yet receptive, she is competitive in the proper spirit: she is driven by
mastery—not to dominate and seize power *over* others but to grasp
the mysteries and challenges of the world. She embodies the partnership Riane Eisler described in the era of the Chalice—now lost
to memory because of the ascendance of the Blade and the dominance
it symbolizes.[3]

Much has changed and is still changing for the girl of eight or
nine. But the most important change is yet to come: the retrieval of
such a partnership—without domination—between men and women,
between peoples of various lands. Too much cultural change in the
name of feminism has turned us toward applauding in females the
"masculine" qualities they display, supporting women in their endeavors to be just like men. But to be like men is to fall victim to
the patriarchy's perversion of social values, to favor competition *over*
cooperation, rationality *over* emotionality, power *over* love, aggres-
sion *over* empathy. The girl of eight or nine is one who unifies the
basic *human* values of cooperation, care, and competence without
distorting them. As in Rosabeth's Maine coastline, the girl reconciles
these elements of human nature instead of splitting them off.

In the alliance between the girl within who possesses initiative
and the woman who embodies mature generativity lies the creative
force we need to become fully ourselves and shape this culture in the
way it so desperately needs to be shaped. Only when we wed girlhood
autonomy to womanly fecundity and re-cognize the connection between germ and soil will we as a culture reclaim our generativity.

Women have long tended the gardens of others. While providing
the context for others' development, they have historically neglected
their own. Women's full development depends on circling back to
the girl within and carrying her into womanhood.

12

WHO I STUDIED,
WHAT I STUDIED,
HOW I STUDIED

 found the twenty subjects who informed my doctoral study of adult development by asking colleagues, associates, and friends to refer women from a variety of backgrounds, explaining in a letter that the study would involve asking women themselves how they thought about their lives. This meant taking a new tack: in the official arena of psychological research, women had rarely been asked to reflect on their own experience, and psychology had got itself into quite a fix as a result. Lacking direct experience, the field had only been able to borrow on abstract concepts, usually drawn from studies of men, to explain female development—a handicap that not only had made women appear to be deficient but also had badly skewed psychological concepts.[1]

The eager response of my referral network was telling: over two hundred women were nominated for the study. Of that group, half returned the Loevinger Sentence Completion Test I sent out to determine which women were self-reflective and psychologically mature. I used this measure of psychological maturity—derived empirically by testing literally thousands of women from a full range of social, economic, cultural, and educational backgrounds—because I was looking for what Leon Edel has called the "figure under the carpet," the underlying pattern that explains and makes sense of a woman's life experience.[2] It seemed to me that women who had reached "higher" levels of development were in a unique position to illuminate my study's questions about the underlying process of maturing, and those who were self-reflective would be most apt to attend to the inner phenomena involved in that process. While Loevinger does not single out self-reflection, I later came to view it not only as the quintessence of a developed person's ego but also as the key to development itself, for it is self-reflection that leads to a comparison between discrepant aspects of experience, and reconciling those discrepancies—a process Piaget called accommodation—is a process that in itself evokes more complex and comprehensive ways of making sense of one's life and living it.

I chose twenty of more than a hundred women whose scores qualified them for the study by spacing them across the life span between ages thirty and seventy-five and aiming at a diversity of social conditions. Women who became part of the study shared with me a certain pioneer spirit: we were verging on unknown territory and would chart that territory together.

Apart from the commonalities of self-reflection and psychological maturity, the study's subjects were quite different from one another, especially considering that they constituted such a small sample. Although primarily well educated and middle class, they came from many walks of life, varying in age, background, education, and social situation. Ten were between thirty and forty-nine; 10 were between forty-nine and seventy-five. Some had grown up during the Depression, others during World War II; some were children of the fifties, others flower children of the sixties. Many had defined themselves as wives and mothers before the women's movement gave them choice in the matter. Some became women of accomplishment way ahead of their time. Many of the women from poor families achieved levels of education and rose to heights of economic wealth unimaginable to their parents.

The women's education and training covered a broad spectrum, ranging from grade school through college to the doctoral level and professional training. Among the group of twenty, two had not finished high school, two had gone to art school, three had bachelor's degrees, seven had master's degrees, four held doctorates, and two were physicians. Some whose parents were doctors, realtors, teachers, and homemakers stayed close to these occupational origins but made departures from their family backgrounds in values and lifestyle. Although seven of the women had been divorced (of whom one had remarried) for instance, none of the subjects' parents had split up while the women were children.

Of the nine who were married, three met their husbands while schoolgirls, six later on. Two of them were married for the second time; one had been divorced, the other widowed. The eleven who were single included a thirty-year-old businesswoman who was engaged and a thirty-seven-year-old pediatrician who hoped to marry and have a family before she passed childbearing age. Fifteen of the twenty were mothers. Two childless subjects had married late; the three others had never married. Six were divorced, two were widowed, and one gave her marital status as lesbian.

Because it seemed essential that this book on women's identity include the perspectives of women who identified themselves as lesbians, when this woman later withdrew her story, I used the network approach again to contact other women to fill the gap. I interviewed four who met the criteria for the original study sample: self-reflection and psychological maturity. I chose the full account of one of these women for Chapter 7.

Many women listed two or three occupations—especially those who were wives and/or mothers. Five were at home; one, a newly remarried mother of adolescents, was a photographer. A homemaker, expecting to return to teaching when her small children were older, studied music. A scientist who had retired early because of physical failings continued to assist her husband in his academic career. A woman over seventy who'd had a successful career as a writer still took on occasional writing projects. One in her late sixties helped direct a ladies' guild art gallery while pursuing an advanced degree through university extension courses. The other fifteen were engaged in various permutations of personal and professional endeavors that included such disparate fields as arts administration, medieval history, divinity, movement therapy, and medical care.

Striking contrasts marked these women's family backgrounds; they represented a variety of European origins. A middle-aged Harvard student grew up in England's Midlands, where her father was an engraver. An elderly doctor's wife living in a stately home in suburban Boston had grown up in the city's slums, where her father, an immigrant from Poland, barely eked out a living as a tailor. A woman in her midforties was brought up by a nanny on a country estate where her father was a member of the landed gentry. A writer in her early seventies was reared in the South by a salesman and a portrait photographer. A secretary in her late fifties remembered her house painter father putting bootblack on her socks when the toes of her shoes wore out. Her experience growing up was diametrically opposed to that of a pediatrician in her thirties who had lived as a child at the height of elegance in New York City, where her grandmother hosted musical salons. I interviewed most of the women in their homes, finding myself variously at a table covered with oilcloth in the simplest small kitchen or amid leather and gilt in the library of a grand Victorian mansion.

The differences among these women make the dynamic they shared—the root identity held by the girl within—all the more remarkable.

To elicit the life studies of the original twenty women, I developed a "map" of topics I wanted to discuss with them. The only "standard" question I asked was the one that opened the interview series: "If we were writing your biography, how would you describe your adult life?" I arrived at it after pondering long and hard to come up with a question free from bias. It turned out to be a question loaded with bias, and that bias came to inform this work in a fundamental way.

Women were often dismayed by that question; many turned to me when I asked it, asking in return, "Adult life? When would that start?" to which I would reply, "When *would* it start?"—and we were off! When I inquired with genuine curiosity about how and when they'd begun to think of themselves as adults, their responses revealed a profound discrepancy between women's self-concepts and the culture's standards of adulthood, yielding, as their narratives reveal, a concept of adulthood quite different from the official definition.

I also asked my subjects whether their experience fell into phases or eras, and, if it did, what differentiated one from another. I suspected that the turning points between them would have to do with changes in their social experience, changes such as marriage, motherhood, and the ages of their children—rather than conforming to the decades of chronological age marked off in segments, as much of the work on men had suggested.[3]

I asked them too what had led them to feel mature and was forced by their responses to reshape my own concept of maturity so drastically that the word *maturity,* implying as it does a kind of stasis, no longer applied. When I invited them to suggest an image for their development, they provided organic, dynamic, mobile images. Standard concepts that cast developmental advances as static points of arrival paled in comparison to these rich metaphors.

When I interviewed the four women who were added to the study after my hypothesis had been formed, I skipped the "map" including questions about adulthood, eras, and maturity, focusing instead on the process of identity development. I asked them several questions about how they had "gotten" a sense of self, and also asked what they remembered about their self-realization as girls. I asked whether there had been a point at which they realized that their lives would not be fitted to the "usual" female pattern. Most important, I asked when in their lives they had most felt themselves. I very much regretted not having thought of this question when I'd interviewed the first group of subjects, for it tapped most directly the core material.

I interviewed each of the women intensively three or four times because I wanted to get beyond the narrative capsule each of us has at the ready. It is this narrative that a researcher is likely to tap during a first interview, no matter how long that interview lasts. Neither phony nor necessarily superficial, such a first-told account simply leaves out the less easily explained aspects of the life under study— the elements that are the psychologist's very topic.

I suspected too that women's development holds complexities beyond what any researcher could glean in a single interview. A self-reflective person is often mindful of various ways to chronicle events. Many a woman in my study felt she'd just pieced together the scraps of her life during the first interview. Having told her story one way, she seemed intent on telling it another way—an opportunity afforded by the next two or three meetings. But the length of time was secondary to the research objective in attaining a complete study of each woman: to build a set of concepts "free" from the patriarchal bias of the standard literature. In a departure from hypothesis-testing protocols that would have fit a set of questions to a preformed schedule, I held myself instead to an absolute standard, interviewing each subject until I understood how she structured her world and how she saw herself within it.

As one interview led to the next I learned that the most productive question to ask was "How?" Although I cannot explain exactly why, this question piqued women's curiosity and led them to inquire into their own lives. I came to regret the questions I introduced with other queries. "Why?" a question that addresses motivation, proved especially problematic. It stopped women short rather than helping them explore the meanings of their present and past experiences. "How" questions helped to hold us to a developmental line of inquiry, one that caught women's attention so that they began to sort through changes in their perceptions of themselves and the world, and the relation between them. It was through providing these "thick descriptions," accounts that included perceptions, feelings, and interpretations, that women came upon the girl within.[4]

Besides taking these descriptions as facts in and of themselves, I found that arriving at a set of concepts that was true to women's experience also depended on dropping the methodological screen that typically separates researcher from subject, as Marcia Westkott suggested in her article "Feminist Criticism of the Social Sciences."[5] Westkott claimed that this convention, widely followed in official approaches to social science research, only distorts the human phenomena under study. She submitted that abstracting social data from the context in which they are generated can only result in a false dichotomy, and she suggested that such abstraction, arising from an approach intended to mask the so-called subjective questions that motivate research in the social sciences, be supplanted by a dialectical method, a dialogue in which the researcher and those researched together shape emergent concepts. This feminist perspective held me in good stead: Had I assumed the patriarchal stance of "the psychologist as expert," the nascent girl within could not have been born. Only by taking women themselves as the authors of their biographies and joining them in making sense of their experiences could I possibly have come upon the girl within.

Using a retrospective approach brought up the question of distortion from selective memory. As George Vaillant has pointed out, "Maturation makes liars of us all."[6] We recast the past through the prism of the present. But it is not the so-called facts of women's lives that are important to the study of development, rather it is the way in which those "facts" are assembled that matters. Arranging the events of a lifetime so that they are all of a piece is an inner, constructive task.* This activity is what tells the listener how the person

---

*This stance derives from aligning myself with the constructive-developmental school of thought, which includes such psychologists as Herbert Fingarette, Jane Loevinger, George Kelly, Robert Kegan, and Lawrence Kohlberg.

constructs her experience, and *that*—the construction of experience, the activity of making sense—was the subject under study. *How* women view their lives and make sense of their life experience is the "truth" that matters most to the developmentalist. As one woman said of looking back on her life experience, "It's like a bas relief, a topographical map where the mountains look all flat until you paint them. The flatness of experience takes on a texture when you throw over it a sepia wash. And then the landforms stand out brilliantly. I reclaim my past through throwing over it the sepia wash of present knowledge."

To analyze the narratives I gathered, I asked myself how each subject structured her narrative. What did her story center on? How did she organize its "chapters"? Where did it start, and what course did it take? What was its pattern? What faded into the background, or dropped out of the picture entirely? What seemed so obvious to a woman that it "went without saying"? What appeared to be the organizing principle of her story, the theme that gave form to her biography? How could the facts of her life be explained?

By sticking close to the marrow in this analytic task, I grounded the study's concepts in the data, deriving concepts from the facts of these women's lives rather than fitting their lives to what ultimately appeared to be ill-fitting "standard" concepts.[7] Only by working this way could I be sure that how the story was told was in essence the story itself. For my purposes, at least, the medium was the message.

As I evaluated my data, it became apparent that the authentic girlhood identity women described—and the loss of this self to a contrived self—was just what D. W. Winnicott had discovered in his analytic work, when he found that emotional injury had caused his adult patients to put their "real" self into cold storage while children and then to proceed in an as-if manner to operate from what he called a "false self," living quite apart from their own emotional experience.[8] Although this phenomenon had been described in the psychiatric literature (a literature about people who require treatment), it had not previously been noted in a nonclinical, psychologically mature population. When they uncovered the girl, the women in my study placed this dynamic in a normative realm.

The process through which the women in my study forfeited the authority of their natural self seemed, too, very much like what Alice Miller had described.[9] Whereas Miller did not link the imprisonment of the self in childhood to one sex or the other, the women in my study showed how the dynamic she identified threatens females in particular. Their stories held clues to just how a woman buries who and what she really is beneath the feminine facade she adopts in youth. In this, my data also underscored the work of Karen Horney—especially as it is interpreted by Marcia Westkott[10]—work that shows how the female personality comes to be lodged in an idealized feminine image rather than in the authentic identity a female possesses as a child.

The life studies I collected also suggested that the remedy Miller prescribed, mourning the lost self, might not be sufficient to restore the abandoned child. In addition to mourning, the women I studied indicated that a woman must break the hold of the false self, often through rage, to revive the girl she's buried in childhood. They detailed the crisis this breakthrough entails, taking Winnicott's, Miller's, and Horney's work a giant step further by documenting and describing a *variety* of natural paths to spontaneous recovery, avenues that turn, interestingly enough, on particular kinds of attachments.

In pointing to relationships as the medium of recovery, their accounts called to mind Sullivan's interpersonal psychiatry and Heinz Kohut's notion of empathic self-objects.[11] Their narratives also substantiated the work of those engaged in feminine empiricism, which perceives women's identity as a "self-in-relation."[12] These analysts contend that women's sense of self is situated in a web of relationships, as Carol Gilligan suggests. Even more important, they underscore the point made by Jean Baker Miller, who asserts that authenticity, itself the goal of women's development, is achieved through relationships of a particular sort—those free from subordination.[13]

The narratives in my study not only fleshed out and connected these analysts' concepts by showing just how a female's natural self is estranged but also extended their work by elucidating the dynamics involved in reclaiming this self: by springing free from subordinate relationships and reaching back to catch hold of a girlhood self long ago left behind, these women came fully into their own as adults. In explicating this process, they both detailed the "how" of female development and demonstrated once again the double-edged character of crisis.[14] By identifying the very experiences that erode and restore an original identity, women who have succeeded in recovering the girl who embodies their primary identity could be considered natural developmental specialists.[15] They are perhaps especially best qualified for elaborating the vicissitudes of the self.

No one ever told us we had to study our lives,
make of our lives a study, as if learning natural history
or music, that we should begin
with the simple exercises first
and slowly go on trying
the hard ones, practicing till strength
and accuracy became one with the daring
to leap into transcendence, take the chance
of breaking down in the wild arpeggio
or faulting the full sentence of the fugue
—And in fact we can't live like that: we take on
everything at once before we're forced to begin
in the midst of the hardest movement,
the one already sounding as we are born.
At most we're allowed a few months
of simply listening to the simple line
of a woman's voice singing a child
against her heart. Everything else is too soon,
too sudden, the wrenching-apart, that woman's heartbeat
heard ever after from a distance,
the loss of that ground-note echoing
whenever we are happy, or in despair.

—ADRIENNE RICH
from "Transcendental Etude"
in The Dream of a Common Language

NOTES

1 REDISCOVERING THE GIRL WITHIN

1. Emily Hancock, "Women's Development in Adult Life" (unpublished doctoral diss., Harvard University, 1981).
2. D. W. Winnicott identified this "interim space" as a zone of the psyche in his work *Maturational Processes and the Facilitating Environment* (New York: International Universities Press, 1965).
3. Robert Bly discussed the significance of this age and the golden ball in an interview by Keith Thompson, "What Men Really Want: A New Age Interview with Robert Bly," *New Age*, May 1982, 30–37, 50–51.
4. This phenomenon, described by Jean Piaget, is called the great cognitive shift by Sheldon White of Harvard University's Department of Psychology and Social Relations. See "Some General Outlines of the Matrix of Developmental Changes Between Five and Seven Years," *Bulletin of the Orton Society*, 20: 41–57.
5. Louise Fitzhugh, *Harriet the Spy* (New York: Harper and Row, 1964).
6. Astrid Lindgren, *Pippi Longstocking* (New York: Viking Press, 1950).
7. E. L. Konigsburg, *From the Mixed-up Files of Mrs. Basil E. Frankweiler* (New York: Dell, 1967).

8. Ruth Sawyer, *Roller Skates* (New York: Viking Press, 1936).

9. Carol R. Brink, *Caddie Woodlawn* (New York: Macmillan, 1935, reprinted 1973).

10. Elizabeth Enright, *Thimble Summer* (New York: Holt, Rinehart & Winston, 1938).

11. Lois Lenski, *Strawberry Girl* (Philadelphia: J. B. Lippincott, 1945).

12. Eudora Welty, *One Writer's Beginnings* (Cambridge: Harvard University Press, 1984), 29, 104.

13. Annie Dillard, *An American Childhood* (New York: Harper & Row, 1987), 11.

14. Gail Sheehy noted in her book *Passages* (New York: E. P. Dutton, 1974), 118, that inside every thirty-five-year-old woman is a girl who was a wizard at word games.

15. Robert Kegan used this term in a beautiful description of the features of this stage in *The Evolving Self: Problems and Process in Human Development* (Cambridge: Harvard University Press, 1982).

16. "Pseudo-schooling" is Nancy Chodorow's phrase. See "Family Structure and Feminine Personality" in *Woman, Culture and Society*, eds. M. Z. Rosaldo and Louise Lamphere (Stanford: Stanford University Press, 1974), 43–66, and *The Reproduction of Mothering* (Berkeley: University of California Press, 1978).

17. H. S. Sullivan named competition and compromise the two hallmarks of the juvenile era in *The Interpersonal Theory of Psychiatry* (New York: Norton, 1953).

18. TV ad, Miss America pageant, September 19, 1987.

19. Simone de Beauvoir, *The Second Sex*, trans. and ed. H. M. Parshley (New York: Alfred A. Knopf, 1953).

20. Jane Wheelwright, *The Ranch Papers* (San Francisco: Lapis Press, 1988), 139.

21. This account can be found in Nancy Peterson, *Our Lives for Ourselves* (New York: G. P. Putnam's Sons, 1981).

22. Lynne Sharon Schwartz, *Disturbances in the Field* (New York: Harper & Row, 1983).

23. The review was "Woman's Root Identity: The Girl Within," *San Francisco Jung Institute Library Journal* 7, no. 1 (1987): 15–18.

24. Gloria Steinem, "If Marilyn Had Lived . . . Who Would She Be Today?" *Ms.*, August 1986, 40–45 *passim*.

2 MEN'S THEORIES, WOMEN'S LIVES

1. Doris Lessing, *The Summer Before the Dark* (New York: Alfred A. Knopf, 1973), 14–15.

2. Marcia Westkott, "Feminist Criticism of the Social Sciences," *Harvard Educational Review* 49 (1979): 429.

3. Erik Erikson, "Identity and the Life Cycle," *Psychological Issues* 1, no. 1 (1959).

4. George W. Goethals of Harvard University's Department of Psychology and Social Relations made this point in a course he taught on the life cycle—a course originated by Erik Erikson himself. The point has also been noted by Justin Kaplan in "The Naked Self and Other Problems," in *Telling Lives:*

The Biographer's Art, ed. Marc Pachter (Philadelphia: University of Pennsylvania Press, 1981), 38.

5. Sigmund Freud, "Some Psychical Consequences of the Anatomical Distinction Between the Sexes," *International Journal of Psychoanalysis* 8 (1927): 133–142.

6. See Carol Gilligan, *In a Different Voice: Psychological Theory and Women's Development* (Cambridge: Harvard University Press, 1982), for a discussion of the male bias in Freud's and Erikson's work, and for what she sees as the superior values associated with female development.

7. By Daniel Levinson in *The Seasons of a Man's Life* (New York: Alfred A. Knopf, 1978) and George Vaillant in *Adaptation to Life* (Boston: Little, Brown, 1977).

8. See Chapter 10 of Marcia Westkott's *The Feminist Legacy of Karen Horney* (New Haven: Yale University Press, 1986) for an explication of this dynamic.

9. This phenomenon is described—without respect to gender dynamics, however—by Alice Miller in *Prisoners of Childhood: The Drama of the Gifted Child and the Search for the True Self* (New York: Basic Books, 1981).

10. Naomi Ruth Lowinsky's term in "All the Days of Her Life" (doctoral diss., Center for Psychological Studies, Albany, CA, 1985).

11. Again, see Gilligan's *In a Different Voice.*

12. See David Bakan, *The Duality of Human Existence: Isolation and Communion in Western Man* (Boston: Beacon Press, 1966), for a discussion of the duality of human experience.

13. Feminine empiricists—a term coined by Lowinsky in "Why Can't a Man Be More Like a Woman?" *San Francisco Jung Institute Library Journal* 5, no. 1 (1984): 20–30, to refer to Jean Baker Miller, Carol Gilligan, Nancy Chodorow, and others—claim that relatedness is primary and fundamental to females.

14. See David C. McClelland, *Power: The Inner Experience* (New York: John Wiley, 1975), 81.

15. On interdependence in the Japanese culture see Thomas Rohlen, "The Promise of Adulthood in Japanese Spiritualism," in *Adulthood,* ed. Erik Erikson (New York: W. W. Norton, 1976). On the symbolic unity of mother and child see Robert Lifton, "Woman as Knower: Some Psychohistorical Perspectives," in *The Woman in America* (Boston: Houghton Mifflin, 1965).

16. In Jean Baker Miller, *Toward a New Psychology of Women* (Boston: Beacon Press, 1976), 40.

17. Thanks to writers such as Riane Eisler, author of *The Chalice and the Blade: Our History, Our Future* (New York: Harper and Row, 1987).

18. Carol Gilligan, "Woman's Place in Man's Life Cycle," *Harvard Educational Review* 49, no. 1 (1979): 437.

19. Mary Brown Parlee, "Psychology," *Signs: Journal of Women in Culture and Society* 1, no. 1 (1975): 127.

20. Mary Brown Parlee, "Psychology and Women," *Signs: Journal of Women in Culture and Society* 5, no. 1 (1979): 130.

21. Fritjof Capra, *The Tao of Physics* (New York: Bantam Books, 1977).

22. Jean Baker Miller, in *Psychoanalysis and Women,* ed. J. B. Miller (New York: Brunner/Mazel, 1973), 403.

23. Marcia Westkott helped to explain the deep roots of this phenomenon in *The Feminist Legacy of Karen Horney* (New Haven: Yale University Press, 1986). She pointed out that women historically have followed a "nurturing imperative" that requires selfless concern. Interpreting Horney, Westkott submits that females develop a character structure lodged in an ideal self, the content of which is drawn from others' expectations. Bent to adapting to the wishes of men, they then mistake the compliant adaptation for their true identities. In these selfless roles, whether external or internal, it is impossible for a woman to realize and come to rely on the authority of her natural self.

24. The academy's study found that about half of all employed women work in jobs that are female dominated, and it states that occupations segregated by sex "are expected to grow more than those that are relatively integrated." It reports that the Reagan administration brought about "reversals of federal civil rights policy" that "are likely to negatively affect women's future employment opportunities." Quoted in the *San Francisco Chronicle*, 13 December 1985.

25. Robert Seidenberg, "Is Anatomy Destiny?" in *Psychoanalysis and Women*, ed. J. B. Miller (New York: Brunner/Mazel, 1973), 327.

26. This phrase borrows from Margery Davies's title *Woman's Place Is at the Typewriter: Office Work and Office Workers, 1870–1930* (Philadelphia: Temple University Press, 1984).

27. Jean Baker Miller's comment at the Askwith Symposium, Harvard University Graduate School of Education, April 1979.

28. Dianne Burden and Bradley Googins, Boston University School of Social Work, "Balancing Job and Home Life Study: Managing Work and Family Stress Incorporations," Boston University Monograph, 1987. To add insult to injury, when a man "helps" with the housework or child care, he is accorded a sympathy and adulation that a woman rarely elicits "in the course of duty."

29. This is one of the findings of the "Becoming a Family" project, headed by Philip and Carolyn Cowan at U.C. Berkeley. The findings will be published in *The Delicate Balance: Partners Becoming Parents* (Basic Books, forthcoming).

30. Ad in the *San Francisco Chronicle* during December 1985.

31. Seidenberg, "Is Anatomy Destiny?" 313.

32. Suzanne Gordon, "Natural Childbirth: Who Needs It?" *San Francisco Chronicle*, 7 November 1985, 25.

33. See Mary Daly, *Beyond God the Father: Toward a Philosophy of Women's Liberation* (Boston: Beacon Press, 1985).

34. June Singer's term, in "For the Woman Who Has Everything and Still Is Not Happy," a paper presented at the Gifts of Age Symposium, U.C. Extension, San Francisco, CA, June 1987.

35. See Lillian Rubin, *Worlds of Pain* (New York: Basic Books, 1976).

36. Barbara Ehrenreich, *Hearts of Men* (Garden City, NY: Doubleday, Anchor Press, 1984).

37. See Talcott Parsons and Robert F. Bales, *Family, Socialization and Interaction Process* (Glencoe, Il, 1955).

38. Seidenberg, "Is Anatomy Destiny?" 310.

39. Ibid., 326.
40. Sylvia Hewlett's title, *A Lesser Life: The Myth of Women's Liberation in America* (New York: Warner Books, 1987).
41. See, for instance, Levinson's *The Seasons of a Man's Life* and Vaillant's *Adaptation to Life*.
42. See Phyllis Chesler, *Women and Madness* (Garden City, NY: Doubleday, 1972), and, for an ironic commentary on this perspective, see the movie, *A Woman Under the Influence*.
43. This is a topic contemporary analyst Jean Baker Miller took up in *Toward a New Psychology of Women*. The theme was earlier addressed by the body of Karen Horney's work.
44. "False self" is D. W. Winnicott's term. See his *Maturational Processes and the Facilitating Environment* (New York: International Universities Press, 1965).

3 ADULT EQUALS MALE

1. For an interesting discussion of the legacy handed down through generations of females, see Naomi Ruth Lowinsky, "All the Days of Her Life" (doctoral diss., Center for Psychological Studies, Albany, CA, 1985).
2. See Pamela Daniels, "Dream vs. Drift in Women's Careers: The Question of Generativity," in *Outsiders on the Inside: Women and Organizations*, ed. B. Goldman and B. Forisha (Englewood Cliffs, NJ: Prentice-Hall, 1981), 285–302.
3. Daniel Levinson, *The Seasons of a Man's Life* (New York: Alfred A. Knopf, 1978).
4. With this substantiation of the lonely sacrifice entailed by a medical career, it is no wonder that women in Matina Horner's research—"Toward an Understanding of Achievement-related Conflicts in Women," *Journal of Social Issues* 8, no. 2 (1972): 157–74—demonstrated a fear of success in responding to the story prompt, "After first-term finals, Anne finds herself in the top of her medical-school class." Who could respond with excitement—or even equanimity—to such a prospect as Katherine describes?
5. An avoidance of selfishness can be seen as a feminine conflict of moral values if one uses the developmental framework Carol Gilligan has constructed. See her *In a Different Voice: Psychological Theory and Women's Development* (Cambridge: Harvard University Press, 1982).
6. Katherine's remarks call to mind Virginia Woolf's "angel in the house" in her essay "Professions for Women" in *Collected Essays*, Vol. 2, ed: Leonard Woolf (New York: Harcourt, Brace and World, 1967), and Adrienne Rich's reference to the "million tiny stitches" involved in women's mothering care for others in her foreword to *Working It Out*, eds. Sara Ruddick and Pamela Daniels (New York: Pantheon Books, 1977), xvi.
7. Sigmund Freud, *Civilization and Its Discontents* (New York: W. W. Norton, 1962), 27.
8. Inge Broverman, Susan Vogel, Donald Broverman, Frank Clarkson, and Paul Rosenkrantz, "Sex-Role Stereotypes: A Current Appraisal," *Journal of Social Issues* 28, (1972): 59–78.

9. Ibid., 75.

10. Carol Gilligan made this assertion in *In a Different Voice*, 5–23.

11. A web of relationships is Gilligan's image in *In a Different Voice*, 62.

12. Gilligan (*In a Different Voice*, 42) has noted the danger women perceive in situations in which they are isolated (as against men's perceptions of danger in connection with others).

13. Nancy Chodorow asserts that "feminine personality comes to define itself in relation and connection." See "Family Structure and Feminine Personality" in *Woman, Culture and Society*, eds. M. Z. Rosaldo and Louise Lamphere (Stanford: Stanford University Press, 1974), 43–66. Researchers at the Stone Center, Wellesley College, coined the term "self-in-relation."

14. Sylvia Perera, *Descent to the Goddess* (Toronto: Inner City Books, 1981), has dealt with the need to contact and express anger in order to become fully oneself. Jean Baker Miller's *Toward a New Psychology of Women* (Boston: Beacon Press, 1976) also makes this point.

15. Marilyn Steele, "Life in the Round: A Model of Adult Female Development" (doctoral diss., Wright Institute, Berkeley, CA, 1985).

4 MARRIAGE: WOMEN'S CRUCIBLE FOR GROWING UP

1. According to Daniel Levinson, in *The Seasons of a Man's Life* (New York: Alfred A. Knopf, 1978).

5 A CHOICE OF ONE'S OWN

1. Sara Ruddick coined the term "Woman's Life Plan" in her essay "A Work of One's Own," in *Working It Out*, eds. Sara Ruddick and Pamela Daniels (New York: Pantheon Books, 1977), 130.

2. The process of assimilation and accommodation, the heart of Jean Piaget's theory and of Robert Kegan's book *The Evolving Self*, is what is involved here.

6 THE DIVISION OF PURPOSE FROM SELFLESS CARE

1. Sara Ruddick's term; see note 1 in Chapter 5.

2. Maggie Scarf discusses this problem in *Unfinished Business: Pressure Points in the Lives of Women* (New York: Doubleday, 1980).

3. This is Robert Kegan's approach, as he has explained in the last chapter of his excellent book *The Evolving Self: Problems and Process in Human Development* (Cambridge: Harvard University Press, 1982).

7 THE POWER OF FEMININE IDEALS

1. W. R. D. Fairbairn has suggested that loving is as important to ego development as being loved. See his *An Object Relations Theory of Personality* (New York: Basic Books, 1952).

8 NATURAL PATHS TO THE GIRL WITHIN

1. See Paula Caplan, *The Myth of Women's Masochism* (New York: E. P. Dutton, 1986).

2. This sort of relationship—one of mutual dependence—appears likely to promote development rather than to restrict it. Among the few psychoanalytic theorists who have considered it in delineating developmental models rather than positing independence and autonomy as the end point of development is W. R. D. Fairbairn, of the British object relations school. In *An Object Relations Theory of Personality* (New York: Basic Books, 1952), Fairbairn set forth a model of development that begins with a stage of infantile dependence and moves toward mature dependence—rather than independence. Margaret Mahler, *The Psychological Birth of the Human Infant* (New York: Basic Books, 1975), has also suggested that the developmental process aims not at the goal of separateness but at rapprochement, a condition in which differentiated individuals actively engage with each other. Jean Baker Miller pointed out the necessity of relationships of equal give-and-take for women's development specifically in *Toward a New Psychology of Women* (Boston: Beacon Press, 1976). Interdependence rather than absolute independence is the end point implied by these theories.

3. See Alice Miller, *Prisoners of Childhood: The Drama of the Gifted Child and the Search for the True Self* (New York: Basic Books, 1981).

9 RECKONING THE RELATIONSHIP BETWEEN DAUGHTER AND MOTHER: TRANSFORMING A CRITICAL TIE

1. Adrienne Rich's title, *Of Woman Born* (New York: W. W. Norton, 1976). See especially chapter IX, "Motherhood and Daughterhood," 218–59.

2. See Bert Cohler and Henry Grunebaum, *Mothers, Grandmothers, and Daughters* (New York: John Wiley, 1981).

3. See Natalie Low, "The Relationship of Adult Daughters to Their Mothers" (Paper presented at the Massachusetts Psychological Association, Wellesley, MA, May 1978), 9.

4. Paula Caplan and Ian Hall-McCorquodale, "Mother-Blaming in Major Clinical Journals," *American Journal of Orthopsychiatry* 55, no. 2 (1985): 345–53.

5. Low, "Relationship of Adult Daughters," 12.

6. Ad in *Working Mother*, April 1987, 53.

7. Ibid., May 1987, 61.

8. Marcia Westkott explained the nurturing imperative in her *The Feminist Legacy of Karen Horney* (New Haven: Yale University Press, 1986).

9. Jean Baker Miller, *Toward a New Psychology of Women* (Boston: Beacon Press, 1976).

10. See Rich, *Of Woman Born.*

11. Marcia Westkott's image, in "Mothers and Daughters in the World of the Father," *Frontiers* 3, no. 2 (1978): 16–22.

12. "Good enough mothering" is D. W. Winnicott's term, from *Maturational Processes and the Facilitating Environment* (New York: International Universities Press, 1965). Janet Surrey has also arrived at this conclusion in

her paper "Self-in-Relation: A Theory of Women's Development," Stone Center Working Papers, no. 13, Wellesley College, 1985, where she explained this as a kind of relational competence.

13. "Good enough daughtering" is Ronnie Levine's term. See her "Clinical Implications of the Mother-Child Relationship: Good Enough Daughtering," a paper presented at the 8th annual national conference on feminist psychology of the Association for Women in Psychology, Boston, MA, March 1981.

14. Ronnie Levine submits that this process, although it is initiated by daughters, can also reaffirm a mother's sense of emotional competence. By receiving, accepting, and tolerating her daughter's emotional communication, a mother provides herself an opportunity for emotional growth. As a result of the effective emotional impact on her mother, the daughter develops a sense of emotional competence in herself. The implication of Levine's clinical work is that reversing a trend of feeling emotionally ineffective removes inhibitions in love, work, and play.

15. "Rapprochement" is Margaret Mahler's term. See her *The Psychological Birth of the Human Infant* (New York: Basic Books, 1975).

16. "Mature, mutual dependence" is W. R. D. Fairbairn's concept. See his *An Object Relations Theory of Personality* (New York: Basic Books, 1952), 39.

10 THE SEARCH FOR MY OWN GIRL WITHIN

1. My experience was just as Alice Miller described in *Prisoners of Childhood: The Drama of the Gifted Child and the Search for the True Self* (New York: Basic Books, 1981).

2. L. M. Montgomery, *Emily of New Moon* (1923; reprint, New York: Bantam Books, 1983), 29.

11 WOMANLY IMAGES OF SELF AND DEVELOPMENT

1. Roy C. Amore and Larry D. Shinn, *Lustful Maidens and Ascetic Kings: Buddhist and Hindu Stories of Life* (New York: Oxford University Press, 1981), 23–25.

2. Robert Kegan's title, *The Evolving Self: Problems and Process in Human Development* (Cambridge: Harvard University Press, 1982).

3. See the masterful investigation of human history by Riane Eisler, *The Chalice and the Blade: Our History, Our Future* (New York: Harper & Row, 1987).

12 WHO I STUDIED, WHAT I STUDIED, HOW I STUDIED

1. Carol Gilligan has explicated this in her book, *In a Different Voice: Psychological Theory and Women's Development* (Cambridge: Harvard University Press, 1982).

2. Leon Edel, "The Figure Under the Carpet," in *Telling Lives: The Biographer's Art,* ed. Marc Pachter (Philadelphia: University of Pennsylvania Press, 1981), 16–35.

3. See Daniel Levinson, *The Seasons of a Man's Life* (New York: Alfred A. Knopf, 1978), and George Vaillant, *Adaptation to Life* (Boston: Little, Brown, 1977).

4. "Thick descriptions" is Clifford Geertz's term. See his *Interpretation of Cultures* (New York: Basic Books, 1973).

5. Marcia Westkott, "Feminist Criticism of the Social Sciences," *Harvard Educational Review* 49 (1979): 422–30.

6. Vaillant, *Adaptation to Life,* 197.

7. This approach is described by Barney Glaser and Anselm Strauss, *The Discovery of Grounded Theory: Strategies for Qualitative Research* (Chicago: Aldine, 1967).

8. D. W. Winnicott, *Maturational Processes and the Facilitating Environment* (New York: International Universities Press, 1965).

9. Alice Miller, *Prisoners of Childhood: The Drama of the Gifted Child and the Search for the True Self* (New York: Basic Books, 1981).

10. Marcia Westkott, *The Feminist Legacy of Karen Horney* (New Haven: Yale University Press, 1986).

11. Harry Stack Sullivan, *The Interpersonal Theory of Psychiatry* (New York: W. W. Norton, 1953), and Heinz Kohut, *The Restoration of the Self* (International Universities Press, 1977).

12. "Feminine empiricism" is a term coined by Naomi Ruth Lowinsky, my former student and present colleague and friend, in "Why Can't a Man Be More Like a Woman?" *San Francisco Jung Institute Library Journal* 15, no. 1 (1984): 22. "Self-in-relation" has been coined by scholars at the Stone Center at Wellesley College.

13. Jean Baker Miller, *Toward a New Psychology of Women* (Boston: Beacon Press, 1976).

14. Erik Erikson stressed the dual nature of crisis when he put forth his theory of developmental crises in *Childhood and Society* (New York: W. W. Norton, 1963).

15. "Natural developmental specialists" is Jean Baker Miller's phrase (personal communication).

BIBLIOGRAPHY

Amore, Roy C., and Larry D. Shinn. *Lustful Maidens and Ascetic Kings: Buddhist and Hindu Stories of Life*. New York: Oxford University Press, 1981.

Bakan, David. *The Duality of Human Existence: Isolation and Communion in Western Man*. Boston: Beacon Press, 1966.

Bly, Robert. "What Men Really Want: A New Age Interview with Robert Bly." Interview by Keith Thompson, 30–37, 50–51. *New Age*, May 1982.

Brande, Dorothea. *On Becoming a Writer*. 1934. Reprint. Boston: Houghton Mifflin, 1981.

Brink, Carol R. *Caddie Woodlawn*. New York: Macmillan, 1935. Reprint, 1973.

Broverman, Inge, Susan Vogel, Donald Broverman, Frank Clarkson, and Paul Rosenkrantz. "Sex-Role Stereotypes: A Current Appraisal." *Journal of Social Issues* 28 (1972): 59–78.

Burden, Dianne, and Bradley Googins. "Balancing Job and Homelife Study: Managing Work and Family Stress Incorporations." Boston University Monograph, 1987.

Caplan, Paula. *The Myth of Women's Masochism.* New York: E. P. Dutton, 1986.

Caplan, Paula, and I. Hall-McCorquodale. "Mother-Blaming in Major Clinical Journals." *American Journal of Orthopsychiatry* 55, no. 2 (1985): 345–53.

———. "The Scapegoating of Mothers: A Call for Change." *American Journal of Orthopsychiatry* 55, no. 4 (1985): 610–13.

Capra, Fritjof. *The Tao of Physics.* New York: Bantam Books, 1977.

———. *The Turning Point: Science, Society, and the Rising Culture.* New York: Simon & Schuster, 1982.

Chesler, Phyllis. *Women and Madness.* Garden City, NY: Doubleday, 1972.

Chodorow, Nancy. "Family Structure and Feminine Personality." In *Woman, Culture and Society,* edited by M. Z. Rosaldo and Louise Lamphere, 43–66. Stanford: Stanford University Press, 1974.

———. *The Reproduction of Mothering.* Berkeley: University of California Press, 1978.

Cohler, Bertram, and Henry Grunebaum. *Mothers, Grandmothers, and Daughters.* New York: John Wiley, 1981.

Cowan, Carolyn Pape, and Philip A. Cowan. *The Delicate Balance: Partners Becoming Parents.* New York: Basic Books, forthcoming.

Daly, Mary. *Beyond God the Father: Toward a Philosophy of Women's Liberation.* Boston: Beacon Press, 1985.

————. *Gyn-ecology: The Metaethics of Radical Feminism*. Boston: Beacon Press, 1979.

Daniels, Pamela. "Dream vs. Drift in Women's Careers: The Question of Generativity." In *Outsiders on the Inside: Women and Organizations*, edited by B. Goldman and B. Forisha, 285–302. Englewood Cliffs, NJ: Prentice-Hall, 1981.

Davies, Margery. *Woman's Place Is at the Typewriter: Office Work and Office Workers, 1870–1930*. Philadelphia: Temple University Press, 1984.

de Beauvoir, Simone. *The Second Sex*. Translated and edited by H. M. Parshley. New York: Alfred A. Knopf, 1953.

Dillard, Annie. *An American Childhood*. New York: Harper & Row, 1987.

Dinnerstein, Dorothy. *The Mermaid and the Minotaur*. New York: Harper & Row, 1976.

Edel, Leon. "The Figure Under the Carpet." In *Telling Lives: The Biographer's Art*, edited by Marc Pachter, 16–35. Philadelphia: University of Pennsylvania Press, 1981.

Ehrenreich, Barbara. *Hearts of Men*. Garden City, NY: Doubleday, Anchor Press, 1984.

Eisler, Riane. *The Chalice and the Blade: Our History, Our Future*. New York: Harper & Row, 1987.

Enright, Elizabeth. *Thimble Summer*. New York: Holt, Rinehart & Winston, 1938.

Erikson, Erik. *Childhood and Society*. New York: W. W. Norton, 1963.

————. "Identity and the Life Cycle." *Psychological Issues* 1, no. 1 (1959).

Fairbairn, W. R. D. *An Object Relations Theory of Personality*. New York: Basic Books, 1952.

Fingarette, Herbert. *The Self in Transformation*. New York: Harper & Row, 1985.

Fitzhugh, Louise. *Harriet the Spy*. New York: Harper & Row, 1964.

Freud, Sigmund. "Femininity." In *New Introductory Lectures on Psychoanalysis*, translated by James Strachey. Standard Edition of the Complete Psychological Works, vol. 22, 3–182. London: Hogarth Press, 1933.

————. "Some Psychical Consequences of the Anatomical Distinction between the Sexes." *International Journal of Psychoanalysis* 8 (1925): 133–42.

Friedan, Betty. *The Feminine Mystique*. New York: W. W. Norton, 1963.

Geertz, Clifford. *Interpretation of Cultures*. New York: Basic Books, 1973.

Gilligan, Carol. *In a Different Voice: Psychological Theory and Women's Development*. Cambridge: Harvard University Press, 1982.

————. "Woman's Place in Man's Life Cycle." *Harvard Educational Review* 49, no. 1, (1979): 431–46.

Glaser, Barney, and Anselm Strauss. *The Discovery of Grounded Theory: Strategies for Qualitative Research*. Chicago: Aldine, 1967.

Hancock, Emily. "Women's Development in Adult Life." Unpublished doctoral diss., Harvard University, 1981.

————. "Woman's Root Identity: The Girl Within." *San Francisco Jung Institute Library Journal* 7, no. 1 (1987): 15–18.

Hewlett, Sylvia. *A Lesser Life: The Myth of Women's Liberation in America*. New York: Warner Books, 1987.

Hochschild, A. *Working Parents and the Revolution at Home.* New York: Viking Press, forthcoming.

Horner, Matina. "Toward an Understanding of Achievement-related Conflicts in Women." *Journal of Social Issues* 8, no. 2 (1972): 157–74.

Horney, Karen. *New Ways in Psychoanalysis.* New York: W. W. Norton, 1939.

———. *Our Inner Conflicts: Constructive Theory of Neurosis.* New York: W. W. Norton, 1945.

Kaplan, Justin. "The Naked Self and Other Problems." In *Telling Lives: The Biographer's Art,* edited by Marc Pachter, 36–55. Philadelphia: University of Pennsylvania Press, 1981.

Kegan, Robert. *The Evolving Self: Problems and Process in Human Development.* Cambridge: Harvard University Press, 1982.

Keller, Evelyn Fox. *Reflections on Gender and Science.* New Haven: Yale University Press, 1985.

Kelly, George. *Theory of Personality: The Psychology of Personal Constructs.* New York: W. W. Norton, 1963.

Kohut, Heinz. *The Restoration of the Self.* New York: International Universities Press, 1977.

Konigsburg, E. L. *From the Mixed-up Files of Mrs. Basil E. Frankweiler.* New York: Dell, 1967.

Lensky, Lois. *Strawberry Girl.* Philadelphia: J. B. Lippincott, 1945.

Lessing, Doris. *The Summer Before the Dark.* New York: Alfred A. Knopf, 1973.

Levine, R. "Clinical Implications of the Mother-Child Relationship: Good Enough Daughtering." Paper presented at the 8th annual national conference on feminist psychology, Association for Women in Psychology, Boston, MA, March 1981.

Levinson, Daniel. *The Seasons of a Man's Life.* New York: Alfred A. Knopf, 1978.

Lifton, Robert. "Woman as Knower: Some Psychohistorical Perspectives." In *The Woman in America*, 27–51. Boston: Houghton Mifflin, 1965.

Lindgren, Astrid. *Pippi Longstocking.* New York: Viking Press, 1950.

Loevinger, Jane. *Ego Development: Conceptions and Theories.* San Francisco: Jossey-Bass, 1976.

Low, Natalie. "The Relationship of Adult Daughters to Their Mothers." Paper presented at the Massachusetts Psychological Association, Wellesley, MA, May 1978.

Lowinsky, Naomi Ruth. "All the Days of Her Life." Doctoral diss., Center for Psychological Studies, Albany, CA, 1985.

———. "Why Can't a Man Be More Like a Woman?" *San Francisco Jung Institute Library Journal* 5, no. 1 (1984): 20–30.

Mahler, Margaret. *The Psychological Birth of the Human Infant.* New York: Basic Books, 1975.

McClelland, David C. *Power: The Inner Experience.* New York: John Wiley, 1975.

Miller, Alice. *Prisoners of Childhood: The Drama of the Gifted Child and the Search for the True Self.* New York: Basic Books, 1981.

Miller, Jean Baker. *Psychoanalysis and Women.* New York: Brunner/ Mazel, 1973.

———. *Toward a New Psychology of Women.* Boston: Beacon Press, 1976.

Montgomery, L. M. *Emily of New Moon.* 1923. Reprint. New York: Bantam Books, 1983.

Parlee, Mary Brown. "Psychology." *Signs: Journal of Women in Culture and Society* 1, no. 1 (1975): 119–38

———. "Psychology and Women." *Signs: Journal of Women in Culture and Society* 5, no. 1 (1979): 121–33.

Parsons, Talcott C., and Robert F. Bales. *Family Socialization and Interaction Process.* Glencoe, IL: Free Press, 1955.

Perera, Sylvia. *Descent to the Goddess.* Toronto: Inner City Books, 1981.

Peterson, Nancy. *Our Lives for Ourselves.* New York: G. P. Putnam's Sons, 1981.

Piaget, Jean. *The Construction of Reality in the Child.* 1937. Reprint. New York: Basic Books, 1954.

Rich, Adrienne. "Conditions for Work: The Common World of Women." Foreword to *Working It Out*, edited by Sara Ruddick and Pamela Daniels. New York: Pantheon Books, 1977.

———. *Of Woman Born.* New York: Norton, 1976.

Rohlen, Thomas. "The Promise of Adulthood in Japanese Spiritualism." In *Adulthood*, edited by Erik Erikson, New York: W. W. Norton, 1976.

Rubin, Lillian. *Worlds of Pain.* New York: Basic Books, 1976.

Ruddick, Sara. A Work of One's Own." In *Working It Out*, edited by Sara Ruddick and Pamela Daniels, 128–46. New York: Pantheon Books, 1977.

Ruddick, Sara, and Pamela Daniels, eds. *Working It Out.* New York: Pantheon Books, 1977.

Sawyer, Ruth. *Roller Skates.* New York: Viking Press, 1936.

Scarf, Maggie. *Unfinished Business: Pressure Points in the Lives of Women.* Garden City, NY: Doubleday, 1980.

Schwartz, Lynne Sharon. *Disturbances in the Field*. New York: Harper & Row, 1983.

Seidenberg, Robert. "Is Anatomy Destiny?" In *Psychoanalysis and Women*, edited by J. B. Miller, 305–29. New York: Brunner/Mazel, 1973.

Sheehy, Gail. *Passages*. New York: E. P. Dutton, 1974.

Singer, June. "For the Woman Who Has Everything and Still Is Not Happy." Paper presented at the Gifts of Age Symposium, U.C. Extension, San Francisco, June 1987.

Smith, Agnes. *An Edge of the Forest*. Farmington, WV: Westwind Press, 1974.

Steele, Marilyn. "Life in the Round: A Model of Adult Female Development." Doctoral diss. Wright Institute, Berkeley, CA, 1985.

Steinem, Gloria. "If Marilyn Had Lived . . . Who Would She Be Today?" *Ms.*, August 1986, 40–45 *passim*.

Sullivan, Harry Stack. *The Interpersonal Theory of Psychiatry*. New York: W. W. Norton, 1953.

Surrey, Janet. "Self-in-Relation: A Theory of Women's Development." Stone Center Working Papers, no. 13, Wellesley College, 1985.

Vaillant, George. *Adaptation to Life*. Boston: Little, Brown, 1977.

Welty, Eudora. *One Writer's Beginnings*. Cambridge: Harvard University Press, 1984.

Westkott, Marcia. "Feminist Criticism of the Social Sciences." *Harvard Educational Review* 49 (1979): 422–30.

———. *The Feminist Legacy of Karen Horney*. New Haven: Yale University Press, 1986.

——. "Mothers and Daughters in the World of the Father." *Frontiers* 3, no. 2 (1978): 16–22.

Wheelwright, Jane. *The Ranch Papers*. San Francisco: Lapis Press, 1988.

White, Robert. "Competence and the Psychosexual Stages." *Nebraska Symposium* 8 (1960): 97–144.

——. *Lives in Progress*. New York: Holt, Rinehart & Winston, 1975.

White, Sheldon. "Some General Outlines of the Matrix of Developmental Changes Between Five and Seven Years." *Bulletin of the Orton Society* 20 (1970): 41–57.

Winnicott, D. W. *Maturational Processes and the Facilitating Environment*. New York: International Universities Press, 1965.

Woolf, Virginia. *A Room of One's Own*. New York: Harcourt, Brace & World, 1929.

INDEX